Ticket to the World

MARTIN KEMP

Ticket to the World

MY 80s STORY

HarperCollins*Publishers*

HarperCollins*Publishers*
1 London Bridge Street
London SE1 9GF

www.harpercollins.co.uk

HarperCollins*Publishers*
Macken House, 39/40 Mayor Street Upper
Dublin 1, D01 C9W8, Ireland

First published by HarperCollins*Publishers* 2022
This edition published 2023

3 5 7 9 10 8 6 4 2

A catalogue record of this book is
available from the British Library

ISBN 978-0-00-858605-8

Printed and bound in the UK using 100%
renewable electricity at CPI Group (UK) Ltd

Dedicated to Steve Strange ... 1959–2015
Who styled so many lives!

CONTENTS

PREFACE

When I first started this book, I had this idea to mark the names of the Blitz Kids somehow. A motif, a little gimmick to remind you just how often they cropped up over the course of the decade. An asterisk or a *[BK]* each time I named one; some small tag to denote 'BLITZ KID'.

To spare your sanity and mine I decided against it in the end. Instead, you will simply have to endure me acting like a proud dad sat next to you at a school play, nudging you in the arm every 40 seconds to whisper in your ear, 'See that one? They're one of ours too ...'

I can't help it. I wish I could but, in recalling all of what's contained in this book, it still astonishes me just how much of the decade we remember as the 80s was formed by such a tiny group.

We went by many names at the start of the decade, when no one knew what to make of us. The Blitz Kids. The Dandies in Hand-Me-Downs. The Cult with No Name.

Eventually we became known as the New Romantics. That was the name that stuck and the name that would echo around the globe as the years marched on.

I still think of the New Romantics as the last great pop culture, even now. It's a cliché to say that we were in the right place at the right time. We were, but I don't think that paints the full picture. It says nothing of our attitude. We embodied the prevailing mindset of that era. It wasn't greed that drove us, but a sense of self. Of individuality. Of learning early that we were one-in-a-trillion life forces with endless possibility at the edge of our fingertips if we'd only just tip forward and make a grab for it.

We were a vision of hope. A vision of ambition. We were brighter than the cameras of our day could capture and we left a hell of a legacy.

80s pop culture changed the world – artistically, technologically, politically, socially. So when you think back and laugh at your backcombed hair, your smeared turquoise eyeshadow, your shoulder pads and your puffy taffeta dress, you should know that it was more than just some weird fashion. However you engaged with it, you were part of the future.

It might feel a lifetime ago now – for some of you, it possibly was – but there's a reason Gen Z are obsessing over Kate Bush and the sounds of 'Running Up That Hill' in the 2020s. There's a reason TikTok is overrun with 80s aesthetic challenges, SoundCloud is filled with synth-pop and YouTube is filled with Rick Astley. They are plundering it in much the same way that the New Romantics plundered everything and anything that had gone before them – to take it and make it their own.

The 1980s made me. I can go pound for pound with anyone who wants to highlight awful outfits, ridiculous hair and pretentious poses. I have crates of photos I'd be happy to leave locked in a vault until 3030. But I loved the 1980s and I want you to love them too.

So here, between these covers, is my attempt to record the decade as I lived it. If you were there, I want you to recall it. To reach out, touch it.

If you weren't, I hope I can do it justice. The lessons the era taught me are the ones I have strived to pass on to my own kids as a father now. To be open, to explore, to welcome everything as it comes to you. To love life as it is but to always push forward onto greater things.

Whether it's just for you, or whether it's for the world at large, the lesson of the 80s is simple: it's all there – and it's all there for you.

MK

HAPPY NEW YEAR

Outside, it was a tired and worn-out Britain. As rubbish piled high on cracked pavements and widespread strikes caused disruption around the country, we had an economy in turmoil. Unemployment was high, jobs were precarious and inflation was out of control. An energy crisis was causing havoc, with petrol prices ramping up and fuel costs causing families to have to decide between heating and eating.

The government had just been rocked by a damning vote of no confidence. Ongoing tensions with the Soviet Union provided a terrible background hum; the ever-present threat of a third world war never far from people's minds.

Even pop culture – our last bastion of fantasy and escapism – had become dark, pessimistic and angry. Glam rock had been run out of town by punks, dressed in studs and black leather, calling for anarchy. Jamie Reid, the young street artist, had stuck safety pins through the Queen's nose for her Silver Jubilee and, like a voodoo doll, it embodied the pain the nation was feeling.

The Land of Hope and Glory was rife with chaos and despair. Up and down the country it felt as if the Winter of Discontent had lasted all year.

But inside? Inside our family home on New Year's Eve 1979, things felt different.

As the prawn cocktail vol-au-vent started to congeal on the Formica kitchen table and the Black Forest gâteau collapsed softly to one side, my mum and dad put their arms around my brother's and my shoulders, and we huddled around our television to count down the chimes of Big Ben.

10 …

Babycham glasses in hand, we had no idea at that point what the 1980s would bring. No idea of the explosion of colour, the flamboyance, the fashion, the sounds and sights of a brand new pop culture that would be ushered in on a wave of futuristic technology.

9 …

Actually, to say we had *no* idea isn't quite right. My brother Gary and I had been given a small taste of what was to come a few weeks before – a sneak preview of the coming attractions – when we'd been booked to play our first proper gig as a new band.

8 …

We'd been hired to play a Christmas party, performing for an audience of our friends. It was a small gig. There couldn't have been more than a hundred people there, if that. But the people who were would be the ones to usher in this new movement.

7 ...

We knew we were all standing on the verge of something amazing, but we could never have predicted just how big it was going to get. In the streets of Soho and the clubs of Covent Garden, a ragtag bunch of misfits were building something. A collective of musicians, artists, writers, designers, fashion students and film-makers were congregating every Tuesday, but it had no name right now.

6 ...

Actually, that might not quite be true either. It was probably around that time we were being referred to as The Cult with No Name – although we'd be called a hundred different things before a proper name settled.

5 ...

Spewing out our amphetamine-fuelled version of a beautiful future, at any other time, in any other place, our plans to take on the world might have come to nothing. The only result, a hangover – washed away the next morning with a strong cup of tea.

4 ...

Instead, our collective would become a nucleus of change for the next ten years. A creative hotbed where all that was good, bad and bizarre about the 80s would take shape and be unleashed upon the world.

3 ...

We knew this new decade was going to be special. We didn't know how exactly but, within a year, things would be completely different. The 70s had been such a heavy, grey time. The 80s had to change. They just had to.

2 ...

Here it comes. The future.

1 ...

Happy New Year!

1980
BLITZ SPIRIT

Post-it Notes | *Moscow Olympics* | The Empire Strikes Back | Pac-Man | *Rubik's Cube* | *Roland TR-808* | *Who Shot J.R.?* | Back in Black | *Alton Towers* | Xanadu | *Vauxhall Astra* | *Reagan Wins* | *Eradication of Smallpox* | *'Going Underground'* | Airplane! | *'Another One Bites the Dust'* | *The Sinking of Radio Caroline* | *24-Hour Rolling News* | Les Misérables | *UK Indie Chart* | *'The Lady's Not for Turning'* | *'Turning Japanese'* | Caddyshack | The Great Rock 'n' Roll Swindle | *Assassination of John Lennon*

The Name

The name came from a Berlin wall.

Not the Berlin Wall. A Berlin wall. A toilet wall to be specific. Our friend Robert Elms had seen it while taking a piss in a nightclub there recently. To us kids of the post-punk scene, Berlin was a growing source of fascination. David Bowie had just released *Lodger*, the last in his 'Berlin Trilogy' – a set of albums that had seen him leave LA for Europe to experiment with the strange new sounds, styles and technology emerging out of there.

A group of our friends had just come back from a trip and were telling us all about it. It might only have been a few hundred miles away as the crow flies, but to a working-class kid from the rough-arsed end of Islington in the late 1970s, Berlin might as well have been the other end of the earth.

As I sat drinking in a dingy old Irish pub talking German graffiti with Bob I had no way of knowing this, but the second he told me what he saw on that wall my life would change forever. At that exact moment, without knowing it, Bob would trigger a different countdown.

Ten years. In ten years' time, I would find myself in Berlin. I would be there with my band – the band we had just invited Bob to see play for the first time – and I would watch the wall come down.

This time the Berlin Wall.

That countdown wouldn't just mark out my own personal journey. It would mark the lifespan of our band too. At the tail end of 1979, we got our name. By the dawn of 1990, it was all but over.

Between those two points, a new pop culture movement would sweep the globe and it would be dictated by the friends we had just played to that morning in Halligan's Rehearsal Room. Music, fashion, film, TV, magazines, art, nightlife. Nothing would be spared. We would change it all. Not just for one band's fandom or a handful of fashionistas. For everyone.

It didn't happen completely by chance, but it wasn't completely by design either. Advancing technology, political unrest, economic turmoil and cultural globalisation would all play their part. Against a grim backdrop of humanitarian horror, nuclear catastrophe and the ever-present threat of war, the glittering culture we were about to create would not only thrive, it would have an absolutely unprecedented effect on global affairs.

And me, a kid from Islington who had only picked up a bass for the first time a few short months ago? I would be standing on the frontlines.

Like I say, there was no way I could have known any of this as I drained the dregs of my snakebite and black and made my way out onto the dismal pavement of Holloway

Road. The only thing I knew for sure at that point was that we had just played our last gig as Gentry. The next time we played again, we would have a brand new name.

The words Bob had read on that toilet wall in Berlin?

Spandau Ballet.

The Showcase

It was perfect. Provocative. Poetic. Even a little bit pretentious. Of course an 18-year-old in a beret and black mascara was going to love it.

Gentry had been a decent name, but it was no hardship to lose it – and it's not like we'd been especially attached to any of the others either. The band had already been Roots, the Makers and the Cut. Names like Gentry, their time had passed. We were five working-class kids from North London, about the furthest thing you get from the actual gentry. It was sarcastic, bratty. That sort of snark had been all the rage during punk, but that rage had had its moment. The tide was starting to turn. We had all loved the shot of adrenaline punk had given us, but its insistence on destruction – always tearing things up and ripping things down – was beginning to wear thin.

For kids like me and my brother Gary, who had grown up playing around nearby bomb sites, levelled-out areas of our neighbourhood that the council still hadn't got round to clearing up after the war, destruction and desolation held limited appeal. At first it had been great to see people like us on stage, kids with spirit, spitting and snarling. It definitely spoke to the fiery young upstart in me, like it did with millions of kids around the world. After a while, though, when you're looking down the barrel of 50 years of the futureless future that punk promised, the fun quickly faded.

The band we had formed, the sound we were making, it was something new, something exciting. The energy and attitude of punk were still there. The hunger to take on the world headfirst was too. But we were no longer interested in turning the place to rubble. We'd worked hard to build this and we liked what we'd built. We were going to make things beautiful and we were going to take pride in them.

That's why we would become Spandau Ballet.

For months, the five of us – me, my brother Gary, Steve Norman, John Keeble and Tony Hadley – had been rehearsing on the sly, on the advice of our manager Steve Dagger, perfecting our sound and our style.

The final gig we'd just played as Gentry had been a showcase of sorts. An audition, really. Not for any record execs or label bosses. For someone much more important than that.

The reason we played that Saturday morning in Halligan's was for the benefit of a guy in the audience we'd invited down. He, along with a friend of his, ran a club night in town that we were all regulars at. A Bowie night, basically, in Covent Garden. Every Tuesday we would take over this wine bar on Great Queen Street and spend our nights taking cheap speed, dancing to synth-pop and mapping out our plans for world domination.

This guy was looking for someone to play that club night's Christmas party. As a band we were so fresh and new that we'd only just that second named ourselves Spandau Ballet. If he was looking for something exciting, that band was us. So he gave us the gig.

Steve Harrington his name was. Or, as we all knew him better, Steve Strange.

Strange

Seeing Steve Strange around town in the 80s was one of those things you couldn't avoid. It was involuntary – like sneezing, or laughing. You couldn't help it. It just … happened.

The first time I saw him, he was standing in the wings at a Generation X gig in '77 at the Marquee Club in Soho. He was further on stage than he was meant to be, beyond the point that even his triple-A access pass allowed.

His look was one I can only describe as Corduroy Space Cowboy. It was like a cartoon character come to life. His huge jet black quiff stood a foot high in the air and came a good six inches out in front too. His Elnett hairspray caught the spotlight and acted like a reflector, as if his head had been dipped in glitter. His giant padded shoulders threw an even bigger shadow on the wall behind him and the smoke from his extra-long Benson gave him a magical glow, as if he had appeared from nowhere – a conjuror's trick that made you gasp in disbelief.

I was supposed to be jumping about to Derwood Andrew's crashing guitars. I was supposed to be shouting along with Billy Idol, but my eyes were fixed on this apparition in the wings.

The Marquee has seen some incredible names up on that stage over the years, from Hendrix to the Who, from AC/DC to the Stones – but I will bet you any money it had never seen a battle of charisma like this before. Without making a noise, without throwing a shape, a man whose name I was yet to learn was stealing the show from bona fide rock gods.

And I shouldn't have been easily distracted. I loved Generation X. I can't tell you how much that band meant to 15-year-old me. Their 7-inch singles sat in pride of place above my record player. I'd taped a session they did for John Peel off the radio and replayed it so many times that the tape itself had stretched and twisted and got caught in its plastic casing. It was totally beyond repair, no matter how many times I stuck a pencil into the spool and tried to turn it. I literally played that tape to death.

But as Billy threw his fists into the air and sang about how 'Your Generation' had fucked it up to a thousand sweating, bouncing bodies around me, Steve stood quietly in the wings, the chrome tip of his King's Road cowboy boot gently tapping, as he took it all in. I was mesmerised.

I wouldn't meet Steve properly for another couple of years, but he wasn't the sort of person you easily forgot. It's weird because he was also the sort of person who never looked the same on any two occasions. One night you might run into him and he'd be dressed like Robin Hood: a green velvet tunic, white tights, pixie boots and an alpine hat pulled down, a cascade of dark curls covering one eye. The next he could be styled as a young Italian priest: a fitted black cassock, row after row of rosary beads tied around his waist, a cape and a cappello romano hat with a brim as wide as his shoulders.

There was one time I bumped into him head to toe in white, with black contact lenses in that filled the whole of his iris, making him look a Martian.

His face was a canvas and every day it had a new design. Friday, a French mime. Saturday, Russian Constructivist. He could paint himself as a Regency prince or a Cubist Picasso, Cleopatra or a kabuki dancer, but every single time he was unmistakably Steve Strange.

Steve ran a club night in town with a friend of his at a place called the Blitz. It was there he first spoke to me.

One night, as I handed over my two quid entry fee, he took my hand and held it in his. Instantly, I felt a connection. The same magnetism that had drawn my eye at the Marquee Club was now devastatingly close and I couldn't escape it. If he didn't let go of my hand I was going to be stuck there all night, blocking the door. There was no way I was going to be the one who broke this up. I couldn't. I was completely at Steve Strange's mercy.

To this day, I still haven't met anyone else quite like Steve. I've met royalty, heads of state, some of the greatest legends of rock'n'roll and Hollywood, but none of them had what Steve Strange had. At least, not in anything like the same amount. He was charisma in its purest form, crystal clear and sparkling.

The whole world was about to fall for him the way I had. I had never been so sure of anything in my life.

'I'll see you later,' he said with a flirtatious smirk, releasing his grip and letting me pass.

I stepped into the Blitz and immediately fell in love.

Billy's

Before I can tell you about the Blitz, I have to tell you about Billy's.

You know how in nature, some of the brightest, most brilliantly coloured creatures spend some time in a dark, dank cocoon? For the Blitz Kids, that was Billy's.

Billy's was a transitional club. The place that transformed the snarling pups of punk into the dazzling visions of beauty that became the New Romantics. It existed underground, in the hot, smoky basement of 69 Dean Street.* Depending on who you ask, Billy's was either the basement of a Soho strip club or the basement of a Soho brothel. Possibly both. Whatever it was, it was like everything else in Soho at that time. Seedy.

This wasn't the Soho of today, where you have ten tidy little streets of post-production studios, Pret A Mangers and private members' clubs. Soho in the late 70s was a mess. By night, you could maybe just about mistake it for somewhere vaguely glamorous, with all its lights and neon. But as soon as you noticed what that neon spelled out, you were left under no illusion.

Every other shop sold sex. Magazines to Super 8 movies, strip shows to cinemas. It oozed from every window. Men skulked from doorway to doorway, while women stood alone on the damp street corners, greasing the tips of their French Gitanes with scarlet lipstick.

---

* Seriously, the single dirtiest address in Soho – which is some going …

Even the streets themselves were grimy; bin bags stacked like mountains and rats roaming the pavement. Every corner and every doorway smelled as though someone (or something) had pissed up every inch of it the night before.

In a way, there's something quite fitting about the fact that Steve Strange – who came from a small coal-mining community in Wales – gravitated towards a dark, dirty hole in the ground like Billy's. He certainly looked at home there.

Attracting a clientele that dressed mainly in black military jackets and biker leathers, there were small signs of flamboyance starting to show. Neckerchiefs would be tied just so. A trilby would be set at a gravity-taunting angle. Collars were studded with diamanté. The colourless costume of punk was growing some sparkle in that smut-filled pit.

The Billy's era didn't last long. Owing to a disagreement with the owner (a large gentleman named Vince; the kind of guy you don't disagree with twice), Steve was looking for a new home for his event within three months. But that had been more than enough for us.

By the time we emerged from that underground cocoon in Soho, we were ready to spread our wings and burst forth – to the Blitz.

The Blitz

According to the sign outside, the Blitz was a nightly cabaret/club–restaurant–bar. While that might have been true on every other night of the week, on Tuesday nights the Blitz became a portal to another planet.

Tucked in off the main streets of Covent Garden, there wasn't much passing foot traffic trying to get in to this otherwise unremarkable wine bar. It was a good job too because the Bowie night that Steve Strange hosted there wasn't really designed for the public. It was barely designed for anyone except the hundred or so souls who gathered there every Tuesday to show off their latest creations.

Positioned almost dead centre between two of London's big art colleges – Central and St Martin's – the Blitz called out to the creative spirits of both campuses who descended each week to debut their latest looks.

That was the key to admission into the Blitz. It wasn't about who you were, who you knew or how much money you had to chuck about. Entry was dependent on how you looked. If you didn't meet Steve Strange's exacting standards on the door then there was no appealing against his decision. No amount of strong-arming or grease-palming could get you in. You simply had to look the part.

To say it took hours to get ready for the Blitz on a Tuesday night understates it massively. As soon as Mum had cooked our dinner at 6 p.m. and I had scraped the plates at 6.15, my brother and I would run upstairs to start doing our hair. After throwing on our clothes and putting on the make-up we furtively stole from Mum's dresser, we would just about make it to the Blitz in time for 10 p.m. But if you think it only took us two and a half hours to get our look right, that was only the home stretch.

Where most people's weeks started on Monday and ended on Sunday, ours went Tuesday to Tuesday. There was nothing else. Our whole week was Tuesday. If we weren't at the Blitz, then we were getting ready for the Blitz. We were planning our outfits. Pounding the pavement from charity shop to charity shop looking for things we could buy or customise. Drawing up designs for shirts, stitching on accessories, pairing them with every other item we owned.

Everything you did while your eyes were open was working towards the Blitz. Then when you slept, you would dream of it too.

The venue itself was nothing special. A wine bar with a WWII theme. Portraits of Churchill loomed large on the walls, alongside olde-time painted mirrors, gas masks and 'Dig for Victory' posters. In the cold light of day the place probably looked more like a corridor than a bar and describing it as having a dancefloor could have had you up in front of Trading Standards. It had a floor and you could dance on it, but that was its limit.

We made the space work for us, but it wasn't some glamorous locale. What made the Blitz was the crowd – and that crowd could be split into two distinct camps (one distinctly more camp than the other).

The group I was part of was the North London contingent, sometimes referred to as the Angel Boys. That wasn't a comment on our good behaviour or our cherubic looks – much as I'd like to pretend it was. It was a reference to the Angel, Islington, where most of us would trek down from. We were a bunch of old soul boys, ex-punks and power-pop kids who were moving on from the scuzziness of that dying scene and were captivated by the flamboyant new fashions, keen to try on whatever was going.

Then on the other side, you had the art students. If passing civilians looked goggle-eyed at us Angel Boys with our blusher and mascara, our pearl earrings and bouffant hairdos – they'd have burst on the spot if they saw some of the St Martin's lot.

Tuesday nights at the Blitz were massively popular with local fashion students as it gave them a place to wear the weird and wonderful designs they had spent the week whipping up. Little did we know at the time, but we were getting early previews from designers and stylists who would go on to have massive influence over the style of the decade. Stephen Linard, Kim Bowen, Lee Sheldrick, Darla Jane Gilroy, Fiona Dealey, John Galliano, Melissa Caplan.

Week after week, they would put together totally new ensembles, drawing inspiration from a completely different set of influences. One Tuesday they might turn up in geisha make-up and a stunning silk kimono paired with a peacock punk mohican. The next, they're dressed in rabbinical robes, looking like they're on their way to conduct a millionaire's funeral.

They would stand side by side at the bar wedged between someone dressed as a Tudor royal who had just discovered taffeta, and a Russian cosmonaut with a passion for pastels.

Everyone's hair was scraped, styled and sprayed into shapes that threw the most fascinating silhouettes. The sort of shapes you didn't learn until the latter years of school. Parallelograms. Rhomboids. I'd put good money on there being a dodecahedron on someone's head on any given night.

As outrageous as some of the fashion students were, the ones who really stood out at the Blitz were the art students who channelled their energy into becoming living, breathing sculptures.

I remember once chatting to Leigh Bowery, the legendary performance artist, at the Blitz one night. He was dressed fully in white. His face was caked in stage make-up half an inch thick and there was candle wax dribbling in rivulets all down his bald head. It gave the effect of Humpty Dumpty after his fall – all except for one detail. Rising out of the centre of his wax skullcap was a full-length tapered candle, alight on the top of his head, its flame flickering away in the middle of the club.

It wasn't a costume. He hadn't come to the club dressed as a candle. He had come dressed a Leigh Bowery. He just happened to also look like a humongous seven-foot candle. That was Leigh.

Sharing a space with these sorts of artists and designers was the best education a budding New Romantic could have in those early days – but it put no small amount of pressure on the North London contingent. Every week, the stakes would get ever higher. The looks were bolder, wilder. The colours, the patterns, the styles were all pushed to the furthest reaches of our imaginations. We couldn't just rely on hairspray and a bit of blusher. We had to hustle if we didn't want to be left behind.

The Look

We didn't have a ready supply of ruffs, chiffon and organza the way the fashion students did, so we had to be resourceful. Charity shops were often the thing to do as there were all sorts of beautifully tailored clothes sitting in those shops. Tuxedos from the 50s that had been bought for a big occasion and only worn once. Exquisitely tailored suits from the 1940s that had fallen out of fashion but kept pristine by owners who cherished them.

These suits were stunning, but in those alone we'd look like kids from *Bugsy Malone*, all dressed up in dead men's

Sunday best. So we accessorised. We'd find bejewelled brooches to pin to the lapels. We'd find cheap beaded necklaces to wear like cummerbunds and bandoliers. We'd pair them with a silk neckerchief or a feather or a leather cap.

For those who could afford it, there was PX. PX was the shop of Helen Robinson and Stephane Raynor, on James Street in Covent Garden. Helen and Stephane were Blitz Kids and would always be there at the club on a Tuesday. Steve Strange could be found at PX a lot too, working the tills and chatting to the customers – even though I'm not convinced he was ever formally employed there. If he was, his payslip must have had him listed as a mannequin, because he was there to showcase the clothes. Wherever he went, he was a human billboard for that shop – advertising outfits Helen and Stephane had let him borrow.

If you really wanted to push the boat out, the most fashionable designers all set up shop along the King's Road, Chelsea. Statement pieces from Vivienne Westwood's SEX shop, suits from Johnson's, boots from R.Soles,* or if you wanted cheaper versions from lesser-known designers, you could find them in Kensington Market.

All of those were way out of my league, though, so for the Blitz Kid who couldn't afford the boutiques, we had Laurence Corner: the army surplus store.

To people of a certain age, Londoners especially, the name will hit you like a ton of bricks. For those who don't know it, the reach of Laurence Corner's influence is hard to overstate. For a time, it was the most famous army surplus store – not just in Britain, but worldwide. It wasn't a flashy shop, by any means. It just punched well above its weight.

---

* Say it out loud a few times.

The famous *Sgt. Pepper's* outfits that the Beatles wore came from Laurence Corner. Keith Moon was a regular. Some of Jean Paul Gaultier's most memorable designs were inspired by the shop's stock and it became such a favourite of so many fashionistas that they gave it the affectionate nickname Yves Saint Laurence.

Laurence Corner also provided costumes and props for massive film franchises like *Star Wars* and *Indiana Jones*, but you didn't need Beatles money or George Lucas money to pick up an outfit there. Fundamentally, this was a place where kids on the dole could pick out eye-catching outfits at a snip. Where students could kit out a full year's wardrobe on a budget.

There was so much stuff left over from the Second World War. Rack after rack of military clothing. If you wanted cheap, characterless khakis to slap on then they were there by the crateful, but plainness was poison at the Blitz so we would seek out the most decorated jackets we could afford. The stuff made for the officers. The generals. The admirals.

The variety and versatility were incredible. There were sailor suits from the Navy. Jumpsuits from the Air Force. Safari suits from desert missions. And it wasn't just British service outfits either. We found items of uniform from all over the world. American. Canadian. Italian. Soviet. French. We didn't come out of Laurence Corner dressed like anonymous interchangeable infantrymen. We looked like an international assortment of superheroes.

Looking back, one of the things I loved most about the Blitz was this lack of uniform. Punk had become a uniform, just like the teddy boys had and the mods and rockers had. With the Blitz, you could try on anything. Literally anything. You could take what you liked from wherever you liked and just … try it. The look would only last for a night anyway, so if it was a disaster, the next week you'd be trying something else on.

Individualism would become one of the defining traits of the 80s. Everyone looking out for themselves, everybody trying to make the most of their own lot in life. In a sense, that was one of the defining traits of the Blitz as well. You weren't just free to be whoever you wanted to be in that club, you were encouraged.

Every single person in that club held themselves like they were the star of their own movie. You never played second fiddle to anyone there. The outrageous outfits were never designed to steal anyone else's limelight. That was the magic of it. You got dressed exactly how you wanted to look and then you went to the Blitz where you had a hundred glamorous extras to back you up. And because we all played that part for each other, everybody got that feeling.

That was Tuesday night at the Blitz. The beginning and end of my week.

The Sound

If Steve Strange dictated the look of the Blitz, then the sound of it was shaped by Rusty Egan.

The first time I stepped through that door and made my way through the smoke – a mix of punters' Marlboros and a wheezing dry-ice machine that sat in the far corner – it was the sound I was being led by. David Bowie's 'Boys Keep Swinging'. As I pushed my way along the room, the shadowy form of Rusty took shape in the DJ booth. Suited and booted, a wedge of brilliant blond hair, Rusty might have been one of the Blitz's more conservative dressers, but his look was always crisp and sharp.

His magic was in his records. In a room where a hundred people were all the stars of their own movies, he somehow managed to find a soundtrack to unite them all.

An absolute master of atmosphere, his sets gave the night a true identity. You didn't come to the Blitz to listen to a jukebox. People weren't getting dressed up in all these wild outfits just to hear the hits they'd heard on the radio all week. We came to the Blitz to be transported to strange, far-off worlds – and we knew that Rusty would be our guide.

Synth-pop from Japan. Krautrock from Germany. Italodisco. He would move seamlessly between Yellow Magic Orchestra and Bauhaus, Nina Hagen and Roxy Music, Giorgio Moroder and OMD.

Such was Rusty's hunger to play the newest, most interesting music he could, he even went so far as to form a band to make music specifically to play on those Tuesday nights. It made sense that he would. Rusty had come of age through the punk era. He'd been right at the heart of the post-punk scene too, playing drums in a band called the Rich Kids, formed by ex-Sex Pistol Glen Matlock.

Everything punk had taught us Blitz Kids – the attitude, the energy, the DIY aesthetic – came so naturally to Rusty that the idea of just creating the music he wanted to hear in the Blitz was a no-brainer.

Back in the mid-70s, if you wanted to make a song, you could only really scratch one out on a guitar. Maybe a piano if your parents had one. The idea of having your own synthesiser back then was a pipe dream. You had to be a genuine rich kid to afford one of those. The decent ones cost about the same as a small house – and were practically the size of one too.

By the turn of the decade, though, a whole new range of affordable, accessible synthesisers started hitting the market. Japanese tech firms like Yamaha, Roland, Korg and Casio were turning an expensive, minority pursuit into a mass-market phenomenon, producing smaller, cheaper synths that were simple to play.

This was actually what broke the Rich Kids up. Rusty and fellow bandmate Midge Ure had taken possession of a synth and were desperate to mess around with it, folding this new electronic sound into the Rich Kids. Glen – a devotee of the classic four-piece guitars/bass/drums set-up – hated it. So the band parted ways, leaving a chunk of unused studio time in their wake.

Never letting anything go to waste in those young lean days, Rusty and Midge snapped that studio time straight up and used it to start a new project, making demos of songs Rusty then spliced into his Blitz sets. Songs that soaked up all the future-forward influence of the club and fed it right back to us.

Midge was a Blitz Kid too, so he knew the sound. The project became a band. That band became Visage. And Steve Strange would become its face.

Rusty was constantly experimenting with sound. Even at his turntables on the night, long after the songs were all locked in and ready to play, he'd bring along a drum machine to add some live percussion to them. They were two synthetic drum pads that didn't sound like drums at all. They made that 'pew pew' disco noise and he would tap them over the top of other people's songs, making it sound like some alien invader had got loose with a ray-gun.

If you wanted classic rock'n'roll, you'd have to find it elsewhere. If you wanted the future, you had to be at the Blitz.

The sound Rusty cultivated in that smoky, sweaty club wouldn't just live in the heads of the hundred or so kids that turned up to dance each Tuesday. That was only the beginning. In the same way Steve Strange's aesthetic and magnetism were bringing the freshest young minds in fashion together, Rusty's music would influence the next big wave of chart hits.

Spandau had already fallen under the influence of Rusty's records, shaking off Gentry's trad power-pop trappings and replacing them with the sort of angular synth sounds we heard those nights in the Blitz.

Spandau's salvation came in the form of a Yamaha CS-10. It was a simple machine. Analogue. Monophonic. That meant it could only process one note at a time, which, in turn, meant you didn't need to be a virtuoso to play it. No chords. No harmonies. This was a one-finger wonder.

Perfectly in keeping with the punk spirit of not knowing how to play an instrument and not letting that stop you, the Yahama CS-10 transformed us from the type of garage band you might have heard in any school music block or pub backroom in the country and made us sound like a troupe of time-travellers.

Take a listen to 'Cut a Long Story Short' and you'll hear what I mean within the first two notes. The earliest incarnation of that song had the riff ground out on a guitar. Catchy, but could have been the work of a hundred different bands. Switching that melody over to a synthesiser was the work of an instant, yet running it through that Yahama flipped the entire thing on its head. That fizzing, wiry, electric squelch laid over the standard rock-band set-up added a whole new dimension. It sounded like it was being beamed in from outer space.

What's weird is, had the technology developed too quickly – if those early synths had raced out of the gate with full polyphonic capabilities, a raft of effects and over-lays, allowing you to instantly create huge sonic symphonies with the press of a key – we'd have almost certainly missed our chance.

Maybe Gary or Steve would have gone down the Rick Wakeman route and become an all-out keyboard wizard, but then we would have sounded just like any number of the prog-rock bands our parents were into – and where was the fun in that? The physical, mechanical limitations of these early machines meant we could only play it punk. As such, monophonic synths provided a slip road for bands like us to join in with the new wave of tech-assisted pop – and let us learn the rest on the job.

We weren't the only ones. Dotted around the crowd on the dancefloor on those early Blitz nights were all sorts of musicians and performers who fancied the life of a pop star and were going to ride this very same wave.

Members of Visage. Ultravox. Bananarama. Sigue Sigue Sputnik. Techno Twins. Haysi Fantayzee. Blue Rondo à la Turk. Marilyn.

But maybe the biggest star of all would turn out to be the kid who sat behind Rusty's DJ booth on coat-check duty, swapping jackets for tickets – then rifling through the pockets when everyone's backs were turned. A stunning, living work of art by the name George O'Dowd.

The Blitz's banner creation: Boy George.

The Blitz Kids

You know a club is special when even its cloakroom attendant goes on to become a global, multi-platinum megastar – but the Blitz didn't just create chart acts like Spandau Ballet and Culture Club. It wasn't just a motley bunch of fashion students, wannabe rock stars and weirdos either. In that club, there were the makings of an entire cultural movement. There were writers, photographers, film-makers. Producers, promoters, painters. Actors, models, graphic designers. Everything you needed to launch a full-scale, multimedia assault on the world.

We even had an in-house hat-maker who went on to become internationally renowned. Millinery doesn't tend to churn out megastars, but Stephen Jones's early works could be seen every week atop the heads of some of the more adventurous Blitz Kids. Someone in a Roman chariot driver's helmet, a huge red brush plume sticking high above the crowd. Someone else in a gigantic black wedding veil, a wire scaffolding wrapped in lace. Stephen himself in a leather biker's cap, outlined in barbed wire.

Stephen's hats would go on to take pride of place on the heads of international icons like Grace Jones, Madonna, Barbra Streisand and Princess Diana, and he has since worked with every fashion house and catwalk model you could care to mention. The famous jewel-encrusted bishop's mitre that Rihanna wore to the Met Gala? That was one of his.

Hat-making might seem like a strange example to give but, for me, the fact it's so niche really encapsulates the overarching spirit of the Blitz. Whatever you wanted to do

– whatever – you could make it happen. If being a pop star was what you wanted, then you could go from the cloakroom to the charts in the blink of an eye. If it was making hats, why not? You could do that too and it wouldn't be long before the royal family was visiting your workshop.

The stage there was set for alchemy, but these things didn't happen in isolation. Everything was intertwined. To take these two as an example: Stephen would make hats for George, who made a fantastic model. George's look made him a cover star, which built both their profiles. When the inevitable record deal got signed, album covers, promo shoots and music videos all needed styling. Stephen creates more iconic headwear, while George commands yet more attention. Before you know where you are the two of them are starring in the video for Culture Club's first No. 1 single, 'Do You Really Want to Hurt Me?'*

That trajectory wasn't just theirs. Everyone at the Blitz was working on everyone else's projects, boosting each other at every turn. The same way that we acted as extras in their own mental movies, we acted as support staff for their artistic endeavours too. The photographers, stylists and writers for all those magazine profiles were sourced from the Blitz. The extras for our music videos were the people we partied with on Tuesday. The fashion students needed us to model their college catwalks? Point us towards the changing room. The promoters need a band to play their warehouse party? Show us the stage.

When Spandau signed our record deal, we needed a producer to make our album, a stylist to kit out our videos,

---

* Shot, in part, at 69 Dean Street, the former home of Billy's ...

a graphic designer to create our record sleeves – and we knew just where to find them.

In an era of jobs for the boys, the Blitz went one better. We had jobs for the boys, the girls and those in-between.

It pains me to skip over the contributions that so many bright and beautiful Blitz Kids made to the 1980s. So much has been written about the club over the years and there are always oversights and omissions everywhere. I'm going to be guilty of it too. If I concentrate on the people who broke out into the mainstream and became household names, I overshadow all the maverick geniuses who stuck closely to the beating heart of clubland and made it all so alive and vibrant. If I focus on the unsung heroes of that scene, whose ingenuity set the bar and propelled the rest of us to raise our sights, then it's hard to give you a full sense of just how far the Blitz bled into everyday life in the 80s.

Volume after volume could be written about the various seeds that took root in the Blitz and the many ways they went on to flower in various unexpected spots throughout the decade. I'll try to trace some of them in more detail as the story goes on, but I can honestly say without each and every one of those Blitz Kids, there is no way I would have enjoyed the career I've had. Everyone played their parts to perfection.

But a group like this always needs a conductor. Someone working behind the scenes to keep the show on the road.

For the Blitz – and for Spandau – that man was Steve Dagger.

The Mastermind

I find it hard to write about Steve Dagger now that I'm older and (supposedly) wiser. Hand on heart, I owe so much of all that is good in my life to that man. Had it not been for him – and whatever brain-damaging toxins were in the home-brewed cider we were drinking the night he instructed my brother to let me join his band – I have no idea where my life would have ended up.

Dagger was my brother's band's manager, at that time called the Makers. I had loved watching the Makers play and had often fantasised about being up there with them myself, but I was Gary's younger brother and I didn't really play anything.

I had a school punk band of my own, the Defects. We weren't going to set the world alight, but I wasn't half dedicated. We rehearsed in the basement of a friend's dad's dry cleaners, all our equipment precariously run through a single electrical outlet. We played songs like 'Cut Your Throat' and 'We Are Defects'. Before rehearsals I would get my mum's kitchen scissors and cut up pairs of my old pyjamas so I could wear the shreds. I'd take chunks out of my hair too, for a truly asymmetric style. I even showed an early flair for accessorising that would put me in good stead for my Spandau days, by taking the wire hangers that were lying around the shop and wearing them around my neck.

Gary was a proper musician, though. When we sat and listened to prog rock, Gary could understand all that stuff. I'd listen to Steve Howe play guitar or Rick Wakeman play keyboards and it all seemed so unattainable to me. These were masters of their craft. Virtuosos. Never in my wildest dreams could I picture becoming that good. How is a kid with a coat hanger round his neck ever going to compete with that?

I had figured the closest I would ever get to the stage myself was as a roadie, lugging the band's equipment on and off. So that's what I did.

Dagger had seen me about at gigs and said he liked my look. Maybe it was the bootlegged scrumpy talking, but he told my brother to kick their bassist out and get me in instead.

'But he doesn't even play bass!' my brother cried.

A fair, and completely correct, objection – but you ignore a man like Dagger at your peril. Within days, Gary was teaching me all his songs on a hand-me-down bass and I turned up to the next rehearsal. I was in.

It wasn't a fluke – as much as it felt like one. Dagger knew what he was doing. He had a real eye for this stuff. A sixth sense. Rather than idolising rock stars and fashion icons the way we all did, Dagger's big inspiration was Andrew Loog Oldham: the guy who broke the Rolling Stones.

Loog Oldham is a fascinating guy and a real trailblazer when it came to shaping the modern music industry. I wish I could do him justice the way Dagger can in the retelling of it, but suffice to say whatever mix of instinct, gumption and hard graft Andrew had to get the Stones eye-to-eye with the Beatles – it was alive and well in Dagger too.

Dagger had the look of an old-time soul boy. The wedge haircut. The slick suits. Blond, good-looking. That alone would have had everyone flocking around him whenever we were out at the Blitz, but Dagger is also an incredible storyteller. People sought him out because he was like a local paper. A Blitz fanzine in human form. Nothing happened on that scene without Dagger knowing about it. He kept hold of every thread, every storyline in that place like a housewife watching her soaps. He knew who everyone was, what they'd been doing last week, who they'd been doing last week. If you ever missed out on anything, the person who would catch you up was Dagger.

This was his business. Or it's what he made his business, at least. He was a people person but he had the eye of an engineer. In that club, he saw all the component parts of a machine. He knew everyone, what they each did, who would work well with who, who would cause a cataclysmic breakdown if they ever crossed wires. God knows how he took it all in, because the sheer scope of that scene has taken me the best part of four decades to get a handle on. But he did it.

Dagger's big idea to launch us was to make us a myth. The standard-bearers for the Blitz. A band that created events. Shows with no tickets. Spectacles spread by word of mouth.

The Blitz was already notoriously tricky to get into. Steve Strange's capricious whim on the door meant that crowds of people had got tantalisingly close to seeing the world we had created inside, but were turned away at the last minute because Steve had suddenly decided that this was No Blondes Hour.

Having been selected to play the Blitz Christmas party for our first gig as Spandau Ballet, we had become the de facto house band of this mystical club night. Already an air of intrigue surrounded us.

Our second show was at Mayhem Studios, Battersea – a sort of proto-warehouse party, organised by various Blitz

Kids. Films were projected on the walls, DJs blared music, drinks and drugs were passed around in copious measure. Hundreds of people were rammed into the room, but hundreds more were left out in the cold.

The ones turned away were left to imagine what had gone on there and it made them all the more determined not to miss out next time. From there, the myth would grow.

Dagger's plan built to a masterful execution on the night of 3 March 1980: our gig at the Scala Cinema. Spandau Ballet would play a set as part of an evening's specialist programming. Alongside a screening of Buñuel and Dalí's classic surrealist short film *Un Chien Andalou* and a poetry reading by our friend Bob Elms, we would play to a strict guest list of friends – and two hand-selected journalists.

Again, this was a Blitz Kids production. Our friends from the club, Simon Withers and Graham Smith, designed the lights and did our photography. Melissa Caplan came down and styled us to make sure we were looking our best.

And we looked fantastic.

The show went over big. We got a double-page spread in the *Mirror* – a feature by Christena Appleyard, which is now credited with coining the Blitz Kids moniker – and a page and a half in the *Evening Standard*. Two for two.

Dagger could have spread the news of this gig far and wide, but had deliberately limited the number of reporters he invited. Not just to add mystique to the proceedings, but to help further the interests of another Blitz Kid: Bob Elms.

The performance poetry was just a sideline. What Bob wanted to be was a journalist. What Spandau wanted to be was the biggest band in the country. Dagger, in full Loog

Oldham mode, saw these two things slotting together. After all, a myth is only as good as the number of people telling it. Dagger needed someone on the inside who could chronicle this Blitz Kids movement and sell it to the press on our terms. Bob was the one with the scoop. The guy could write and he had exclusive access to this hot new youth culture, which set him strides apart from the rest of Fleet Street.

So rather than invite an *NME* journalist down to the gig, Dagger told Bob to write a review, then cold-call the *NME* with it. Tell them, 'This is the review you're going to run.' Sure enough, they did.

With one ingenious flick of his wrist, Dagger had broken Spandau into the mainstream music press and Bob Elms into the cut-throat world of journalism.

This was only the start of Dagger's masterplan, though. Press clippings were nice, but they were just a stepping stone to what he knew was the inevitable next step.

The call.

Lift-Off

London Weekend Television had heard about the gig. They were sorry to have missed it. These Spandau Ballet boys and their Blitz Kids crowd sounded interesting. Was there any way they could do another? This time for the cameras?

The producer was Janet Street-Porter and she was making a series of films for LWT with Danny Baker about youth culture called *20th Century Box*. From what she was hearing of this Scala gig the other night, she thought it would make a good show. Were we interested?

Television. We were unsigned, had played the tiniest handful of gigs and now we were getting on television. Dagger was a fucking wizard.

From there, the tidal wave was unstoppable. Newspapers, magazines, camera crews, radio DJs; they all wanted to be there. Record labels, venue bosses, moneymen. The Blitz Kids were going to have to fight for their space, but they were the ones these people had come to see – and the Blitz Kids would never let an audience down.

At the time, the UK had just three TV channels and none of them broadcast for 24 hours. Between the news, Open University and the odd soap opera, there really wasn't much airtime to spare in 1980. So when footage of our Scala gig and the curious creatures who populated the crowd was broadcast, audiences could have been forgiven for thinking that another civilisation from beyond the stars was trying to make first contact through their TV sets.

The strange thing is, we never watched *20th Century Box* when it went out. Not because we were too cool to bother with it – we'd have been glued to the screen if we'd been around to catch it – but because we were otherwise engaged. We'd just been given our first foreign gig.

Saint-Tropez. For two weeks.

I've often described our time in Spandau Ballet as being like a ten-year holiday to Benidorm. Five mates who went off for a little bit of an adventure, and ended up spending a decade having the craziest time of our lives.

The reason I picked Benidorm is that, before the band, it was the only place I'd been abroad – on holiday with Mum, Dad and Gary. Even now, having travelled the world, it never really occurs to me to pick somewhere fancier for my simile. Now, like then, the idea that someone in Saint-Tropez had even heard of us – let alone liked us enough to actually pay us to come and visit – is too much for my mind to handle.

Saint-Tropez was not the sort of place the English working class ended up by chance. It was a retreat for the moneyed elite. Where the international jet-set parked their yachts for the season before heading back to their mansions and palazzos. It wasn't where kids from Islington council houses popped for a visit.

Did they make a mistake? Did they mishear that we used to be Gentry?

Our trip, I must confess, wasn't a sophisticated one. We tootled down to the South of France in a stinking-hot minivan: the five of us in Spandau, a few of our Blitz crew (Simon on lights, Graham on camera, Bob with his reporter's pad) and what felt like five hundred bags of Batchelors Savoury Rice foisted on us by parents who didn't know what we were going to be able to eat out there.

It was a good job too because the only thing we found when we opened our fridge in the apartment was a single bottle of poppers.

The contract was to play two sets a night at the Papagayo Club and the rest of the time was our own. Steve Norman and I spent it in our skimpies, lying out on the beach soaking up every last ultraviolet ray we could. Tanning wasn't really the fashion at the start of the decade (the 70s had been too grey and depressing for anyone to ever cultivate one) but it would become a big part of the 80s look. Ray-Bans, bronzed skin and blown-back beach hair – Steve and I were some of the style's earliest adopters that July.

I was always a little sad that Simon Withers' beach look didn't take off, though. Every day he turned up to the beach in his full-body leather bondage suit from Seditionaries, refusing to let a single sunbeam touch his skin. He insisted he would be disowning his culture if he stripped off and joined us.

Moving from beach to bar, to stage to bed and back became my life for two blissful weeks, but the trip wasn't just a jolly. Having only played a handful of highly curated events as a band, that intensive string of gigs really helped the band to tighten up. Playing once a month, we were at risk of just becoming a spectacle of style and sound. Saint-Tropez was where we developed our chops as a group and it put us in extremely good stead for what came next.

For when Steve Dagger got back home to London, he found some messages waiting for him on his side table. *20th Century Box* had been broadcast in our absence and now there were a few people waiting on him to call them back. Island, CBS, EMI, Virgin, Polydor and Chrysalis. The major labels were here and they all wanted in on it.

The Deal

When we signed our record deal, Gary carved out three conditions that ended up being absolutely instrumental to Spandau's success – and that of the wider New Romantic movement. I have no idea if he had a sudden flash of Steve Dagger Svengali-style inspiration, or whether he was just being cheeky and accidentally lucked out, but it doesn't really matter. It all worked out in the end.

As well as Chrysalis agreeing to cover our album and single costs, our contract stipulated that the band would also need an allocated budget for three things:

– Clothing
– Videos
– 12-inch single remixes

The clothing probably speaks for itself. We weren't just a band that threw together some songs and started playing. Our success was tied up with the Blitz and the Blitz wasn't solely a music venue. The look was vital and we couldn't rely on Laurence Corner forever. We wanted money to spend at PX, Willie Brown's and Axiom.

Music videos were a thing in 1980, but they weren't 'A Thing'. They wouldn't properly explode until the following year, but making sure that we had the money available to lock in a top-tier creative team for our videos was a return on investment for the label that made Gary look positively clairvoyant.

As for the 12-inch single remixes, I have no idea what possessed Gary to do that. This was not something that white-boy bands did. 12-inch remixes were the preserve of reggae and dub, of disco and funk. There was no precedent of that sort of thing with rock and pop bands like ours, but we were creations of the club scene and I guess Gary wanted to pay something back to clubland.

Me, I just wanted to sign a contract. I wanted to be standing in a studio, recording future radio hits. I wanted to be on *Top of the Pops*, posing for the camera. I wanted to be waiting in the wings of Wembley Arena as a voice boomed over the speakers, 'Ladies and gentlemen … The greatest rock'n'roll band in the world … Spandau Ballet!'

I didn't know how or why a 12-inch single remix clause would help with that, but it sounded like fun – so I was on board.

Top Five

Ironically, 'To Cut a Long Story Short' had taken a long, long time to wind its way from Halligan's Rehearsal Room to the Top 40. As fast as everything had been moving for us – whipping our way from that first showcase, to the Scala, to Saint-Tropez in a flash – a year in your teens can feel like an eternity when you're waiting for something. Especially at a club where the looks were changing every single week, where no one stayed still, constantly chasing the next new thing. It felt like, after a year, we should have a whole new sound, a whole new set of songs.

I was terrified we'd dragged our heels in signing a deal. Chris Blackwell from Island Records had originally offered to sign us right after that very first Spandau gig at the Blitz Christmas party and I could have killed Dagger with my bare hands when I found out he'd turned it down. His insistence on holding out for a bigger, better deal always felt like a dangerous game to me. There was nothing stopping anyone stealing our style and getting in ahead of us, and the club scene was nothing if not cut-throat.

Those synthesisers that had sounded so fresh, so vital in November '79, they were so easy to play and getting ever cheaper. With every day that passed, we were losing our advantage. Every time I saw Gary Numan or the Human League on *Top of the Pops* I got this gnawing feeling we'd already missed our moment.

Parallel scenes were beginning to pop up all over the country. Every city had a Blitz equivalent. The Rum Runner in Birmingham, which brought forth Duran Duran. The Warehouse in Leeds would give us Soft Cell. The

Crazy Daisy in Sheffield where Phil Oakey found Susan Ann and Joanna. Crocs in Rayleigh that spawned Depeche Mode.

I was convinced we'd waited too long when our debut single was released at the end of October 1980, but there were all these signs that started to tell me that – shock! – I might be wrong.

Peter Powell, who had been one of the broadcasters who came down to that *20th Century Box* show, had been playing our song on Radio 1. Rotation was good. None other than Bryan Ferry – a style god who took a back seat only to Bowie – had described the record publicly as 'witty' and 'smart'. News from the clubs was good too. Chrysalis's promoters had been getting a very positive response from DJs and dancers in nightspots around the country.

Could it actually be happening? Could we really break the charts?

It was a slow, steady build. It took a couple of weeks to make our way into the Top 40. It was a few more to slide up to the top 20 and start nudging up against the top 10. But on 6 December 1980 – one year and one day since we'd played Steve Strange's Blitz Christmas Party – we had done it.

'Spandau Ballet ... at No. 5 with ... "To Cut a Long Story Short".'

What a way to end the year.

1981
JOURNEY TO GLORY

Wedding of Charles and Diana | 'Tainted Love' | Raiders of the Lost Ark | *Brixton Riots* | *DeLorean* | Only Fools and Horses | *Death of Bob Marley* | 'You Cannot Be Serious!' | *Bucks Fizz Win the Eurovision* | *First London Marathon* | 'Ghost Town' | Donkey Kong | *Last Fight of Muhammad Ali* | 'Stand and Deliver' | 'Don't You Want Me' | Midnight's Children

The Kiss of Death

By 1981, the Blitz was no longer. Like everything beautiful in this world it burned bright and burned quickly. Steve picked up his pixie boots, Rusty collected his records and they went on to start a new night on Henrietta Street at a club called Hell.

What killed the Blitz? For my money, it was the same man that inspired it. David Bowie.

Both Billy's and the Blitz had begun life as Bowie nights. Though they were never officially billed as such and Rusty played all sorts of artists throughout the night, you only needed the swiftest glance around the room to see that we were all children of Bowie.

Everyone there had grown up watching this strange, shape-shifting phantasm. Even in his earliest days there was something otherworldly about Bowie, strumming his acoustic guitar and singing us songs of Major Tom. When he emerged a few years later as Ziggy Stardust, the androgynous alien rock star with a rusty red mullet, flared jumpsuits and haunting pale face, we were all obsessed.

Then the evolution into Aladdin Sane, with his striking lightning flash face. Then the Thin White Duke, the dashing aristocrat, supremely tailored and slickly coiffed.

If Bowie had been sent to us from another galaxy, then the Blitz was clearly the colony he'd established on Earth. So it made sense that word of the club would eventually reach the man himself.

Looking back at pictures of that night, it's weird to see just how ordinary Bowie looked. A plain grey suit. A plain white shirt. His hair a sort of semi-natural gold. If he was wearing make-up then it was uncharacteristically subtle. If it hadn't been for the reaction he'd stirred, you'd be forgiven for thinking he was the club's owner coming down from the office with change for the till, or someone's dad coming to pick up their kid.*

There was a reason for the formal wear, though. Bowie had come on business. He wasn't there to drink Schlitz, dance to Visage and chat with Barry the Rat. He had come to recruit a cast for his video 'Ashes to Ashes'.

'Ashes' had been a sort of renaissance for Bowie. His 'Berlin Trilogy' might have been critically acclaimed but he hadn't exactly been setting the charts alight in the late 70s. 'Ashes to Ashes' would change all this and give him his second UK No. 1, but he wanted the video to make a statement.

He selected four Blitz Kids – Steve Strange, Darla Jane Gilroy, Judi Frankland and Elise Brazier – who would each get 50 quid to come and star in his video. He gave them instructions to meet at the Dorchester Hotel at 5 a.m., then whisked them all down to the beach at Pett Level for a shoot.

---

* A cool dad, but a dad nonetheless.

48

The resulting video was huge. The most expensive music video that had ever been produced at that point, the whole thing exploded. But as massive as 'Ashes to Ashes' proved to be, it marked a grave turning point for the Blitz.

Us Blitz Kids had known for a while that the scene we had created was getting big. A blessing from Bowie cemented that – but it also killed it off. Mainstream acknowledgement usually means death for any young counterculture. For us, the killer kiss had come with that video. The Blitz style wasn't just the curious subject of an LWT documentary or a *Newsnight* report anymore. It was now tied inextricably to Bowie's biggest single.

Those nights couldn't continue after 'Ashes to Ashes'. The whole thing just looked like a tribute act.

Bowie soaked up a lot of their credit in 1980, but Darla Jane, Judi and Elise were every bit as responsible for the success of that video. Steve Strange was too. So in 1981 they decided they wouldn't let it happen again. The Blitz Kids were going to break loose from the club that gave us our name and out into the wider world to take what we knew was rightfully ours.

Top of the Pops

Even after the Blitz was over, my week still started and ended on a Tuesday because, until 1987 at least, Tuesday was the day the UK charts were announced.

The five of us and Dagger used to gather together in a wine bar called Serendipity up Camden Passage to wait to hear how our latest single had done that week.

Obviously chart positions are important to any band. You want to know if your new single has cracked the top 10. You want to know if you have outsold Duran Duran or Culture Club or Heaven 17. You want to know that you still have fans out there who would turn up if you went out on tour. But the real reason you cared about your chart position was because of the call that would come next.

Top of the Pops.

For bands, booking *Top of the Pops* was like making it to the FA Cup Final. I've heard all sorts of musicians who played the show remark about how tiny the studio was when they got there – even other members of Spandau – but I never felt that. It was small, sure, but every TV studio is small. Every set I've ever set foot on has always been smaller than it looked on the telly, and people always remark on it – so let me tell you right here and now: studios are always smaller, duller and darker than you imagine.

They're also incredibly mechanical places. For all the fun you saw on *Top of the Pops*, with kids dancing down the front and cuddling up close to the host to get themselves on camera, there was also an army of ruthless cameramen cutting about, stopping at nothing to get their shots. I cannot tell you the number of kids I witnessed trying to dance to the Thompson Twins or Haircut 100 and getting yanked about by their jumpers to make way for a cameraman swooping backwards across the studio floor. I wouldn't even want to hazard a guess at the number of toenails lost due to dollies rolling over unsuspecting audience members' shoes.

None of that ruined the magic for me, though. Being in that studio was like climbing inside of our telly to put on a show, and I loved it. I don't care who pretends they were too cool to be impressed by *Top of the Pops*. Yes, there were cooler, more credible shows, but *Top of the Pops* was one of those milestones that meant something to everyone. In a business that can be so insular and obsessed with metrics and measurement that normal people (rightly) don't care about, landing *Top of the Pops* was an achievement that anyone could understand.

I remember when we told Mum and Dad we were doing *Top of the Pops*. They called everyone they knew. Friends, family, neighbours, old school friends – even though they needn't have bothered. *Top of the Pops* was already unmissable appointment television.

When we told Mum and Dad we were doing *The Old Grey Whistle Test*?

'Ooh, no. That's on too late. We're not staying up for that.'

Booking *Top of the Pops* wasn't a given. Securing yourself a good position on Tuesday's chart would increase your chances, but it was by no means a guarantee. Conversely, some bands got extremely lucky and were drafted in as understudies when bigger acts fell through, which would often do wonders for their sales the next week.

If you'd made the top 20, though, the *Top of the Pops* call likely would come through that same night. And though the show wouldn't go out until Thursday, you had to get to work straight away.

We were so rushed with our first appearance in late 1980 for 'To Cut a Long Story Short' that we were still buying stage equipment and instruments on our way to the studio. We met some of it there, taking it all out of its packaging for the first time for the show.

When we were asked back for our second single, 'The Freeze', the band was much more settled. You can tell from my performance that I had got the measure of things. Because those performances were mimed and I didn't have to concentrate on actually hitting the right notes and the right time, I went off on one.

As our old pal Peter Powell introduced us and Tony stood stoic in the centre of the stage, I got myself right at the front of the stage and started going to town on my completely unplugged bass. My thumb goes hell for leather on those strings and I was stamping so hard on that stage, I was at risk of drowning out the bass drum on the backing track.

It was such a fun performance. Tony had this rugged little beard for that single and dressed like he'd come straight from a matinee of *Much Ado About Nothing* at the Globe. Steve Norman looked like a notorious French jewel thief in his dark glasses and beret. Gary clearly couldn't decide between styling himself as a Bedouin or one of Dexys Midnight Runners, so did both. I boldly mixed a burgundy doublet with bright red trousers, while John played it safe with classic black, because when you're stuck behind a drum kit all your effort gets wasted.

However, if you think *Top of the Pops* was just a case of dolling ourselves up and playing up to the cameras, there was a lot of work that went on in the run-up to that show. The strangest of all being the infamous *Top of the Pops* tape swap.

The Tape Swap

When Spandau first started having hits in the early part of the decade, the trade unions were still pretty powerful. Thatcher obviously did her level best to make sure that wouldn't remain the case as the years rolled on but, before she could really take her axe to them, there were a lot of rules in place. Even on *Top of the Pops*.

Especially on *Top of the Pops*.

The previous year – in the spring of 1980 – the Musicians' Union had gone on strike against the BBC. Rampant inflation in the wider economy was forcing the BBC to make budget cuts and they had proposed lining up some of the BBC orchestras for the chop. *Top of the Pops* – which still had an orchestra of its own back then – got caught up in the negotiations and was pulled from the schedules that summer as a result.

Luckily for Spandau, it coincided with our stint in Saint-Tropez but the teenage pop fans we'd left behind in Britain got stuck with a summer of *Are You Being Served?* re-runs in its place.

There's only so much of Mrs Slocombe's pussy a nation can endure, so the disputes were soon ironed out and *Top of the Pops* returned that autumn with a few big changes – thanks to a new producer, Michael Hurll.

Taking advantage of all the upheaval, Michael decided to modernise the show. These changes turned *Top of the Pops* into the glittering neon disco that so many fondly remember, as well as binning off the TOTP orchestra – which was something newer bands increasingly had no use for.

The Musicians' Union had to suck up those orchestra job losses, but in return they insisted that if bands were going to mime on stage, they would have to record backing tracks specifically for the show. If the track's original musicians were going to miss out on a payday playing live, they would get that money returning to the studio to re-record their parts instead.

As a plan, I can see how this would make sense for pop acts. I can also see the union's side of all this. For years they had a decent handle on all this stuff. Then, at the turn of the decade, they were blindsided with a triple whammy of changes.

There was a massive cost of living crisis, causing jobs like theirs to suffer early and suffer hard. A new Tory government had been elected that wasn't particularly interested in safeguarding the arts at the expense of the economy, and was extremely anti-union. On top of all of that, rapidly improving (and rapidly cheapening) synthesisers were threatening to destroy one of the last remaining avenues of profitable work – playing on pop music shows – completely.

But for Spandau, a band that already played all our own instruments, it made no sense. The Musicians' Union was asking us – forcing us – to rush record a worse version of a song we'd already spent months perfecting in the studio. Who did that serve?

Still, rules was rules and we had to obey them, otherwise we didn't get to play *Top of the Pops*.

Straight after we got the *TOTP* call therefore, we would block in a three-hour session in a studio (we used the Olympia in Barnes) to go through the whole rigmarole of setting up our gear, wiring up the mics and loading up the mixing desk, being ready to record at a second's notice, in case anyone from the Musicians' Union came down to check on us.

All we actually did was make a copy of the song onto fresh new tape from the original masters and then piss the rest of the time away chatting.

Putting my feet up in Barnes studio for three hours once every couple of months was no big deal. It was faintly ludicrous that we had to jump through hoops like that, but if it helped keep talented, creative artists in work in the long run, then I was more than fine with it.

At the end of those three hours, when we handed over a duplicate of the single they could have bought in Our Price, everyone involved knew what had happened, and pretending that this process was all working smoothly already felt unsustainable. Change was clearly coming. It was just a matter of when.

The Bible

At the end of the 70s, music journalism was in a dull place. Obviously we all still hoovered up every issue of *Sounds*, *NME* and *Melody Maker* – and savoured any scrap of pop culture news that made it to the proper papers – but the relentless focus on big, establishment acts was starting to stagnate.

Punk had brought a much-needed breath of fresh air to the industry in the form of zines: scrappy little self-published mags written by, and for, fans of the scene.

Zines like *Sniffin' Glue*, *London's Burning* and *Ripped and Torn* were never intended to be serious contenders for the mainstream press. *Sniffin' Glue* was typed up on a children's typewriter; its mistakes got scribbled out and its headlines were handwritten in felt tip. Issues were put together by hand by its writers, who would lay out thousands of photocopied pages in a circle all around them, rip a line of speed and then start doing laps of the room with a stapler.

The energy the zine scene generated was immense but, as always, punk tended towards destruction. The moment *Sniffin' Glue* sensed its scene was going mainstream, the editor (Mark Perry) shut the whole thing down and encouraged readers to go off and make their own zines instead.

That was the thing with punk. It encouraged creativity, but never longevity. It can be fun to build something just to break it, yes. Doing something purely for the thrill of it, with no thought of what lies beyond, is one of the great thrills of life. But when everything else in the country was being broken or crumbling down around us, having to watch every last thing we loved get torched was getting boring.

We needed something new – and, moreover, we needed it to last.

A black and white zine was perfect for the punk scene but it could never do justice to the striking style of the Blitz. It was so colourful, so alive. You can reflect the snarling, fuck-it-all-to-hell attitude of punk by scribbling and doodling and swearing on a photocopied pamphlet. But the New Romantics, to whom visuals were everything, would require something more glossy.

One magazine that had been trying something new was *Smash Hits*. Its founder, Nick Logan, had previously been the editor of *NME* and had grown equally bored of the rut that music journalism had fallen into. He'd had an idea for a magazine that unashamedly celebrated the colour, energy and spirit of modern pop.

Smash Hits had launched in 1978 and was a pretty immediate success.* A couple of years into the new project, though, Logan had got itchy feet again. He was getting the growing sense that this new wave of pop culture he'd been interested in covering wasn't just about bands.

The young people in clubland, who spent their entire weeks gearing up for a club night, weren't just there for the music. They were there to meet with people who were interested in everything. Writing. Photography. Film. Fashion. Art. These young people needed a magazine – a bible – that covered it all. So he created *The Face*.

It was one of a trio of new style magazines that would come to dominate the cultural conversation throughout the 80s. *The Face*, *i-D* and *Blitz* – each with their own ties to that very club.

The Face would make an early hire of Bob Elms, whose coverage of the New Romantics offered a true insider's view from the heart of the scene. *i-D* was co-founded by Perry Haines, a Blitz Kid who had graduated from St Martin's and wanted to create a street-style journal that challenged the cordoned-off world of high fashion. *Blitz*'s fashion editors were two pillars of the club night's style: Iain R. Webb and Kim Bowen.

I landed my first cover of *The Face* in March 1981 to coincide with the release of Spandau Ballet's debut album, *Journeys to Glory*. The feature inside was on the band but

---

* Although it would truly hit its stride in the mid-80s, when it regularly shifted as many as 800,000 copies a fortnight.

the cover? The cover was mine all mine. I was the face of *The Face*.

With these new magazines now being stocked in newsagents the length and breadth of the country, the New Romantic style was consolidating. What had once been a disparate collection of club nights was quickly becoming a single national trend.

And once it had gone national, there was only one place left for it to go.

International.

Paris

Photoshoots soon became as much a part of my life as the music. I never considered it to be modelling, as such. Being a model felt like it would be a whole other job, the way that being an actor was, or being a greengrocer. Getting my picture taken was just part and parcel of being a pop star.

The offers were so constant and so casually made that I thought nothing of accepting any that came my way. That's how I ended up agreeing to take a trip with Steve Strange and our friend Paula Yates to Paris. It was early '81 and Paula was working for *Cosmopolitan*. Her editors wanted a little New Romantic flair for their next issue, so the three of us were going to go and get our picture taken in front of the Eiffel Tower.

A simple enough assignment – or so we thought.

When we landed in Paris it was the middle of Fashion Week so, naturally, there wasn't a single hotel room available in the whole of the city. Luckily, you're never stranded for long when you're with Steve Strange. Steve always knew someone. His little black book made *War and Peace* look like a beach read. No sooner had he put in a call to some mystery acquaintance of his than I found myself standing in the lobby of the most outrageously expensive hotel on Place de la Concorde being handed this huge golden key by the receptionist. God knows how, but Steve had just blagged me, him and Paula the presidential suite.

Suddenly, we were the city's most important guests. We decided to make the most of our temporary VIP status and head out to the biggest club in the city, Privilege.

As we were away from home, we could reprise some of our signature looks without fear of rolled eyes. Steve dressed in his classic forest green velvet and pixie boots, looking like Peter Pan in his sullen teenage years. Paula didn't look that unlike his sidekick, Tinkerbell, an absolute vision in a gold lamé Antony Price dress – a single piece of fabric that wrapped its way beautifully around her body. I had put on what I had come to describe as my Mad Monk's outfit: a brown crimplene dress that I'd customised to give off more of a sexy Benedictine robe vibe.

Privilege had this big winding staircase that spanned two storeys. Playing up for the *Cosmopolitan* cameras, I thought it might be cute after a few drinks and a slap-up dinner to scoop Paula up in my arms and carry her up these stairs. She was tiny – as light as a bird – but unfortunately I somehow ended up catching my heel on some hanging part of her dress and got so tangled up in it that I managed to topple the pair of us. Paula fell down the stairs and, with one end of this Antony Price creation wrapped around my ankle, she ended up unravelling her way completely out of it, eventually coming to a halt – naked as a newborn – at the other.

Peter Pan came flying up the stairs to sort us both out, and bundled us all up and out of the way of the lenses.

After such an embarrassing display, we had no choice but to quickly and copiously drown ourselves in more champagne, all of which left us a little worse for wear when we arrived back at our big fancy suite in the not-so-early hours of the morning.

We crashed into bed and were woken what felt like minutes later to the sound of phones ringing, doors banging and a succession of Parisian hotel staff telling us we needed to vacate le room.

No amount of pleading could spare us. We would have to pack up our bags and our hangovers and haul our arses off somewhere else. Our Parisian fairy tale was over.

As I slunk out of the suite that I never should have had, who do I come face to face with but the person responsible for turfing us all out at that ungodly hour. Richard Nixon. Disgraced former President Richard Nixon, to give him his full title, but at that moment in time he wasn't anywhere near as disgraced as me. I can only imagine what he made of the sight of us spilling out of his suite. Me with my mascara, stubble and champagne breath; a tiny beautiful blonde pixie filing out behind me; then Steve Strange bringing up the rear, his face still thickly coated in Christian Dior pan make-up.

Actually, I noticed Nixon had a fair amount of slap on himself. I assume it was in readiness for some sort of TV appearance he had there that day, but who knows? Maybe he was riding the New Romantic wave too.

After all, America was next on our list.

The 21

I still have a Melissa Caplan piece in my wardrobe. I got it out recently to show my son, Roman, and I promise you the pair of us could have spent hours trying to figure out how you'd go about actually putting the thing on. It was part Japanese Samurai, part Egyptian Pharaoh and it came in about eight different sections. Visually, the thing is awe-inspiring. A genuine work of art. As a practical piece of clothing? I'd still be in my pants now, trying to crack its code.

But even though I no longer have the memory of how to operate that outfit, it brings back crystal-clear memories of Melissa.

Melissa Caplan was one of our earliest stylists and one of the designers we took out with us to New York in 1981. Dagger, who was always thinking ten steps ahead of us, had decided that rather than sending Spandau Ballet out to break America alone, he'd send a whole consignment of Blitz Kids.

At the time, I think I'd have had more luck getting my head around one of Melissa's outfits than I did this idea of Steve's. The five of us were barely drawing a wage from the money we'd been making as a band, and now he was suggesting we pay for a dozen-plus fashion students and models to join us on a trip to New York?

Even worse than getting a cut of our cash, they were going to be getting a cut of our attention too?

Obviously Dagger was a million per cent right. The opportunities he had seen in this New York trip had passed me by completely. As he knew (and I learned), the whole strength of the Blitz scene was how it functioned together. The music, the clothes, the look. What people were responding to so viscerally was the whole package.

It's not as if the fashion designers were strangers to us either. They were friends – good friends – who had started a radical new creative enterprise: Axiom.

Axiom was exactly the sort of initiative that encapsulated the spirit of the Blitz. A fashion collective headed up by our friend Jon Baker – known to all as 'Mole' – Axiom was made up of around 20 designers, couturiers, artists and photographers who worked together to stock and run a shop of the same name. Actually, by 1981, Axiom was two shops. The outpost on the fashionable King's Road in Chelsea was proving to be so successful that Mole was able to open a second location on Soho's fabled Carnaby Street.

What Axiom did for fashion wasn't that dissimilar to what Rusty Egan did for music. Whenever Rusty needed a particular sound to slip into his setlist, he didn't wait for some avant-garde German knob-twiddler to make it for him. He went and made it himself. Whether it was a Visage demo or creating some extra ambience with his synth drums, Rusty rolled up his sleeves and took care of it.

The genius of Axiom was asking why fashion had to be any different. If you had a design in mind that you wanted to see on the street, why wait? You didn't need permission. You just needed to do it.

Axiom gave upcoming designers that shot. Mostly made up of fashion students (but not exclusively), the shop was somewhere they could take the items they'd been whipping up in their workshops and start selling them. They met each Thursday evening to drink, smoke and plan, and the designs that were in their heads one week would be on hangers in Axiom the next.

It all made so much sense. Why should these talented young creatives pin their hopes on someone deigning to come down to see their end-of-year catwalk show at St Martin's, crossing their fingers they might be offered some junior assistant job on the bottom rung of the ladder at a fancy fashion house, where they'd hand over all their brilliant designs to be absorbed, diluted and spat out in some more commercial form, stripped of their individuality?

Fuck that. If they had the tools to turn their designs into items, the moment was now. These looks were already blowing up the pages of magazines like *i-D* and *The Face*. Not all of us Blitz Kids were so handy with a needle and thread, and we wanted to look as sharp as they all did. The market was there. The drive was there too. So why waste any more time?

Axiom played home to a number of our friends. Melissa, who styled our early videos. Simon Withers, who'd done Spandau's light design at the Scala and Papagayo. Chris Sullivan, the Blitz's best-turned-out dandy, who would later design our suits for the 'True' video.

It even included a friend of ours who had a very short-lived and under-discussed career in fashion, which became eclipsed when she swapped it for an international career of singing superstardom: Sade.

In another time, Spandau and Axiom might not have had anything to do with one another. Two separate disciplines sharing a similar spotlight. But not now. This was our time. We were all in this together.

I had no idea what to expect from America. I had never been before and had only seen New York on TV. Half of the image in my head was *Kojak*; the other half was *Top Cat*. I was completely clueless. But whatever culture shock I was in for arriving in New York City for the first time, New York City was about to get an even bigger one.

Our gang became described in the press as 'The 21', as there were 21 of us and we had an average age of 21.* We were young, we looked like nothing else and we were ready to take America by storm.

Hitting the streets in outfits styled by Melissa, Simon, Chris and others from Axiom, the pictures really do make it look like an invasion. Even if New Yorkers were used to seeing films being shot on their streets, there wasn't a movie on earth that had a bunch of characters like us.

The event the trip was hinged around was a showcase gig in a venue called The Underground. Axiom would stage a fashion show to start; Spandau Ballet would play a set to close – but the press out there couldn't wait. They were desperate to know everything they could about us. We'd barely had a chance to take any photos of ourselves before the press were doing it for us.

Spandau were whipped from pillar to post, with appearances at record stores that had already been selling hundreds of copies of our albums on import only. Andy Warhol's magazine *Interview* wanted to do a feature on us. Invites for parties at penthouses and nightclubs around Manhattan were coming in constantly, while press conferences soon became multimedia previews.

Things hadn't been quite so easy for the designers. Customs officials had given Melissa a hell of a time at

---

* That was the line at least; I'm not sure it was in anyone's interests to count too closely.

border control going through all her outfits one by one (they probably had the same trouble I did figuring out how on earth they actually went on). Simon Withers reckoned he was close to getting deported when he saw the border guards' reactions to some of the military-influenced pieces he'd packed – their eyes widening yet further when they saw just how many stamps his passport had from East Germany.

But under Dagger's masterful eye, everything was soon smoothed over and we were all getting ready for our big show.

Big Night Out

Of all the drugs that were taken in the 80s – and there was a wide array, depending on who you were and where you went – the one that defines the decade is cocaine.

Because it goes arm in arm with that mega-moneyed yuppie culture, and because it heightens every single one of the egocentric, arrogant and decadent impulses that the 80s indulged, it was destined to become the decade's drug of choice.

That's not to suggest that the 80s invented cocaine. You only had to look at your standard record company exec in 1980 to see that plenty of cocaine had already been consumed. If you weren't careful, though, you could quickly find yourself in the centre of an all-encompassing snowstorm.

I remember the first time I saw just how prevalent it was in the music industry on an early business trip with the band, taking a flight with some label types.

A short while after take-off – almost the second we reached cruising altitude – the guy next to me flipped down his little tray table, pulled a bag of coke from his pocket, chopped out a line in full view of everyone and then used this small silver straw he had on a chain round his neck to hoover it up. Not a discreet little sniff either. A huge ripping great snort.

I've always found it funny that he was happy to take cocaine at top volume, in plain sight, but didn't want to risk getting snapped at by the stewardess for having his tray down before the captain had extinguished the seatbelt sign. Or perhaps he was just waiting until the plane levelled out so his line wasn't at risk of sliding off his table and into his lap.

Whatever it was, this kind of open drug-taking was all par for the course.

If cocaine had a challenger for the crown, then there was a new drug coming up through the decade: something called MDMA. As a powder, it picked up in popularity in the early 80s. In pill form, as ecstasy however, the drug would dominate the end of it with the Second Summer of Love and the growing rave scene.

Spandau were always more of a drinking band. We weren't always brilliantly behaved, by any means, but we never went in for the drugs in the way some of our contemporaries did. Seeing the state some of them were in in the middle part of the decade, I reckon we dodged a massive class-A bullet – but there's no denying they were a huge part of the business in those days.

Weirdly, I had my first experience of both coke and MDMA on the same night – almost entirely accidentally.

It happened the night of our show in New York, as the headline act of The 21. After we played, we were greeted by the usual crowds you get after a showcase like that. Everybody smothers you, everybody wants to shake your hand and tell you that they loved your band. It can be an overwhelming experience, with voices coming in from all angles, taps on the shoulder spinning you in circles. In the cut and thrust of it all, a drink was shoved into my hand. Champagne. Only the good stuff for the heroes on stage. I chucked it back, handed the glass off to someone and got back to getting my arse kissed.

By this point in our career, I was pretty familiar with the feeling of adrenaline. I knew the sort of buzz I got from playing a gig. As much as it was amazing to be in New York and to be going over so well with the crowd here, I couldn't see anything about this place that made it so fantastically special that I should start to feel as if I was actually levitating.

So what the fuck was going on with my feet?

I hadn't immediately noticed that I couldn't feel my feet touching the floor because I had become transfixed by the glowing tip of a woman's cigarette.

This woman wasn't talking to me. She wasn't even in our circle. She was right across the other side of the room, but somehow my eyes had zoomed in on the pulsing embers and they were all I could see. When I eventually decided to leave, that was when I felt like I was floating. Heaven knows what I looked like to anyone in the room who was watching me try to walk, but I felt as if the soles of my shoes were about three feet off the ground and my head and neck were brushing across the ceiling.

Whatever shape my body was in, something was very obvious to the member of our road crew who took me by the hand and hauled me off to the bathroom.

'Your drink's been spiked,' he said. 'Hang on.'

I stared at myself in the mirror. I looked like Steve Strange with his Martian contacts in. My pupils were so big, so black, it looked like someone had ripped two holes in the fabric of the universe and put them where my eyeballs should be.

'What was it?' I asked, dreading that he'd say the word 'heroin'.

'MDMA,' he said. 'It's a new drug. A bit like LSD.'

It was the first I'd heard of it, but it at least explained why gravity had decided to take a coffee break.

'Listen. Look.' He drew my attention to a long white line that had appeared on the lid of the toilet seat. 'This will sort you out if you need to come down. OK?'

'What was it?' I asked again, again dreading that he'd say the word 'heroin'.

Maybe it was because MDMA was such a new thing that even roadies didn't yet know how best to counterbalance its effects, but I'm not convinced this line did the trick of levelling me out. It was cocaine.

I don't particularly want to glamorise the world of drugs. I have seen friends struggle with addiction of various types and it is awful to watch. I also know that some of the stuff we were offered back in the day is nowhere near the chemical composition of what's on the market now. So I offer the next few paragraphs purely for the historical record. This was my experience.

When I left the bathroom, I was told to get my stuff together as we were leaving the party. We were off to Bond's to see a gig. Blondie. I had always loved that band and Debbie Harry was one of the hottest stars in the world

– in every sense of the word. I couldn't miss this. I just couldn't.

Now, my memories of that night are strangely clear but they're also a little … let's say limited. Like Privilege in Paris, Bond International Casino also had a huge staircase winding its way from the entrance to the dancefloor. The sort of thing you'd see in a Disney film; an ostentatiously grand feature.

My head was still swimming. I wasn't sure how or when I would ever feel normal again, but I could at least feel my feet on the ground. I knew when I was taking a step. Which made it all the more weird to me that every time I did, I felt a flash of light and heard a note ring out like a fanfare announcing my arrival. I took another step and, again. Light. Sound.

I looked down at my feet. The flash of light was still there, all round my shoe. I couldn't see the note, but it was still ringing in my ears. I took another step. And another. Was that … 'The Star-Spangled Banner'?

I stepped again. It was! The staircase was a giant piano! And it was playing the American national anthem!

Fearing I must still be hallucinating, I went back down to the foot of the stairs, only to hear the notes play out in reverse. This wasn't my imagination. I didn't know 'The Star-Spangled Banner' backwards. This was the steps. They were playing along and if danced on them, I could make beautiful, beautiful music.

It would be years later that I saw the film *Big*, where Tom Hanks plays out a slightly more PG version of this same incident. His trippy, out-of-body experience comes thanks to a weird end-of-the-boardwalk curse, rather than accidentally ingesting a cocktail of narcotics in a gay club in Union Square, but the similarities are uncanny.

Did someone watch me spend the entirety of a Debbie Harry gig in 1981 prancing up and down a set of musical stairs, making each step sing as I giggled delightedly like a child trapped in the body of an adult, then sell the screen-play to Hollywood?

Can it be a coincidence that FAO Schwarz put its iconic walking piano on display in 1982 – the year after I put on this impromptu performance for the patrons of Bond's – a venue just a few short streets away from their flagship store?

And am I, Martin Kemp, really the inspiration for one of cinema's most beloved, heartwarming scenes (therefore, arguably, responsible for the enduring box-office success of multiple Academy Award winner and beloved global icon Tom Hanks)?

As I say, I don't want to glamorise drugs. But it's import-ant to get all this on record.

Video

Smoke rolls over the cobbled street. A blinding light shines from way over yonder. As synths start to swirl and drums ring out – snares echoing like gunshots – a horse trots slowly forward. A woman, clutching a fur coat to her chest, runs out into the cold night air.

Then comes the voice.

Dressed in a trenchcoat, looking every inch the film noir detective, Midge Ure walks towards the camera with an upturned collar and an immaculately sharp moustache.

Mysterious shadows are cast upon the church in shades of midnight blue, as he takes his place underneath a statue and sings out into the frosty dark.

As the second verse starts, the scene changes. Colour suddenly floods the frame. The cinematic widescreen starts to shift. Boundaries we hadn't even noticed were there expand, transporting us somewhere completely different. An ambassador's reception? A royal banquet? A Bullingdon Club social?

What is this? Where did the woman go? Where is that horse?

It is hard to explain the exact feeling I had when I first saw Ultravox's video for 'Vienna'. The jumble of cinema, drama, music and lights was exhilarating. All I knew is that I loved it and that Spandau should be doing it too.

We had already shot a couple of videos by this point, but nothing like this. Our first, 'To Cut a Long Story Short', was filmed in the London Dungeon and saw the five of us dressed in tartans, playing our hearts out for the camera. There were tiny hints of a story in there, I suppose. A few shady looking characters playing a game of cards in a corner. A couple of women dancing in black lace by candle-light, surrounded by the bars of the cells. But mostly the focus was on us: five good-looking lads belting out their song.

Our second video, for 'The Freeze', was a bit more abstract but still fairly simple. Tony directed most of the singing to a stunning model draped across a chaise longue, while the rest of us played on behind a backlit screen.

This had been the way of things up until now. All anyone expected of a music video, right from the earliest days of the Beatles, was some footage of the band playing their song. Simple promo clips. Even 'Bohemian Rhapsody', which often gets cited as the first modern music video, is basically just a very engaging concert performance. Fundamentally, it's Freddie and the boys playing the song under hot stage lights – and occasionally directly over them too.

That's not to say that a lot of thought or love hadn't gone into any of these videos. It had. Shooting our first video was a dream come true and we took every last second of it seriously. Whether it was getting Melissa Caplan in to style us in our tartan tabards, or forking out for a fancy velvet pirate's jacket from PX, we knew the styling was essential. That's why we also had our studio sets echo the graphic motifs that Graham Smith worked into our record sleeves, to ensure a cohesive visual through-line from single to album to video.

But 'Vienna'? That video influenced just about everyone who made a music video in the 1980s – whether they knew it or not. What Ultravox had produced for that track wasn't just a promo clip. It was a movie. Shot on 16mm film, it looked like something you would see in a cinema, not on *Top of the Pops*.

What's more, the video didn't represent the band. It represented the song. It took the imagined world that Midge was singing about and painted it up on the screen for everyone to share in.

The really fascinating thing about 'Vienna' is that it almost didn't happen. The record company was really against putting the song out at all – even as a single.

If you weren't around in early 1981, I should make it clear just how huge a hit 'Vienna' ended up being. It spent ages on the charts and was No. 2 for a full month. It was kept from the top spot first by John Lennon (understandable, as his assassination had just rocked the world), then by Joe Dolce (less so, but the 80s – I admit – weren't perfect).

'Vienna' remains Ultravox's biggest and best-remembered hit but the record label released it so reluctantly back in '81 that they point-blank refused to stump up any extra cash for an accompanying video. So the band took matters into their own hands and paid for it themselves.

As you've seen already, decisions like this came easy to Blitz Kids like Midge. If there was something you wanted to see in this world, then it was up to you to make it.

I don't think it's an exaggeration to say that the decision to self-fund that video was a watershed moment in pop culture history. I can only really speak for myself and Spandau when I say how completely obsessed we were with 'Vienna', but you only need to look at the list of bands and artists that went on to hire the video's director, Russell Mulcahy, over the next few years to see the impact it had.

Russell was an Australian who came to London to shoot a music video and got on so well here that he decided to stick around. He was quickly inundated with job offers too. As well as blowing our minds with 'Vienna' he'd already directed videos for the Stranglers, the Human League, Paul McCartney and the Vapors' breakout hit 'Turning Japanese'.

As Midge was a pal from the Blitz, it wasn't a struggle to get Russell on board to shoot our next single, 'Muscle Bound'. Unlike Ultravox, we had a guaranteed budget from the record label to make it – so we dragged Russell up to the Kirkstone Pass in the Lake District and got ready for the shoot.

Originally, we'd arranged to be there for a two-day shoot but our plan quickly came unstuck as the area was hit by an unexpectedly massive snowfall. It made the setting look absolutely incredible, but filming absolutely impossible.

Locked in a little pub, those two days soon became four. From a creative point of view, the extra time (both thinking and drinking) gave us the opportunity to expand our ambition for the video, allowing us to map out a mini-epic of our own. A movie in the three minutes that could happily go toe-to-toe with 'Vienna' in terms of spectacle, intrigue and impact.

From a financial point of view, well … you'd have to ask the record label about that. That expanded ambition came with a slightly heftier stack of receipts, but I maintain it was money well spent.

In those days, the money for music videos tended to come out of a label's PR and marketing budget. The reason for that was the video would get sent around to TV stations all over the world in the hopes that they'd be tempted to stick the video on whatever music shows they had. This wasn't simply a way of driving record sales in multiple markets; it also saved the label having to fork out for five plane tickets and five hotel rooms every time we needed to do a morning TV spot in Amsterdam or Germany or Australia.

The shift, post-'Vienna', for making mini-epic movies as music videos saw a big upswing in production costs. You weren't just shooting a mimed performance on videotape that landed in the can in a few hours. Bands now wanted 16mm film for multi-day shoots across a series of locations with a whole cast of extras. 'Muscle Bound' looked more like an early *Game of Thrones* trailer than a standard pop promo, and it was hugely exciting.

This all came at a price, but now that the visuals were an essential part of the pop-star package, it wasn't something you could afford to scrimp on. You had to be riding horseback through the Lake District across recently thawed rivers. You needed to hire a trio of dwarves to act as mystical mages. The dozen mallet-swinging peasants on the call sheet were essential to the plot.

Even though the finished product came in at well over twice the agreed budget, 'Muscle Bound' was exactly what we wanted. Ultimately, things must have balanced on marketing's books too because the label let us shoot more videos, and let us shoot them with Russell again.

It's a miracle we were able to continue to hire him another half-dozen times over the next few years, though, because looking over Russell's CV today, it's possible he was the hardest-working person in the whole of the decade.

Among the era-defining videos he's shot – still held up as icons of the age – are: 'Rio' for Duran Duran, 'I'm Still Standing' for Elton John, 'Total Eclipse of the Heart' for Bonnie Tyler and 'Gypsy' for Fleetwood Mac.

Russell also went on to make one of the great cult movies of the 1980s, *Highlander*.

But as much of an impact as all of those might have had, it was another Russell Mulcahy video that would have the biggest impact. Not just on 80s pop culture, but pop culture as we know it today.

The first video to be played on a fledgling new TV channel that would define a generation. The debut song on MTV: 'Video Killed the Radio Star'.

MTV

As a statement of intent, you could not have commissioned a better one than 'Video Killed the Radio Star'. It was an almighty power move straight out of the gate – a potent shot of punk spirit, with a New Romantic chaser.

Yes, we're going to kill your radio star, but we've brought you this bold and brilliant replacement.

To start with, MTV was only available in the States, but that wouldn't make it any less valuable to us. The UK wasn't particularly well served with music programming (though things would change on that front soon), but we got by alright with *Top of the Pops* and *The Old Grey Whistle Test*.

What was great about MTV was that, even if we couldn't watch it ourselves, it opened a direct line into the living rooms of America. Before that, it had taken years of touring that vast country to make even the tiniest dent in it. Bands told tales of having to grind from club to club, city to city, state to state. To have any chance of being able to say you had 'broken' America required a detailed five-year plan, a punishing schedule that had you back there constantly working.

MTV didn't eliminate that process entirely, but for a few golden years it gave British bands a vital head start on it.

When it launched, the station was dedicated solely to playing music videos, 24/7. In its first day, MTV played over 200 videos. That's a phenomenal turnover and it relied on them repeating a number of songs throughout the day.*

* 'In the Air Tonight' by Phil Collins was played five times in the first 24 hours. So was 'You Better You Bet' by the Who.

If MTV was to have any hope of holding anyone's interest, it would need a constant influx of new material. There's only so long you can keep watching the same day's programming again and again.

It was an ambitious enough goal, made infinitely more difficult by the fact that American music videos were – by and large – terrible. For the most part, they were uninspired, drably shot performances or cobbled together from existing concert footage. They were lucky screensavers hadn't been invented yet, or those animations would have run rings around early American music videos.

The UK, on the other hand, had already got quite a bit of practice in at making innovative mini-movies. It's no coincidence that 'Vienna' was played that first day of broadcast. Nor that four of Russell Mulcahy's videos made the cut – including the opening spot. The pop promos we Brits were cutting were exciting, eye-catching short films. They had drama and intrigue and sexy models.

As a result, that first day on MTV was absolutely littered with UK artists. Of the first five videos played that night, four were British: the Buggles, Rod Stewart, the Who and Ph.D. There were dozens of others throughout the rest of the day too. Bowie.* Iron Maiden. Phil Collins. Kate Bush. The Specials. Cliff Richard. Robert Palmer. The Vapors. Elvis Costello.

Up until now, we had been making music videos mostly because we could. They were fun to do, they played to our

---

* One song they showed twice was Bowie's 'Boys Keep Swinging', the song Rusty Egan was playing the night I first stepped foot in the Blitz.

strengths and the record companies weren't complaining because the budget was there to be used. But the birth of MTV gave us purpose and a sense of direction. Now we had a reason to make them unmissable.

America was the biggest music market in the world and it was crying out for quality videos. MTV didn't have anything like the domestic supply it needed to survive. While they got to work on fixing that, the channel would have to rely on imported British videos by the crate load to keep itself on air.

I suppose, under the circumstances, we could have tossed off any old rubbish and they'd have stuck it on air, no questions asked. I'm sure some bands did. It was a buyers' market, but it was also a gold-plated opportunity. A cheat code to success in America.

All we needed was a dynamite video.

Le Beat Route

Of all the videos we shot over the years, I still think our best is 'Chant No. 1'. It's not the most ambitious, nor is it the most expensive, but there's something about it that captured a very particular moment in time.

The shoot took place in a newly opened club on Greek Street called Le Beat Route. After the Blitz ended in 1980, this was one of the Soho clubs we Kids migrated to.

If the Blitz had been a celebration of the feminine side of our souls – its music mysterious and ethereal; the materials all taffeta, lace and silk – Le Beat Route was distinctly masculine. It left behind all the futuristic, androgynous, sexually ambiguous stuff and replaced it with straight Zoot suits. The jackets were long, the shirts were bright and while the hair remained pretty big, it wasn't sculpted into gravity-defying shapes anymore.

Le Beat Route's owner, Steve Lewis, had been looking back over to America for inspiration rather than Europe. His dancefloor writhed with muscle and sweat and funk. James Brown. Kid Creole and the Coconuts. Indeep. The Valentine Brothers.

Gary had been looking the same way for inspiration too. You could hear it on the Spandau track 'Glow'. 'Glow' was a song we'd recorded a bit too late to include on the *Journeys to Glory* album, but we were so keen to release it we stuck it out as a double A-side with 'Muscle Bound'. Listening back, you can hear how it bridges the gap from Spandau's early synth-pop to something like 'Chant No. 1', with its slinky guitar intro and its full-on blast of horns.

At this point, I felt as though the band was still completely connected to the club scene and could be relied upon to play something that people wanted to dance to on a Friday night. It helped that Le Beat Route's DJs on a Friday night were fellow Blitz transplants Ollie O'Donnell, Chris Sullivan and Steve Mahoney, but that wasn't really a coincidence. In the middle of '81, we were all still as tapped into the sound of clubland as we had been back in Halligan's Rehearsal Room. Soho still represented what was going on in Spandau, and Spandau still represented what was going on Soho.

The resulting video is a real who's who of the scene at that time. We didn't intend to assemble an all-star cast. We just had Dagger put the word out and invite our mates down, but if you keep your eyes peeled you'll see faces that went on to litter the charts over the next few years. Haysi Fantayzee, Blancmange, Ultravox, Swing Out Sister. There were early cameos from some soon-to-be multi-platinum sellers like Sade and Culture Club. And the brief snapshot that everyone now tries to hit pause on YouTube for: George Michael.

Much like Spandau had become the flag bearers for the Blitz, the band that would emerge from Le Beat Route was Wham! It was the club where Andrew first came up with the lyrics for 'Wham Rap!'. 'Club Tropicana' was written specifically to re-create the spirit of a night out there. And – although I wouldn't learn this for another year – it was also where my future wife had been busy practising dance routines, getting ready for the *Top of the Pops* performance that would later steal my heart.

Being the band that symbolises a specific scene is a real honour but, in all honesty, it doesn't always feel as if we actually had that much to do with creating it.

The arrogance of youth will tell you that it's all your doing. You look out from the stage and see the heaving crowd and think 'They're all here for me' – but that's not the whole story.

I've always maintained that the best moments in Spandau were the ones where it didn't even really feel like we were in a band. It was when we felt like we were part of the audience. It didn't matter who was up on stage making the music. That was just one small part of it. A technicality. A trivial detail. What was important was the atmosphere – and that was being created by everyone. The boundaries between band and audience fall and you all become one. The scene is what makes it.

That's why I think 'Chant No. 1' is our best video. It's not lavish, it's not high concept and I definitely don't get the most screen time, but it represents that scene in that specific moment – and that is like trapping lightning in a bottle.

What makes the memory so pronounced in my mind now is that, while we had managed to hit the sweet spot with Chant No. 1, our star was about to start waning.

Our upcoming schedule was going to start splitting us away from the club scene. We were flying all over the world now. Our weekends were spent promoting records or playing Saturday-morning shows across Europe. No matter how late we went to bed or how early we got up, every engagement felt like it was keeping us away from the heart of things. Every night we were checked into a fancy hotel somewhere was a night we wouldn't be out with the Blitz Kids, soaking up more influences.

We were drifting off into our own little bubble. The Spandau Bubble. And while the Spandau Bubble could be an amazing place to be, the constant churn of 80s culture meant that we were soon going to start floating away.

Fashions were developing without us. Sounds were maturing. Technology was ripping ahead at such a rate that the most innovative productions might already be passing us by.

Steve and Rusty had already left Hell and were headed for Club for Heroes on Baker Street. Soon they'd be launching the Camden Palace.

The Blitz family – while all extremely active – had no spiritual home anymore. As the Blitz house band, it had left Spandau more than a little unmoored. Without the Blitz, who were we?

Everyone else was out in the wilds of Soho finding their niche. All we were about to find – like so many bands before us and since – was that our second album would struggle. Massively.

1982

DIAMOND

Falklands War | ET: The Extra Terrestrial | *Prince William Is Born* | *Ra-Ra Skirts* | *Ozzy Osbourne Bites the Head off a Bat* | *Channel 4* | *'Come On Eileen'* | TRON | *First Successful Artificial Heart Transplant* | *Commodore 64* | *The Haçienda* | *Barbican Centre* | The Dark Crystal | *'Eye of the Tiger'* | Jane Fonda's Workout | The BFG | Fast Times at Ridgemont High | *Reagan's War on Drugs* | *España 82 World Cup* | Thriller | *ZX Spectrum* | *'Physical'* | Combat Rock | Sophie's Choice | *Malibu*

The Playback

Immediately after the success of 'Chant No. 1' in the summer of 1981, Spandau were on a high. We had returned with a single that spoke to the heart of Soho, pushed our sound in a new direction, given us our best chart position so far and – crucially – was selling by the tonne.

But our fortunes would soon change.

Our next single, 'Paint Me Down', stalled a bit in the charts, only reaching No. 30. Promotion hadn't been helped by a rather risqué video we'd shot for it that *Top of the Pops* declined to play. As well as the police getting called to the shoot because some passers-by had confused our semi-naked dancing on Parliament Hill for an early morning Satanic ritual, it also contained quite a lot of flesh.*

---

* One of the signature visual motifs of our director Russell Mulcahy was to drip paint suggestively down people's bodies. You're more likely to have seen the technique appear in Duran Duran's 'Rio', though, because nobody ever played 'Paint Me Down'. In part, because the white paint dripping down Paula Yates's naked back in it could have been misconstrued.

'She Loved Like Diamond', the next single, didn't even make the Top 40 – even though we kept our clothes on for that video. We were having to fight to cut through but, in all honesty, I should have known that this was in the pipeline. Our playback had been a disaster.

When you finish recording an album, you stage a listening event called a playback. It's where label managers and record execs and maybe a few journalists and tastemakers are brought down to your studio to be given a first listen. The way it should work is that you put out some wine and nibbles, do a bit of glad-handing with the big-wigs, blow a bit of smoke up the right behinds and then knock everybody's socks off with your amazing new record.

The *Diamond* playback didn't quite go like that.

It started off fine. 'Chant No. 1' had everyone sitting up in their seats. Spandau had got funky. Brass, bongos, a big bass groove. Even a little hip-hop thing going on at the end. This was something different.

Tracks two, three and four carried on in much the same vein. It all seemed to be going down well.

Then we got to Side B.

I'll get in trouble with Gary if I call the second half of *Diamond* shite, so I won't. But it isn't our best work. I actually don't mind it quite as much as the reviewers and the record execs seemed to, but I can also see why they reacted the way they did.

The mood in the studio as seven-minute songs like 'Pharaoh' and 'Missionary' played out was absolutely leaden. Not a smile to share between anyone. Clearly people couldn't think of anything nice to say about this second side, so they slipped out the door before they had to.

It's well known that second albums are difficult. The received wisdom is that your first album is the product of your entire life's experience. Every influence you've soaked up, every little melody you've whistled. Without knowing it, you've been crafting this first album in your head for 20 years. The whole reason you formed a band in the first place was to bring this set of songs into the world, so by the time you eventually sign a deal and reach the studio, these songs are so ripe they're ready to burst.

Then the slate gets wiped completely clean and you have six months to make another. From nothing. And good luck trying to snatch a quiet moment in between all the touring, TV appearances, radio promos and parties to write anything new. Churn out more of the same, people think you're a one-trick pony. Anything too different and you alienate your fan base. The clock is ticking too. You need to get this next album down before everyone gets bored and moves on. Your rivals are waiting in the wings to take your spot – and besides, you can't back out now. You signed a contract.

So if you've ever wondered why follow-up albums are never as good as the first, that's why.

Poor Gary was under extraordinary pressure. As the band's sole songwriter the whole Spandau enterprise lived or died by his hand. I think a lot of *Diamond*'s second side was a product of that pressure.

We also had a problem in that Richard Burgess, our producer, was getting extremely busy. As was the way with Blitz Kids, his fingers were in a million other pies and he was being pulled in all sorts of directions. His own band, Landscape, were in the charts with 'Einstein a Go-Go'. He was working on R.E.R.B with Rusty Egan.* He was producing singles for Hot Gossip (Perri Lister was another Blitz Kid).

As the minute-long fade-out of 'Missionary' twanged its way to the end, we knew it hadn't gone well. The label didn't have faith in it, we were swiftly losing faith in it and now our fans weren't buying it. A perfect storm. Of shit.

It looked to all the world as if it was over. We'd had a few good years, put out a few good tracks, but that was that. Time to quietly see out our contract and fade into obscurity.

Spandau had one last roll of the dice, though. There was a potential final single we could possibly salvage from *Diamond*, but we were going to need a miracle if we were going to pull it off.

Thankfully, we knew a miracle worker. The man who made the 80s ... Trevor Horn.

The Remix

It is impossible to imagine what the 80s would have sounded like if it hadn't been for Trevor Horn. As well as giving MTV its flagship song, 'Video Killed the Radio Star', Trevor's pioneering work behind the production desk gave the decade some of its most celebrated albums.

Masterpieces like ABC's *The Lexicon of Love*, Frankie Goes to Hollywood's *Welcome to the Pleasuredome*, Grace Jones's *Slave to the Rhythm*. He produced for Pet Shop Boys, Simple Minds, Paul McCartney. He created the Art of Noise.

* R.E.R.B. = Rusty Egan Richard Burgess.

ABOVE: Modelling my new Phil Oakey-style asymmetric haircut, 1979. Taken by Gary in my parents' bedroom before a Human League gig at the Marquee Club.

BELOW: The Saturday-morning rehearsal that changed our lives, 1979. Our unnamed band playing in front of Steve Strange and some faces from the Blitz. Gary is leaning over the brand-new monophonic synth.

RIGHT: Boy George hanging out in the Blitz, 1980. That tiny weekly club night changed so many lives and became part of British pop culture history.

BELOW: The North London contingent mixing it up with the art school crowd. Christos Tolera, Barry without his rat, Stephen Linard and Steve Strange hanging out in the Blitz.

BELOW: Lee Sheldrick, Melissa Caplan, Kim Bowen and Robert Elms at the Blitz, planning their next moves as Rusty Egan plays Germanic electro rock on his turntables.

ABOVE: The video shoot for our first single, 'To Cut a Long Story Short', 1980. A few weeks later, the record was No. 5 in the charts and had sold over half a million copies.

BELOW: The Blitz Kids take New York City, 1981. That evening a few of us went (or tried!) to see Blondie at Bond's, before the following night's Spandau gig at The Underground, downtown Manhattan.

ABOVE: Steve Strange and me hanging in the VIP bar in Camden Palace, 1983. Steve was so much fun, and he taught me to accept everyone for who they are.

BELOW: In the back of a stretch limo on our North America tour, while 'True' was at No. 4 in the *Billboard* charts, 1984.

ABOVE: Rocking a Willie Brown suit I borrowed from Steve Strange for a promo trip to Portugal, 1982. I still have it!

ABOVE: Rock stars, Wembley Arena, 1984. All our plans, all our dreams, had come true. Night after night playing to sold-out arenas. Our feet had left terra firma – but when would we come back down to earth?

BELOW: Recording the Band Aid single, 'Do They Know It's Christmas?', 1984. The song changed the face of charity and the way bands worked with one another over the coming years.

ABOVE: The biggest gig of all time, Live Aid, played either side of the Atlantic, with two billion people watching on TV – but I had to sneak off half-way through to spend time with Shirlie!

RIGHT: Bob and Paula Geldof's wedding at their home, 1986. A meeting of chart rivals and old friends, with the enigmatic Paula stealing the show as always.

ABOVE: Another photoshoot for another pop magazine, Lisbon, 1987. Life was starting to feel like a merry-go-round we couldn't jump down from.

BELOW: Shirlie and me marrying in St Lucia, 1988. We went by ourselves; both of us had had enough of being centre of attention, and we knew we needed to do this on our own.

BELOW: Me and my Harley Moon at home, 1989. My family were keeping me together as Spandau was coming to its end.

Gary and I held a joint birthday party a
the Blitz, 1981. One of Steve Dagger
masterplans to align the band with th
incredible new pop culture

And he breathed life back into Spandau Ballet just as we were starting to choke.

Chrysalis, our label, were reaching the end of their tether with us. After being made to sit through the *Diamond* playback, then watching two successive singles drop like stones, they were all but ready to cut us loose. Dagger convinced them to lift one last single off the album, despite the downward trend. 'Instinction' was his pick. It was Gary's too – but Dagger wanted it remixed.

Given that we had contract-stipulated history with 12-inch versions and dub mixes, we were no strangers to doing alternative versions of our songs. The label were no strangers to paying for them either, but this remix would be different.

Trevor was the most in-demand producer of the moment. Despite having a career as a writer and performer himself – both in the Buggles and a two-year spell in prog rockers Yes – it was his productions that were really catching fire. Songs like 'Poison Arrow' and 'The Look of Love' by ABC had introduced this lush new sound to our ears, one that mixed orchestral arrangement and high drama with cutting-edge polyphonic synthesisers.

The Lexicon of Love album they came from was all anyone in the music industry wanted to talk about around then and is still considered a visionary piece of work today.

It's a clever title too. From the outside, *The Lexicon of Love* sounds like it's a reference to language and romance. To those in the production business, though, there's a second reading.

The Lexicon was a very particular piece of production equipment. A little box, about as big as a cassette recorder, that all the producers of the day were using. It was a relatively new device that allowed you to create this whole range of huge, rich reverb sounds; an effect that's the hallmark of almost every 80s record that ever spoke to your soul.

Reverb had existed before that. It was just an unbelievable hassle to create.

There's a famous story about Simon & Garfunkel recording 'The Boxer'.* In order to achieve the almighty reverb they got on that snare drum – the one that sounds like a cannon being fired – they had to take the drum kit out of the studio and set it up at the far end of the building, snaking a load of mics and wires all the way down the corridor. They then sat the drummer right next to an open lift shaft and had him smack the snare with all his might so they could record all the echoes as the sound reverberated up and down the length of the building.

With a Lexicon plonked on top of your mixing console, though, you could now re-create that entire set-up with the flick of a switch. The man hours that saved meant the scope of what was possible to record in even the most basic session had blown wide open. And the producer who was making the best use of this technology was Trevor Horn.

Trevor went through the *Diamond* album meticulously, listening to each track and disregarding most of them. He could afford to be picky and, boy, was he. After all that, the only one he said he'd be interested in doing anything with was the second track, 'Instinction'.

Bingo. We were on.

---

* A song that Spandau covered in 1990; the last thing we recorded before we split.

With Trevor on board, we had a shot at turning this ship around but we were going to need to do a root and branch reworking of it – which meant we all needed to be on hand in case we had to re-record our parts.

I was, to put it mildly, absolutely bricking it.

I have always had shortcomings as a musician. I'm not trying to be modest; I really do. The first day I picked up a bass was my first day in the band. I was trained up by my brother to know what notes to hit and when. I didn't have any intention of messing around with my delicate system.

The trouble was, Trevor's a bassist too. That's his instrument. He is also a weapons-grade genius. The prospect of being plucked off the sofa and forced to play bass for Trevor Horn caused rivers of sweat to run down my back. I had never known nerves like it.

I had good reason to be scared. The precision with which Trevor worked is now the stuff of legend; something probably best demonstrated by the work he later did on Frankie Goes to Hollywood's first single.

Frankie signed to Trevor's record label and he took charge of producing their seminal debut single, 'Relax'. Holly Johnson's vocals feature on the track, obviously, but the rest of the band's contribution to it? Nothing. Not a single note of theirs survived.

Trevor was so domineering in those early 'Relax' sessions, he thought nothing of junking everything the band had played and drafting in Ian Dury's backing band, the Blockheads, to see if they could do it more to his liking. The Blockheads were some of the tightest, best-respected session musicians in the business. Famously shit-hot guys. But even they couldn't make Trevor happy. So their contribution got binned too.

In the end Trevor played most of it himself. Which means most of Frankie Goes to Hollywood don't even appear on their own biggest hit* – and such was his power, all you could do was nod and say thank you.

There's no real arguing with a talent like Trevor. His understanding of music is second to none. When he worked on 'Instinction', he was somewhere between a surgeon and a sorcerer. He pulled that song apart entirely, showed us the living insides of it, then sprinkled magic fairy dust all over it and left it sparkling. It was hypnotic to watch.

Our sessions with him were not without their problems, though. Trevor's love of technology and his mastery of all these incredible new machines was a blessing and a curse. It had left him thinking like a robot. Everything he could hear in his head had the precision of a LinnDrum. Everything was measured precisely, electronically. No room for error. No space for slippage.

'You have to change your drummer,' he said to us one day, with no apparent sense of the enormity of what he was asking of us. 'He's not playing as good as he can. You've got to get rid of John.'

Trevor Horn had single-handedly brought the band back to life. Now he was tossing a hand grenade right into the middle of us.

Change our drummer? Kick John out of the band?

Aside from my immediate reaction that John was a friend and founding member, I, personally, knew I could never let him go.

The bass player, more than anyone else in the band, has

* I actually have some experience of this; a story for later …

to work in closest step with the drummer. Everyone has to listen to each other, but we needed to interlock. We are the rhythm section. The backbone of the band. If Tony fluffed a high note or Steve squeaked a sax solo, it would be embarrassing, but nothing we couldn't glide past.

If the rhythm section dropped a beat, on the other hand, the whole show could come tumbling down. Were John and I to come loose, everything could fall apart.

I hadn't worked with another drummer. I didn't know if another drummer would work with me. This wasn't just a question of technique. Trevor was asking us to undergo a heart transplant. To remove the one we had and to put in something new. Something unknown. And what? Just hope it would take?

The thing was, though, given the run of luck we'd had recently, maybe he wasn't wrong? Our records were tanking. Our videos were being passed over. Guys from our own label had walked out of our playback. Spandau were sick. Maybe a new ticker was what we needed?

But kick John out of the band?

As technology continues to progress, making its presence felt in so much of our modern culture – whether it's CGI in movies, autotune in pop music, Photoshop in photography – I take heart in the fact that one thing hasn't changed. Technology is still mostly used to aid human invention, not replace it. Maybe the day will come where everything we do is AI generated and the grand tradition of popular music has been handed over wholesale to robots – but I think there'll always be a place for the human heart in pop culture. Imperfections. Character. Personality. These things are what make it. They're the things people embrace.

And as an artist, there is nothing more satisfying than knowing whatever you did – however successful it ends up being – you did it yourself.

We thanked Trevor for the remix. He had done us proud. After a run of terrible chart positions, the 'Instinction' remix was a hit. Top 10. The call came in from *Top of the Pops* and we were back in position – and just in the nick of time too. With no more singles left on that second album, we would need to record a third if we wanted to keep the momentum up.

Now we had a reason to record more music and the drive to try something new. The 'Instinction' remix might not be a song you could have played at the Blitz, but now there was no Blitz. Everyone had moved on – so we would have to too.

But not with Trevor. We stuck with John.

The Walkman

I said previously that everybody who came to the Blitz acted as if they were the star of their own movie playing out in their heads. There, they relied on Rusty to provide the soundtrack for them. But in 1982, after the Blitz had broken open and let its style spill out onto the street, who would provide the soundtrack for those movies now? The answer was simple.

You.

The Sony Walkman was this new portable cassette player out of Japan. This little device – this impossibly tiny box – allowed you to carry your music with you. You were no longer tied to any one location. You could slip on your headphones, head out the door and go anywhere in the world with your very own soundtrack blasting.

The change the Walkman introduced was actually quite a subtle one. Headphones had existed before now, so this wasn't the first time you'd been able to listen to music that nobody else could hear. Transistor radios had been portable for decades too, so you could listen to music on the move but you were left at the mercy of DJs.

The Walkman's power was in letting you control both what you heard and where you heard it. You were now totally in charge – and what could be more 80s than that?

It made pop culture a 24/7 pursuit. If you weren't listening to music yourself, then you were mapping out mixtapes to make for your mates, your boyfriend or girlfriend. This wasn't like throwing together a Spotify playlist, where you can add something on a whim, take it back out and shuffle the order around to your heart's content. Making a mixtape was a proper undertaking. You had to commit.

Not only did you have to juggle songs so they would fit neatly on the two sides without wasted space at the end, you had to sit and oversee the entire production of it. The idea of spending the 60 minutes of a mixtape's length actually recording it, waiting for each song to finish before you could line up the next might seem alien to a teenager today, who can do all this with a tap or two. But it was alien to us then too.

This was a whole new way of interacting with pop music. People had never known anything like it. It was the start of a pop culture that you could customise. You could discover the bits you loved, discard the rest and curate the experience that you wanted to have – not what anyone else told you you had to have. Even down to the tracks on an album.

I'm certain this helped fuel the strident individualism of the 1980s. The experience of music up until that point had been a shared one. Uniform. Now with the Walkman, that experience was completely disrupted. Everybody could work on their own terms, so everybody would work on their own terms.

The introduction of Walkmans and the proliferation of mixtapes caused a lot of anxiety in certain quarters, though. Specifically, the BPI: the British Phonographic Industry. Much like the Musicians' Union, they were terrified that this new technology would eventually wipe them out – which is why they launched the 'Home Taping Is Killing Music' campaign.

Personally, I couldn't really see why the record labels were worrying so much. To me, it seemed like a good opportunity to sell twice as many records as they had been doing.

Because the quality of a Walkman was relatively poor, music fans didn't want to rely on just listening to a cassette. The novelty of being able to take an album with you wherever you went was great, and a decent trade-off against any loss of sound quality you suffered. But the Walkman was never really a replacement for the feeling you got when you stuck a record on the hi-fi system at home. In the living room or in your bedroom, swimming in the sound that flooded out from the speakers; that was something you couldn't replicate with those tiny little foam earpads.*

---

* The true genius of the Walkman? The only way you could escape the hiss and high-end leak from the headphones of the person sat next to you on the bus was to get a Walkman of your own to drown it out. And so the chain continued …

We noticed our fans started buying copies of both, getting the albums on vinyl and cassette. One for the pleasure of hearing the record as close as possible to the sound we created in the studio; one for the portability opportunities the Walkman offered.

That was undeniably a huge luxury, especially at a time when unemployment was high and the economy was languishing. But pop culture was so exciting, so full of life at that time – it was what people wanted to spend their money on. If the rent was paid and you had enough on the table (which was by no means a given in 1982), this was what you went for next.

This also doesn't take into account the fact that a third format was entering the ring too. One that seemed to work with lasers and holograms. New albums were starting to be pressed on compact discs and while the equipment to play them was prohibitively expensive for the general public, the record labels all had one.

If I could commission a painting of any moment of my life, the first time I was played a CD has got to be a contender. The artist was Phil Collins. The album, *Face Value*. And when that iconic drum fill from 'In the Air Tonight' came crashing through the speakers with no trace of vinyl crackle? I reckon the face I pulled would be enough to get me hanging in the National Gallery. Or the Science Museum.

Besides, if the record companies were really interested in stopping music getting out, they should have been paying more attention to the bands.

There was a bar near Chrysalis Records' office off Oxford Street called Pink Flamingos that served only cocktails. Once a week, Spandau would end up there for a few

Mai Tais or a Coco Loco or two. Then, a little woozy,* we would pay a quick visit to the label, heading into the office to raid their record stocks before leaving.

This wasn't stealing, I want to be clear. The distribution department was more than happy to give copies of these records to us, loading us up with armful after armful of the label's latest releases.

'Have you got this one? What about this? Make sure you don't miss this one! They're going to be big!'

They piled us high with everything they had; miles more music that I could realistically listen to. I confess there were a couple of times when I'd take that huge haul, nip around the corner to Reckless Records, or whatever second-hand record shops were nearby in Soho, and flog them on.

The shops got some up-to-date releases in mint condition, the record label had given this stuff away and we got a bit of pocket money to cover our cocktail tab.

Not the most outrageous rock'n'roll swindle of all time, I grant you, but I probably dented their bottom line with that wheeze more than any pop fan at home who swapped a copy of *Diamond* for *Rio* with their mate.

---

* OK, sometimes more than a little woozy. I once had to carry John into Chrysalis in my arms like a lifeguard and leave him on the sofa in reception to have a quick kip.

The Wag

If you were to map out the Blitz as a Venn diagram, with all the different artistic disciplines laid out as a bunch of overlapping circles, you'd be hard pressed to find a formation that adequately captured everyone who attended those Tuesday nights.

But the one person you could always place with total certainty – because he was always right in the centre of everything, a finger in every last pie – is Chris Sullivan.

If the Blitz Kids had a general, it was Chris. Always impeccably put together, in my mind the signature Sullivan look was a double-breasted suit with slicked-back hair, spats, a cane and a monocle. Not the sort of look you'd immediately associate with a Welsh working-class boy – but then neither was Steve Strange's.

Chris had the air of a Soho dandy of the old school. A man who kept standards alive, even in an era when the finest tailoring you were likely to see of a normal night in that neighbourhood was a flasher's trenchcoat.

In fact, it was his taste in clothes that had originally brought him over to London – indirectly. Growing up in Merthyr Tydfil, the ever-present threat of getting his head kicked in for dressing up the way he did meant Chris was inspired to regularly organise minibus trips to Newport, where he and a small gang of like-minded friends could enjoy a scene where things were a bit more fashion forward.

It was there, in a club called Scamps, that he first met Steve Strange.

Over time, those minibuses from Merthyr became coaches. Trips to Newport became trips to Bristol. Then

Bristol became London and before too long Chris Sullivan was suddenly something of a travel agent-slash-nightlife impresario.

In those early days he worked for the cost of his own travel and nothing more. The fact that he was finding (and later creating) spaces for him and his friends to enjoy the types of nights that they wanted to enjoy was all the payment he desired.

He continued to fill that role at the Blitz too, where he took unofficial charge of our weekend party-crashing schedule. Chris was always the one who had word of a party happening somewhere in the city on a Friday or Saturday night, and we would all line up behind him to join in. Me. Gary. Dagger. Bob Elms. Sade. Barry the Rat. Christos Tolera. A few rotating others.

He was also the instigator of the one big fight that ever broke out at the Blitz. A night that, for sheer absurdity alone, deserves its own mention here.

The Blitz wasn't the only game in town. There was a rival club up by Tottenham Court Road tube station called Studio 21. It had also spawned out of the post-punk scene, but I would argue that the Studio 21 crowd hadn't split off from the punks quite as cleanly as the Blitz Kids had.

A case in point: Studio 21's ringleader was a bloke called Jock McDonald. Jock was in a band called the Bollock Brothers – which, personally, I think gives a good indication of where their heads were at.

They ran themselves more along the lines of the Malcolm McLaren/Vivienne Westwood/Philip Sallon style that had developed out of the Sex Pistols scene. Part punk, part pirate, with lashings of tartan thrown in for good measure.

If you keep Adam Ant in mind for Studio 21 and Boy George for the Blitz, you'll have a rough idea.

Anyhow, Sullivan had said or done something to wind Jock McDonald up one night. A little skirmish had sparked which Chris tried to bring to a swift end by cracking Jock right on the bridge of his nose with his forehead. Strangely, that only inflamed the situation. Jock left, threatening that he'd be back and went off to round up the rest of his band of Bollock Brothers.

Sure enough, they returned and what followed was like something from a Western movie, if there had been a catastrophic mix-up in the costume department. There were buccaneers fighting spacemen. Cowboys scuffling with clowns. Fellas who looked like Braveheart throwing fists at bikers. Elizabethan courtiers tossing chairs and tables. It was absolute carnage. But it was also the sort of fight that only someone like Chris Sullivan could start.

As one of the leading lights of the Blitz, it stood to reason that Chris was forever trying his hand at something new. A real Renaissance man, he did a bit of everything. He once said to me at Le Beat Route one night: 'I fancy a bit of what you've got, Mart. I think I'll start a band.' Within weeks he had started the Latin funk salsa pop band Blue Rondo à La Turk.* Within a few more he had got himself on *Top of the Pops*.

His paintings were the album's artwork. He co-wrote the music and all of the lyrics. He wrote magazine features alongside Bob Elms at *The Face*. He designed suits for the

* Blue Rondo ended up being unexpectedly and immediately huge in Brazil. Their single 'Me and Mr. Sanchez' was used as the theme tune for Brazilian TV's 1982 World Cup coverage.

Axiom collective and was one of the catwalk stars for our New York show at The Underground. He DJed at Le Beat Route on Friday nights, at Whisky a Go-Go on a Saturday and when the Blitz called it a day he joined Steve Strange and Rusty Egan in starting their new night at Hell on a Thursday (a night that ended when, according to Chris's recollection, all the patrons took LSD, flipped out and smashed the venue to bits).

The jewel in his crown, though, his lasting legacy to the scene, has to be the Wag Club: one of the most beloved Soho institutions of all time.

If 1982 was the year Spandau Ballet lost touch with clubland, then I'm glad we lasted long enough that I got to catch the Wag Club. It opened in April, Chris and Ollie O'Donnell having taken on the lease to Whisky a Go-Go on Wardour Street a few months earlier.

Chris maintains, I believe, that Wag wasn't an acronym for Whisky a Go-Go, that the name refers to something else but, whatever the case, the club itself certainly became something completely new.

It started as a Latin-tinged funk and soul night, but it wasn't the sort of place that you'd go to dance like Le Beat Route. Chris was a wit. He loved to talk. A scholar of the art of conversation. He wanted to make sure the Wag Club was a place where he could foster a community, rather than try to go up against the standard-issue discos.

He wanted the music to be a conversation piece, which is why he followed all of the newest, most curious trends wherever they took him. Sometimes that was along the road our fellow Blitz Kids took: putting on gigs by Bananarama, or a really early gig that his old Axiom collaborator Sade played with her new band.

Other times he was a million miles away from the Blitz sound. Within months of opening, the Wag had hosted the first hip-hop event in the UK – The Roxy Road Show – where Chris had flown in a crew of 25 DJs, MCs and hype acts from New York.

It was kind of like a student exchange trip; the second leg of The 21 in New York. We had taken our music, fashion, photographers and Blitz scene out to storm Manhattan. Now Chris sent New York a reciprocal invitation to bring their most exciting club scene to Soho. Artists like Afrika Bambaataa came over, Fab 5 Freddy, Grand Wizard Theodore, Jazzy Jay. The breakdancing troupe Rocksteady Crew. Rope-skip stars the Double Dutch Girls. He put them all up for the weekend and suddenly hip-hop had an early home in London.

Over the years he'd go on to give groundbreaking gigs to acts like De La Soul, Queen Latifah, Eric B & Rakim and Grandmaster Flash.

Naturally, the club became the talk of the town. The guest list was hotter than the surface of the sun and before too long David Bowie was down there scouting it out for music video potential.* Bowie's blessing didn't kill the Wag off the way it did the Blitz, though. The Wag would stay standing at the vanguard of the Soho scene until the turn of the century, only closing its doors in 2001.

It was an incredible place and continued on the legacy of those bits of the Blitz that Chris Sullivan symbolised so well – but I never got to spend anything like the time there that I had been able to at our previous haunts. Partly that was because we were always off in some other country.

---

* Not a joke; one of his videos for 'Blue Jean' was shot there.

Partly, though, it's because I wasn't able to be part of the scene the way I once had. Our profiles had changed. People didn't treat me like I was Martin from the Blitz anymore. Now I was the bass player from Spandau Ballet.

The Wag had a star-studded celebrity clientele – huge A-list names, a million times more recognisable than me – and it accommodated them amazingly. Chris was always the consummate host. Like Steve Strange he could glide between prince and punter without missing a step.

I know it wasn't the Wag's fault that I was feeling this way, but the Wag was where I first noticed I was starting to feel it.

I was becoming famous.

Fame

I don't know who I'm quoting when I say this – thousands of people probably – but fame is a funny old thing.

I really don't want to bore you with a lot of self-pitying tripe about how hard it is to be famous. It's got as much good and evil in it as anything else in this life. Handled correctly, it can be wonderful. Taken too seriously, it can be horrendous.

I've been lucky in that my own relationship with fame started early – long before I was famous myself. As a young kid, I hated attention. I was so shy as a toddler that I didn't speak for years. I let Gary do all of my talking for me, even when I needed to go to the toilet. It got worse as I got older. I would get so embarrassed if I was ever out with my mum and saw anyone I knew. Even friends of mine from school. They could be walking down the other side of the road and I would hide behind her legs, burying my face deep into a buttock to avoid being seen. I hated it.

I started to shake that shyness off around the time I started attending drama classes at the Anna Scher Theatre. It was near us in Islington and priced specifically to attract working-class kids from the area. Getting me through the door that first day was no small feat, but as Anna gradually built up my confidence I soon couldn't wait to take my ten-pence piece there on a Thursday evening for classes.

Anna's school was a regular haunt for casting directors who wanted young actors for film and TV projects. As a pair of brothers, Gary and I got some decent roles out of it. This wasn't what made us famous. We weren't child stars like the Olsen twins or Macaulay and Kieran Culkin or anything, but as a result of those early jobs, I got to work with some fairly famous faces of that time: Tom Conti, Leonard Rossiter.

Acting alongside them, I never really got starstruck. I was so obsessed with acting, the prospect of getting to learn from them superseded that.

Watching these actors up close is what taught me my formative lessons about fame. It quickly became clear to me that these people were actors first and foremost because they loved the work. However famous they might have been, that fame was simply a by-product of doing a job they loved.

It seems so obvious to me now as an adult – but if I hadn't learned that lesson early, there's every chance I could have ended up very confused and unhappy in 1982.

In 1982, there was this feeling among the former Blitz Kids that fame was something you could turn on and off like a tap. In fact, it wasn't just a feeling. It was kind of true. There were enough eyes on the London clubland scene we had created that if you had an idea for a project, you could make it a reality without even lifting the phone. The Blitz had created such a well-oiled multi-armed media machine that you'd bump into someone at Le Beat Route or the Wag or Club for Heroes or the Camden Palace, mention your plans in passing and the wheels would be in motion before your head hit your pillow.

That sort of fame isn't really fame. It's notoriety. Having useful contacts, being well connected. People know you and they trust you. That can lead to all sorts of things.

It's when it steps up a level that things start to get a little more dicey.

I spent the 80s in an extremely well-known band. We travelled the world and commanded huge audiences in arenas and stadiums in major cities all around the globe. At the time, that felt like the height of fame to me and it's probably most people's image of it too. I've made my way through airports with paparazzi bulbs flashing and fans thrusting autograph books into my hands as security minders keep pushing me onwards. I've stepped into the back of a black limo as a screaming girl has fainted in my wake. I've walked a red carpet to a barrage of reporters' questions on my way to shake hands with royalty.

That sort of fame is intoxicating. It's not always great. There are days, weeks, months when you're not in the mood for it and wish that it would all get bent and leave you be. Yet something about it remains enticing; you find yourself returning for more.

However, there's another level after that.

Around the turn of the century I did a few years on a British soap opera, *EastEnders*. Because we filmed that on a set without an audience, I never really got a sense that as many as 18 million people were watching me some nights. At least not at the start. When my episodes started airing, and my storylines became the most talked-about thing around water coolers the following morning, my entire gauge for fame was thrown off-kilter.

I was walking along Tottenham Court Road one day when the true extent of the fame that brings was revealed to me. Some guy jumped out in front of me, then punched me in the stomach as hard as I've ever been punched in my life. Sent the wind straight out of me and could have cracked one of my ribs if it had been an inch higher.

I thought I was being mugged. I thought someone had recognised me off the telly, figured I had a few quid stashed about my person and that I'd be happy to part with it given the right encouragement. That's why he was setting about me with the body blows.

But, no. His reason for punching me, Martin Kemp? 'I fucking hate Steve Owen.'

That sort of fame is horrendous. It's invasive, unwarranted and makes you want to retire from public life forever. Draw your curtains, order takeout every night from now until forever and never show your face again.

I said earlier that Boy George was the biggest star to come out of the Blitz. I stand by that description insofar as stars are bright and flashy. In terms of success, though, there's a number of different metrics to measure by. Global airplay. Record sales. Career longevity. Critical acclaim. Artistic credibility.

Being a recognisable face is part of it, but there's a household name that also came out of the Blitz who beats Boy George on points in practically every way. The

Blitz Kid that is tattooed on Drake not once, but twice: Sade.

I have such immense respect for the way Sade handled her career and fame. She's always described these days as elusive, but she was never particularly interested in standing out – even at a place like the Blitz. She was there because she wanted a good night out, not because she was looking to be a star.

When she came to New York with us as part of The 21 as a designer but had to do a little modelling for the Axiom show, she loathed it. She started her career as a backing singer for the band Pride, before she ever came to the forefront herself. And, much like Spandau did before our first gig, she rehearsed music with her band without telling a soul until they were ready to debut it fully formed.

A bunch of us went to see one of her earliest gigs up a club in Basildon called Raquels. We were expecting her to be good, but the band was already brilliant.

Of course, she wouldn't have booked the gig if she wasn't. She had no interest in just being out there. Like the actors I met through Anna Scher, she wanted to be good at what she did. The fame just followed.

There's a number of reasons I've always been thankful for my early training with Anna Scher as a kid. I've always said Anna was responsible for the angel in me, and Steve Strange was responsible for the devil. The lessons I learned about fame in those years served me well and they're ones I've drilled into my kids too.

Fame can be wonderful, but as someone who has seen it from both sides, I can tell you that chasing it for its own sake is a dangerous, destructive thing. I can give you the names and numbers of people who have the battle scars to prove it. Fame is only ever useful as a pass to the next thing you want to do. It is a key. A way to open doors.

And the doors it can open are huge.

The Second Invasion

They called 1982 the Second British Invasion.

The First British Invasion of America had been in the 1960s, when London was swinging and America wanted everything we had. The Beatles, the Stones, the Kinks. Dusty Springfield, Tom Jones, the Who. Sean Connery made his debut as the dapper British spy James Bond. Jean Shrimpton launched the miniskirt. Twiggy was the face on every magazine.

It was clear that America, for all its cultural might, was not afraid to have its head turned from time to time if the UK could offer something interesting – and in 1982 we had plenty on show.

The previous year had been critical. With UK acts producing so many dazzling videos, with over-the-top production and effects, British music had been on heavy rotation on MTV. This led to something of a snowball effect. Appearing on a cutting-edge channel like MTV meant your song would get lodged in the heads of taste-making Americans. Those people would then not only buy your records, they would request those same songs on radio for when they weren't near their TV.

This opens you up to another, much larger, audience. Before you know it, these radio requests mean you're play-ing in cars, malls and diners in every major city in the States. This leads to even more record sales.

Any band who had the foresight to insist that their label cough up for 12-inch club mixes of every one of their singles really cleaned up too, because if you had a promo vinyl pressed and ready to go, your records would be played in the nightclubs too.

With a stand-out video, a radio edit and a six-minute club mix of your single, for a while you had the entire American market sewn up.

Americans – with their dull, cumbersome videos – didn't sit idle for long. They very quickly caught wise to this formula and would soon be churning out their own Super Bowl-sized superstars by the end of the following year. Madonna, Prince, Michael Jackson – they would all be taking us on at this same game in late '83 and blowing us out of the water in '84. But for a good few years, while America was still lacing its shoes, the Brits got to run riot.

'Don't You Want Me' by the Human League is widely considered to be a critical tipping point. That song, from Sheffield's finest, spent three weeks at the top of the *Billboard* Hot 100 and, from there, us limeys just wouldn't leave the charts alone. 'Tainted Love' by Soft Cell. 'Cruel Summer' by Bananarama. 'I Ran (So Far Away)' by A Flock of Seagulls. 'White Wedding' by Billy Idol.

America was mesmerised by our androgynous fashion too. 'Sweet Dreams (Are Made of This)' by Eurythmics is one of the defining records of the decade and still sounds as arresting and immediate as it did back then – but it threw MTV bosses for a complete loop. There's a story that the station management demanded to see a copy of Annie Lennox's birth certificate before they would play the video so they could determine whether she was a man or a woman.

Boy George created endless headlines and column inches too, with magazine covers openly asking, 'IS IT A BOY? IS IT A GIRL?' – but if the Blitz had taught us anything, it was that our generation didn't particularly care. They loved the look, they loved the sound, and 'Karma Chameleon' would go on to be one of the biggest records of 1983–84.

Gary said he had a conversation once with John Taylor from Duran Duran, who told him: 'It's a fair split, y'know? We own America, you own Europe.'

Even though we were the first of the Second British Invasion bands to go out there with The 21, it sometimes happens that when you're the first to open a door, you get left holding it while a hundred thousand others walk through ahead of you. I'm not complaining about how we fared in America. 'True' is still one of the most played songs on American radio. Gary picked up an award not too long ago to commemorate its 5,000,000th play on the airwaves.

My back-of-the-envelope maths tells me that if you stacked all those individual rotations end to end, at 5m30s each, that's roughly 52 years of consecutive radio airplay. The song itself was only released 39 years ago, so somehow it became massive enough to cause time itself to warp.

Duran weren't wrong. We never did really break America in quite the way they did, but we didn't do too badly, all things considered. I'm quite happy to settle for disrupting the space–time continuum.

The Camel

Bands were easy come in the early days of the Blitz, but they were also easy go. I know because I think I might have accidentally been responsible for the break-up of Visage.

It happened when they were over in New York, about to unveil their second album for the Americans. Steve Strange would call me every night, wherever he was in the world, and offload his latest mad scheme.

'Martin,' he called down the line. 'I've had a great idea. I'm going to turn up for the party on the back of an elephant.'

Transatlantic calls weren't always the clearest things in the early 80s, but I could have sworn he'd said the word 'elephant'. I definitely couldn't figure out what the alternative was if I'd misheard.

'An elephant?' I asked.

'An elephant,' he said.

As Steve called at night, a lot of the times I spoke to him I caught him absolutely off his nut. I mean, he was barely ever on his nut, even stone cold sober, but I knew never to pour cold water on any idea of his. In part, that was because I never wanted to crush or question his creativity. Everything Steve had ever achieved was a result of him thinking big, being wild, doing something that just would never have occurred to anyone normal.

But mostly it was because I knew that telling him 'no' would only make him dig his heels in.

'Steve,' I told him. 'Great idea.'

The next night, I got another a call. Bizarrely, it turned out there'd been a slight hitch in Steve's plan to hire a 12ft pachyderm and stroll it down the one of the busiest streets in America.

'Martin,' he said, 'we couldn't get an elephant. So we're going to get a camel instead.'

'Steve,' I told him. 'Great idea.'

A little later, the phone rings again.

'Martin,' he said. 'Midge is not very happy about me going to the club on the back of a camel. He's saying, "Let's just do it as a normal band would do it. No camels. This is ridiculous."'

I was trapped in the middle of an argument between two bandmates – 3,000 miles away and five hours out – about wildlife. Again, I knew that siding with Midge was only going to make Steve more determined. If I told him I could sort of see Midge's point, there was every chance Steve would hire half a dozen flamingos to flank him too.

You won't need me to tell you what ended up happening. There's photos of it if you want to see it. Steve turned up for the launch that night, looking every bit as Steve Strange as you'd expect, riding side-saddle on this huge, magnificent-looking camel.

Midge would leave Visage not long after. They cited creative differences, which, in a way, I suppose it was. You can't get much more creatively different than thinking, 'I should hire a taxi to get to the club' versus 'I should hire a camel.' But I know the truth. In trying to play the nice guy, letting Steve getting everything he wanted, I split up Visage – and I'm very, very sorry.

In my defence, though, those pictures looked great.

The Alternative Scene

Remember I mentioned that the Blitz started life as Billy's in a basement below a strip club in Soho? It blows my mind to consider this, but as we were all dancing to Bowie and Roxy Music below that strip club, another era-defining institution was getting its start in the room above. One that would see an entirely new breed of comedian doing for comedy what Billy's did for music and fashion.

Comedy had been suffering from a similar malaise. All of our generation's heroes had got their start back in the 60s. We had Bowie, they had Peter Cook. We had Roxy Music, they had Monty Python. The firebrands who had got us all interested in our respective art forms were revolutionary and game-changing, but they had all been going for over a decade at this point and there was no new blood coming up behind them.

The Comedy Store gave the next generation of comedians that chance. Starting, like Billy's did, in the shadow of Thatcher's election in 1979, the night would serve as the birthplace of alternative comedy: an anarchic mix of cabaret, stand-up and sketch that hit audiences right between the eyes.

Among the comedians who developed their craft in that same Soho club were Ben Elton, Rik Mayall, Ade Edmondson, Dawn French, Jennifer Saunders, Alexei Sayle – and many, many others.

In much the same way that the Blitz span itself off from Billy's, a core group of those comedians at the Comedy Store splintered off to start a night of their own. The Comic Strip.

The Comic Strip was a huge hit. After becoming the subject of a half-hour documentary, it soon broke out of clubland and into the country at large. The comedy equivalent of a record deal is a six-part series, and theirs would be a flagship bit of programming for the newly launched fourth channel on British TV, Channel 4.

They were such hot property that as well as producing *Comic Strip Presents* ... for Channel 4, a cluster of the same comedians were making another show simultaneously for the BBC that went out that very same month, debuting a week apart.

While our two scenes had both started off in the same salacious setting of 69 Dean Street, we mostly ran parallel with the alternative comedy lot. However, there were a few points where we would overlap. There was a reunion of sorts on 5 June 1985: a day where the proprietors of one of Soho's seedier strip clubs could be truly proud of all they had inadvertently produced.

That was the day when MTV decided it would branch out into non-music programming, which meant the Second British Invasion was now being fought and won on two fronts. Because MTV's first foray into comedy programming introduced America to *The Young Ones*.

Wham! Bam

It was a regular Thursday evening in the Kemp household. Mum had served up dinner, I had hoovered it up and was now rinsing my plate off in the sink so I could rush through to the living room for *Top of the Pops*.

I settled into my usual spot, sat on the carpet with my back up against the arm of the sofa, legs out in front of me. There were a couple of groups on tonight's episode I didn't want to miss. Culture Club were No. 1 with 'Do You Really Want to Hurt Me?' and I was curious to see what Boy George had up his sleeve. Blancmange – who had come down to Le Beat Route to be in our 'Chant No. 1' video – had 'Living on the Ceiling' tucked inside the Top 40 too, so I was interested to see that as well.

I'd also heard a bit about this new band Wham! that Mike Smith was currently introducing, opening the show with their new single 'Young Guns (Go for It)'.

Had I had my wits about me, I might have recognised the singer as one of the other kids who had also been in our 'Chant No. 1' video – the Greek lad with the shiny red suit and the dark curly hair. But I didn't. Because my wits were currently in my lap, along with my jaw.

Who. Was. That?

The camera had just swung by this girl on stage, in a long white dress with a zip up the side and this choppy blonde haircut that I could not stop staring at. It was immediate infatuation.

This wasn't the first time this had happened. It had happened once before, many years ago. I must have been about six years old when I first saw Cilla Black on the television. I was so smitten with the singing lady on screen that I stood up, walked towards the telly and planted a great big kiss on it, to peals of laughter from Mum and Dad.

I had enough sense now, at the grand old age of 21, not to try to kiss the telly (not while my parents were looking, anyhow) but the urge to do so was overwhelming.

I should offer my apologies to Blancmange and Culture Club here, because I'm sorry to say that I didn't pay the slightest bit of notice to their performances that night. If Hall & Oates, Diana Ross and Shakin' Stevens happen to be reading, the same goes for them too. My head was filled with one thing and one thing only. The girl in white. I couldn't see anything else.

For the next few weeks, I was obsessed with her. Gary, the band, my friends, everyone I saw had to endure me asking about the girl on *Top of the Pops* in the white dress with the zip up the side and the choppy blonde hair. Had they seen her? Did they know her? Did they know anyone who knows her?

I was starting to worry I might spend the rest of my days doing this, talking to people who – at a certain point – would probably just assume I was talking about a ghost. Me, a tragic figure who had lost his young love, forever asking if they'd seen this girl in white.

Luckily, I would soon get my chance to meet her as the band was invited to the opening of a play called *Yakety Yak*, starring our friends – and fellow showbiz brothers – the McGanns. I would have turned up to the opening of an envelope in those days if it got me a free drink and a fistful of peanuts. I ended up getting a whole lot more than that, though, because who should be there but the girl in white.

Shirlie was her name. Shirlie Holliman.

Before I sank too much free wine I steeled my nerves and went over to talk to her. At the end of '82 I was starting to wean myself off the make-up a bit. You can never come off make-up cold turkey. Everyone just thinks you've fallen gravely ill if you make the jump from full-face to bare-face in the course of a day and it craters your confidence. So I was in the process of winding things down. A little mascara, a little blusher. Just to keep a bit of my glow.

It went well. I didn't fall over. I didn't garble my name. I gave her my number and I told her to call me.

And she didn't. Not for ages.

It was three weeks before the phone rang. I was in my bedroom and my mum called up, 'It's Shirlie on the phone for you.'

Shirlie wasn't calling under her own steam, though. She wasn't even calling from her own phone. She was in another boy's bedroom. George Michael's. George was making her do it. He had been the one who dialled my number. He'd waited for the ring, then handed the receiver over to Shirlie when my mum picked up. A regular little matchmaker.

We arranged to meet. I suggested that we go to the hottest new club in town, the Camden Palace. She agreed. The date was set. It was a bit of a ploy on my part; what they call the 'home turf advantage'. You see, the Camden Palace had just opened and I knew the guys who were running it. Steve Strange and Rusty Egan.

All the club nights they'd run, since the Blitz, played to great acclaim, and they had been making a decent bit of money out of it too. By the summer of '82 they were ready to make a real go of things. Take what they'd built and turn it into a serious business. Everyone knew they were due a proper payday for all they'd given the London scene so no one begrudged them going mainstream. That was where all of us were heading.

The look for Camden Palace had evolved again. Now the thing to wear was bright-coloured Johnson suits; much more of a 50s style with the peg trousers and the wide-shouldered jackets. There was a trace of Blitz look left in the make-up that most of us were all now gradually dialling back.

My other reason for picking the Palace was that I knew the VIP Room would be filled with some other pop stars I knew. It was like the green room that *Top of the Pops* should have had. I could all but guarantee there'd be a bunch of familiar faces in there and, as a *Top of the Pops* star herself now, I figured I could introduce Shirlie to a taste of the life behind the velvet rope.

The plan was perfect. I was floating on air as I made my way along Camden High Street. Right up until I spotted Shirlie in the queue and noticed that she wasn't alone. She had brought a mate with her. A wingman. A guy.

George Michael.

In the fullness of time I came to appreciate that, of all the spare wheels you can have cramping your style on the first date with your future wife, George Michael is far from the worst. In fact, George (Yog to his mates) would become one of my closest friends. A fierce supporter of Shirlie's, a rock for me in my darkest hours and the sweetest, funniest, most generous man that music ever knew, I would spend 30 years with him as a vital part of my life.

But that night he was a right pain in the arse.

All I wanted was a tiny bit of privacy. A few stolen minutes to try to score a snog off Shirlie. But every time I thought I'd managed to shake him loose, up he'd pop asking if we were alright, if we wanted to dance, if we had drinks. I'd have felt sorry for the poor guy, forced to traipse around the Camden Palace alone, waiting for his mate to hurry up and seal the deal with the bass player from Spandau Ballet, but he just wouldn't take the hint.

Eventually, we snuck out onto the emergency stairwell to get a moment to ourselves, the sound of the club thumping dully through the fire escape doors. Here I was. Alone with the girl in the white. Kissing.

1983
TRUE

M*A*S*H* *Finale* | *Pound Coin* | Risky Business | *Um Bongo* | Return of the Jedi | *Shergar Kidnapped* | Super Mario Bros. | *'Total Eclipse of the Heart'* | *David Copperfield Makes the Statue of Liberty Disappear* | *'Let's Dance'* | *Thatcher's Second Term* | *'Billie Jean'* | Trading Places | *Chicken McNuggets* | Blackadder | *'Blue Monday'* | Octopussy | La Cage aux Folles | *'Sweet Dreams (Are Made of This)'* | Scarface

Moving Out

Auntie Sheila wasn't actually my aunt; she was just a friend of my mum and dad's. But, in the way that all kids of my generation were apparently taught to do, we always called her Auntie.

She was a housekeeper and there was one particular house, near Highbury Park, that she was always tending to. My earliest memory of the other side of Islington – the posh side – was there.

Auntie Sheila was left watching me one day so brought me along to this house with her while she worked. When we stepped into this house, my eyebrows nearly flew off my face. I could not believe what I was seeing. To me, I was standing in a mansion. The rooms were huge. These people had a snooker room. In their house. I must have spent hours walking around the edge of that table, my sticky little kid's hand grabbing the green baize cushion like it was a banister, letting my fingers be tickled by the felt-like fabric as I went, pushing balls around and dropping them into the pockets.

Knowing the area now as an adult, I'm sure that house was nothing grander than a standard middle-class terraced. But in my mind, at that age, I was walking round Buckingham Palace and you couldn't tell me any different.

Our council house on our side of Islington, on Rotherfield Street, was worlds apart. A tiny Georgian building, we lived on the middle floor: a rent collection station below, my cousin Vivian and her family above. It had this derelict basement that reeked of mould, squeaked with mice and plagued my nightmares. Our only toilet was outside, a little outhouse at the foot of our yard, alive with spiders and other creepy crawlies which turned night-time trips for a piss into terrifying adventures.

Don't get me wrong. I was perfectly content in that house. I had never once so much as considered that we might be poor, even though we were and I would occasionally catch Mum crying on the odd weeks we couldn't afford meat for our meals. I had everything I needed in my mum and dad – and if I had to go and take a bath every other week in the pube-infested public baths at Thebarton Street because we didn't have a bathroom of our own, well, that was just the way things were.

The council eventually moved us out to a much nicer place on Elmore Street when I was 14. Bigger rooms. More floors. Our own bathroom. The constant smell of fungus replaced with pot pourri.

I was still living at Elmore Street with Mum and Dad in 1983. Spandau had two albums out and a third getting ready for release. I had been a regular fixture in the Top 40 for years now. My face had made the cover of the coolest magazines in the country. I had visited more countries in the past few weeks than I had ever expected to in my whole life.

Yet here I still was, wolfing down the dinner my mum had made me, asking to be excused so I could take up my place propped against the sofa to watch *Top of the Pops*.

This wasn't uncommon for an unmarried working boy at that time. I loved living with my mum and dad too. They were the best parents a boy could have and they were loving that they had a set of pop-star sons. When private cars came to collect us for TV and drivers made their way to the door to knock for us, there was a ripple of excitement throughout the street. Fans who found out where we lived would gather outside our gate, trying to catch a glimpse of me or Gary through the window. Dad used to like to twitch the curtains, pretending to be us, seeing if he could fool some fans into letting out a scream.

The biggest perk for Dad I reckon was getting to drive our Porsche 911s. Gary and I had both bought one – his red, mine blue – and Dad would take it in turns to drive them to work at the print shop,* parking up in full view of his colleagues, playing it so cool like him and his alternating sports cars were no big thing.

Many of the Blitz Kids had moved out of their parents' house the second they hit adulthood, but many of them had gone to live in squats on Warren Street and Great Titchfield Street. The idea of them sounded very artsy and creative, but I had been a semi-regular visitor to those squats and they scared the shit out of me. As someone who

---

* Dad would insist he did this purely for our benefit, that it was vitally important that the engines be 'turned over' regularly and wouldn't hear a word of thanks for this selfless act.

grew up living in and around some of the still-levelled streets targeted by German air raids, I knew a bomb site when I saw one and these squats more than met the requirements.

It was amazing to me that these people I saw out on the town night after night, who took such care to get their outfits looking perfect, took so little care with their clothes at home. Marilyn, Boy George, Stephen Jones, Stephen Linard, Grayson Perry, Kim Bowen, John Maybury and countless others all shared squats at various points and they looked like a smash and grab in a charity shop. Everything strewn on the floor, everything trodden on, make-up on every available surface.

As the band's sole songwriter, Gary had been able to move out a bit earlier as he'd also been getting his publishing money. He had moved up to the edge of Highbury Park, not far from where Auntie Sheila's old job used to take her. His new flat was filled with all these gorgeous antiques.

Antiques were something Gary had always had an eye for, even from our earliest days, trudging up and down the shops on Camden Passage and the King's Road. Now that his songs were all over the radio, racking up gold and silver discs as well as big royalty cheques, he could have his pick of them.

Finally, in 1983 Spandau were enough of a success that the band's cash wasn't just going on plane tickets, pocket money and my backstage cheese plates. We were seeing the fruits of our labour pay out. I now had enough to buy a place of my own.

Or, I should say, of our own. I had been seeing Shirlie a lot more recently. She had moved out of her parents' place and was living in her friend Gail's spare room, which only had a single bed. It's not that I minded being close to Shirl – the closer the better as far as I was concerned – but getting squashed right up against the wall didn't make for the most restful night's sleep. The odd disturbed night wouldn't be so bad if my entire life wasn't a succession of them, touring, staying out until all hours, then getting wrenched out of sleep first thing to go and do some radio interview somewhere.

The time had come. I would buy a place, for me and Shirl. Up by Highbury Park. The posh side. Our new ends. I would live the dream. A boy from council housing who made good and got himself on the property ladder.

Was I betraying my early punk roots? Was this me joining the rat race? A homeowner?

I bought the top-floor flat in a building that had been converted from the old post office, overlooking the park. Its red-brick facade meant it stood out from all the other houses on the street and the big, black Georgian front door looked so stately.

Gary was just up the way. Sade was nearby too. A definite Blitz contingent was laying down roots here, so I was sure I wasn't straying too far from the light.

And wasn't this the point? In just a few short years, our ideas of creating a pop culture that was productive, that built the sort of future for ourselves that we actually wanted to live in had come to pass.

We had dreamed it and we had made it.

The only question now was how to decorate it.

Kids' TV

Our drummer John was once asked what he did for a living and I will never forget his answer: 'What do I do for a living? I play music to little kids.'

There were points in 1983 where it felt like that's all we did.

They were just all so bloody early these shows. And bright. And loud. Saturday mornings in your early twenties are a bit of a struggle at the best of times. When you've only managed to get two hours of sleep after rolling in at 4 a.m. from some after-show party, before some plugger is calling you up and yelling at you down the line to get your arse along to Television Centre – it's a bit of a struggle.

As bad as that hangover sounds, you can triple it when you're placed under hot studio lights with a bunch of screaming pre-teens surrounding you. Saturday-morning telly was not a place where you found us at our brightest.

That said, I didn't suffer quite as badly as some of the stars who went on there. Children's TV in the 80s could be a hostile environment for bands. The clip that's most famous from that era is the one of Five Star appearing on *Going Live!* in 1989. A kid called Eliot phoned up the show and was put through live on air to ask Five Star a question. His question? 'I'd like to ask Five Star why they're so FUCKING CRAP!' He then continued swearing at them while someone in the studio control room faded his line down and Sarah Greene tried to pick the show back up – all the while, the camera is trained on Five Star's confused and crestfallen faces.

A similar thing happened to Matt Bianco (the band that spun themselves out of Chris Sullivan's Blue Rondo à La Turk), when a 'fan' called up *Saturday Superstore* to ask them why they were such wankers.

I had a similar moment of my own.

I'm there, a bit worse for wear, wondering where in the world we might be flying to later, whether I've got my order in for my cheese plate on the rider – the important stuff. Mike Read took a caller on the show, a young girl called Samantha, who asked to speak to me in particular. This show was going out live and she asked me, 'Have you got any favourite positions?'

I did the sort of gulp Wile E. Coyote does when he realises he's just run off the edge of a cliff and is now just waiting for the drop.

'Favourite positions?' I asked.

Please tell me this is a wind-up. Please let this be Dagger trying some insane publicity stunt. Or one of Duran Duran pulling a prank to score an easy headline off us. Anything. Please, anything. Just don't let me have to talk about the Kama Sutra on kids' TV.

'Erm, possessions,' Mike Read said calmly. 'Any favourite possessions.'

'Possessions! Oh! Right …'

This is why music videos were such an almighty blessing. If you threw yourself into making a blockbusting music video you could occasionally spare yourself the torture of kids' TV. It wasn't just the early mornings you avoided. It wasn't just the kids with sloppy diction either. With a music video you stayed in control of the way your band looked.

British kids' TV was pretty good for that, I have to say. As gruelling as those shoots could sometimes be, the production team on the UK shows generally made you look presentable – even if you had the whisky sweats.

European kids' TV, though? God almighty. The crap shoot to end all crap shoots.

Take all of the drawbacks of doing kids' TV in Britain and add to the list: hours of international travel, multiple different language barriers and the inexplicable directorial style of European TV producers.

It was so weird watching some of our TV performances that went out in Europe back then. We'd spent so long crafting our looks, the way we had learned in the Blitz, only to find that the director of Belgium's answer to *Top of the Pops* had superimposed a big clown's face over Tony's as he sang 'The Freeze', which followed him wherever he went.

Or, worse, they didn't even put a camera on you. At least Tony appeared as a well-dressed clown. Sometimes I didn't even get a limb on air.

Sending a video instead, you got a lie-in and you looked pristine. Honestly, in about 90 per cent of cases, I'd have been happy to swap all my TV performances for pre-recorded music videos. *Top of the Pops*, I'd obviously make an exception for. *The Old Grey Whistle Test* too.

And now there was a new music show that had just started on the recently launched Channel 4 that every band with any sense was queuing round the block to get on. A show that wasn't designed for kids, so much as kids like us. *The Tube*.

The Tube

The Tube had debuted in the launch week of Channel 4 in late 1982 and had only been on air a few weeks before everyone was clamouring to get on it.

Hosted by Jools Holland and our old mate Paula Yates, *The Tube* was a youth culture phenomenon. A TV show that wasn't pitched at children, or families, or chin-scratching crusties, but one that was made for our generation. Raucous, colourful and brimming over with cheek, it was as if someone had forgotten to invite any grown-ups to help make the show.

That didn't always make for the slickest television, but there was a life to *The Tube* of the sort that only comes from knowing that the whole thing could come crashing down at any second. TV without a safety net.

Unlike *Top of the Pops*, *The Tube* let bands play live and their appearances weren't contingent on good chart positions. They'd take chances on new bands, weird bands, unsigned bands.

In what now seems like a symbolic passing of the baton, the Jam used the first episode of *The Tube* to give their final TV appearance. In a later episode a now-unrecognisable early version of 'Relax' brought Frankie Goes to Hollywood to the attention of Trevor Horn (and hundreds of outraged viewers, who complained about all the debauched dancing, skimpy bras and gun-pointing).

1983 was the year *The Tube* gave an up-and-coming American artist called Madonna her UK TV debut, and also gave soul legend Tina Turner a platform to stage her big career comeback with Heaven 17.

It wasn't just music, there was comedy too – from many of the acts that had cut their teeth in the Comedy Store club above Billy's. On any given show you might see Alexei Sayle stomping around the stage shouting about Doc Martens, or French and Saunders pretending to be giggling pop fans trying to steal the spotlight from Jools.

Rik Mayall started off one episode by stumbling out of the pub next to the studio, pretending to vomit onto the pavement* and then getting the name of the show wrong. This went out at 5.30 p.m. and, according to Jools, enraged one viewer in Oxford so much that they didn't bother complaining to Channel 4. They called the police directly.

The whole show was a shambolic, anarchic scrapheap – and it was amazing. Paula's interviews with star guests were outrageously flirtatious; Jools would drag the camera crew through the corridors and into acts' dressing rooms to chat. In 1984, a band surprised producers by inviting a striking miner onto the stage to rant about Thatcher during their song. Unfortunately, the guest was so unexpected that no one had been told to turn on the mic he was ranting into – so nothing but silence was broadcast. It created a significant backlash as viewers at home were under the impression *The Tube* had chickened out, censoring the miner's remarks. It's entirely likely it was genuinely a production cock-up, though. The show was riddled with them.

I have very clear visions of our appearance; specifically visions of my jacket. That was a real stand-out piece. A

---

* It was a mouthful of cream of chicken soup.

gorgeous long-tailed coat, custom-made from an ornate jacquard fabric I'd picked out at Liberty, the legendary department store at the top of Carnaby Street.

The whole band were decked out in similarly luxe material, each of us dressed like items of furniture you'd find in Barry Manilow's Vegas hotel suite.

I don't know if we inspired her to follow suit, or if it was simply a case of great minds thinking alike, but I found out recently that Paula used to go to the upholstery department in Liberty to pick out their brightest, boldest prints. They presented her with a selection of their more striking patterns – including one that was made up of pictures of fruit and vegetables – and asked what she was intending to make. An armchair? Some curtains?

'Oh no,' she replied, 'this is being made into a dress.'

The Tube came to a slightly sticky end in 1987 when Jools called a bunch of watching children 'fuckers'. It was in a promo trailer, broadcast live, not just pre-watershed but right when all the kids had tuned in to watch cartoons. 'Be there or be ungroovy fuckers' was the line and it caused a national scandal.

It all seems so quaint now, but saying 'fuck' on telly was a big deal in the 80s. Bob Geldof's infamous outburst during Live Aid was such a shock that it's credited as being the thing that properly kick-started the donations. No matter how viscerally the conditions in Ethiopia had been described to the audience at home before then, the thing that spurred people into action was hearing Bob Geldof snap at David Hepworth, 'No, let's ... fuck the address – let's get the numbers.'

After that, the money started pouring in at a rate of £300 per second.

Nowadays, Miriam Margolyes will go on *This Morning* with Phil and Holly, swear like a docker and the lot of them will fall about in a fit of giggles, shrugging while they're apologising.

Obviously calling kids 'fuckers' hasn't put an end to Jools Holland's career completely, but as for *The Tube* – that was it. The damage was mortal. A sixth series wasn't commissioned and the decade lost its greatest show.

Roland

While America had a whole TV channel dedicated to playing music videos 24/7, Britain in the early 80s didn't even have a channel that played anything all day. BBC1, BBC2 and ITV all stopped broadcasting overnight, picking back up slowly on weekday mornings with a bunch of specialist programming.

Breakfast TV as we know it today only arrived in 1983, when both the BBC and ITV launched morning shows within a fortnight of one another, sparking an instant ratings war. *Breakfast Time* on the Beeb was the early leader, with hosts Frank Bough, Selina Scott and Nick Ross drawing in a loyal viewership. TV-am over on ITV struggled to get a foothold, until a few months in when it introduced a new host. A puppet called Roland Rat.

Roland Rat was such a huge success when he debuted to keep kids entertained on their Easter holidays, that he is credited with turning around the fortunes of TV-am. The success was so enduring that, after three years, the BBC poached him, and Roland began working his magic for the other side.

As well as his TV work, Roland released singles, albums, straight-to-video films. There were cuddly toys, T-shirts, HP Roland the Rat spaghetti shapes (a gourmet rat long before Pixar had the idea for *Ratatouille*). He was the star of an early ZX Spectrum video game, *Roland's Rat Race*.

But here's something you might not know. Roland Rat was a Blitz Kid.

OK, technically, Roland wasn't. But the guy with his hand up his arse was.

David Claridge was the creator, operator and voice of Roland Rat and in 1980, you would have found him alongside Spandau, Sade and Bananarama knocking back Schlitz and dancing away to Yellow Magic Orchestra.

I didn't particularly know David, so when the Blitz night dissipated and people moved off to their next haunts – Le Beat Route, Whisky a Go-Go – David moved across to the Hell Club on Henrietta Street, but not with Steve, Rusty and Chris. While they took the Thursday night there, David took the Wednesday night for a much more unusual event.

I'm not sure there's a word in English that comes close to describing The Ancients at Hell. Even the Germans – who have a word for everything – would probably have to cobble together something new for the occasion. David wasn't just taking fashion inspiration from the bygone centuries, like the New Romantics were. He was taking the music too.

The flyer for The Ancients promised Bach and Bauhaus, Mozart and Magazine, Chopin and Clock DVA – the most ambitious span of music contained in any one night I've ever seen. Four hundred years of music crammed into one room on one night, while he dressed in breeches, a doublet and a massive, massive ruff.

But even a night as eclectic as The Ancients didn't quite contain the many interests of David Claridge. Another post-Blitz night of his was called The Great Wall and was based around the fashion and music of the Far East. I never made it down there myself but I know Boy George often went as he famously dabbled with the geisha aesthetic throughout the Culture Club years.

And even that didn't quite cover it either. He also started another night called Skin Too, which was a rubber fetish night (one that caused him quite a bit of embarrassment when the tabloids uncovered it a few years into Roland's ascent to superstardom).

I don't want to take anything away from David in floating this next little theory of mine. Creating a superstar rat puppet was not anything we expected to emerge from the Blitz, so clearly his success was all his own – but I've always been curious about the inspiration for Roland.

For all the talk (mine included) of how it was people like Steve Strange and Rusty Egan and Chris Sullivan who most heavily influenced the direction of the 80s, I think there's a case to be made for someone else who rarely gets mentioned. Someone I know for a fact had a foundational influence on the ideas and enthusiasm of almost every single person in that room – but is often brushed over in the retelling.

It's quite possible that the single most consequential figure at the Blitz – and, by extension, of a huge swathe of 80s pop culture as well – was the club's resident speed-slinger: Barry the Rat.

Booze and Blues

Of the four quid or so I'd turn up to the Blitz with in my pocket, two of them would go to Steve Strange on the door. A handful of the remaining shrapnel would end up behind the bar for as many bottles of Schlitz as it would get me, but one pound would always be reserved for Barry the Rat.

Barry would do you three blues for a pound and everybody I knew in there paid him a visit. You basically had to. Conversations moved at what felt like a thousand words a minute on those Tuesday nights so you had no chance of keeping up with them if Barry hadn't fuelled you up. Besides, as I'd inevitably sink my bus fare home on beers, the long walk home to Islington took a hell of a lot longer if you weren't buzzing off your head.

The nickname 'Barry the Rat' didn't come from him being a telltale or a bastard or anything. It was much simpler than that. It came from an actual rat that he'd bring along to the Blitz that would sit on his shoulder and scurry around his mohair jumpers. You didn't ask questions. If you asked Barry about his rat, you would then have to ask Princess Julia why she was dressed as a day-glo Lily Munster or Leigh Bowery why he was wearing eight pairs of reading glasses as a hat.

You let people be people at the Blitz. That was the joy of it.

I'd be interested to hear an economist's take on the financial impact of the Blitz. When I was on the dole in those days, I sunk a decent chunk of my weekly allowance in there. The art students from Central and St Martin's were hardly living lives of lavish luxury either, but what little they had would be poured into booze and blues there. And what was the upshot? An explosion of rich, creative work that had national and international resonance.

Spandau Ballet, Sade, Culture Club, Bananarama, Visage, Haysi Fantayzee, Marilyn, Animal Nightlife, Sigue Sigue Sputnik, Blue Rondo à La Turk and all sorts of others. Dozens of albums – and hundreds of millions of copies of them – had their roots in that club.

That was just the music. We don't even need to count the contributions made by John Galliano at Givenchy, Dior and his own label. That cabinet full of BAFTAs and Emmys Michelle Clapton won for her costume design in seven series of *Game of Thrones*. Or the international exhibitions staged by sculptor and artist Cerith Wyn Evans.

Again, I'm not looking to glamorise the use of drugs or drink. However, purely in terms of return on investment (surely one of the 80s' key metrics) the profit percentage made from the relatively tiny amount we spent on Barry's speckled blues must have been astronomical. Thatcher would never have dared to admit it, but Barry the Rat was a titan of industry. A self-starter who made an overwhelmingly positive impact on British culture and society by selling speed to students.

I'm being flippant here, obviously – but the tension between the Conservative government of the day and this new wave of alt-establishment subcultures on both sides of the Atlantic produced some sparks of incredible brilliance.

Sadly, that tension also led to some much darker things too.

A Simple Handshake

From what I can remember, the whispers started getting louder in the spring of '83. No one quite knew exactly what it was but people had been getting terribly sick. They'd been dying. Men, anecdotally. No one I knew personally – not yet – but there was a chilling similarity to the stories that our friends kept telling.

Subcultures and fringe communities often get described as little families. For many within these groups, that is exactly how they function. What start out as social gatherings of like-minded people who share a certain interest or outlook eventually grow to provide the sort of support network we're always told a nuclear family is supposed to. I was lucky enough to have both: a loving set of parents at home and the extended Blitz Kids family outside of that. For others I knew, who – for a variety of reasons – didn't have families they could depend on, the friendships they formed would take their place.

In eras of political turmoil, economic hardship and general national gloom, these sorts of networks are a wonderful thing.

In times of true crisis, they are utterly indispensable.

Whether or not having ties to the creative industries and club scenes meant that I heard more about AIDS earlier on, I don't know. I can't imagine I had much of a head start on anyone, what with me floating off in the Spandau Bubble so often. But if there's one group of people who definitely knew more than I did, when I did, it was politicians.

Everything I was hearing at street level was so serious and frightening. Medics had been doing everything they could to understand this new disease, to prevent it from spreading out uncontrollably. There was no way their reports weren't reaching government desks. Yet politicians on both sides of the Atlantic preferred to stick their heads in the sand and refuse to address it.

When sexual contact and drug use were identified as likely points of transmission, they did nothing. As the problem grew and the cries got louder, they still did nothing. They did less than nothing. They let fear and hatred flourish, afraid of the example it might set to show some compassion or humanity towards the predominantly gay patients.

To think that four years later, in 1987, the simple act of shaking a patient's hand as Princess Diana did was seen as a groundbreaking gesture. That was still the stage we were at then.

With no statements from the government or much in the way of mass media reporting, we had to work on whatever dribs and drabs of information made their way to us through word of mouth. Undoubtedly a lot of it was ill-informed and dangerous – but, in the absence of anything else, what could we do? All we knew were the stories of what had happened to friends of friends of friends. Then friends of friends. And, in time, friends.

The shockwaves AIDS sent through the music business ran deep. The industry famously ran on sex, drugs and rock'n'roll and had built up a voracious appetite for them throughout the 70s. Almost overnight, a lot of that appeared to evaporate. Budgets once reserved for such expenditure got reallocated to luxury goods instead: fancy restaurants, fine wines, the latest gadgets and gizmos. With the rampant consumerism and yuppie culture of the 80s getting into full swing, it seemed like a sensible substitute.

It wasn't a solution, though. It did nothing to solve the root problem. All it did was drive the sex and drugs that people were still having out to the fringes where they could be more easily ignored. And that ignorance was deadly.

The spectre of AIDS haunts the entire decade. Eventually it would take people I knew. People I loved.

I was fortunate enough to be able to retreat from the ugly reality of what ignorance and government inaction were causing whenever I needed to. Not all of my friends were so lucky. With no families to turn to and a state that did not care whether they lived or died, they were forced to support each other.

It often falls to artists to pick up this slack. There is nothing unique about the 80s in that respect. Countercultures and marginalised communities have always joined forces when the ruling classes hang them out to dry. It's a massive responsibility to lay at the feet of artists and it comes at a huge emotional cost, but that's what these friends – these families – do for each other.

When the extent of the epidemic became clear towards the end of the decade and a public education programme finally took the place of a rumour mill, the damage could start to be controlled.

But things would be awful for years to come. Our decade's great shame.

◊ ◊ ◊

No. 1,000

Dagger was calling. He had news. Good news.

I should have known what it was before I picked up the phone. A call that early in the morning. In my hotel room. On that day. With all that hooting and hollering outside in the corridor. I guess I just couldn't quite let myself believe it had happened.

We were No. 1.

I don't know where I was on Dagger's call sheet, but I must have been underneath our drummer because when I opened my door, who came whizzing past me, joyriding up and down the length of the corridor on the chambermaid's cleaning trolley, but Keeble.

Like I say, I should have known. Dagger had been keeping us keenly up to date on daily sales figures for 'True' and they were all pointing this way. The first afternoon it had sold 30,000. On another, he told us we had cleared 70,000 in a single day. Those sorts of numbers could only mean one thing, but I was still knocked head over heels to hear it.

No. 1.

Obviously Gary deserves the lion's share of the credit for writing the song, but the omnipotent hand of Dagger had been in it too. After all, it was his idea to go to the Bahamas.

After the doldrums that *Diamond* had thrown us into, we had got ourselves completely in our own heads. We had always been a bit guilty of trying to second guess our audience, give them something they didn't quite expect, keep evolving our sound – but as soon as 'Paint Me Down' and

'She Loved Like Diamond' died on the vine, we had started to spin out.

Our arch rivals, Duran Duran, meanwhile were riding high on their second-album effort *Rio* – which had spawned smash singles like 'Save a Prayer', 'Hungry Like the Wolf' and the title track. Their videos saw them sailing on yachts, windswept in their Antony Price suits, laying claim to the world. I was still living at home, having my mum run me up frilly shirts on her sewing machine. We were obsessing over it, trying to figure out how we could claw our way back ahead of them.

Dagger saw that we wouldn't get any clarity stuck where we were, which is how we ended up at Compass Point Studios in the Bahamas for the *True* sessions.

Here's my great secret about 'True', our only No. 1 hit: I don't play on it.

Having parted ways with Richard Burgess and failing to properly click with Trevor Horn, we were on the lookout for a new producer. In the end, we found two: Steve Jolley and Tony Swain. Jolley and Swain had been working with our fellow Blitz Kids Bananarama on songs like 'Shy Boy' and 'Na Na Hey Hey' (and would go on to do the beloved 'Cruel Summer' and 'Robert De Niro's Waiting' too), but it was the stuff they'd previously produced for the band Imagination that really interested me.

The bass sounds the pair of them had crafted for songs like 'Body Talk', 'Just an Illusion' and 'Music and Lights' were so great, I felt as though Spandau could do with some of it too. Those Imagination lines weren't played on a bass guitar, though. They're played down low on a synthesiser.

When it came to discussing what we could do with this six-minute pop-soul song that Gary had written, I thought this would be the moment to float it. 'Let's use a bass synth for this one!' I suggested, then headed out to lay by the pool while Jolley and Swain sorted that all out for me. Why would I mess with the experts?

Obviously it became Spandau's biggest hit – and I don't play a note on it. Most stupid of all, I was the one who wrote myself out – so I only have myself to blame.* In my defence, though, as much as we all loved that track in the studio, 'True' wasn't an immediate choice for a single. Not because it wasn't good but because it was so long. The album version is over six minutes. Even the single edit is about 5.30. That's not standard for a pop record.

Radio around the world is geared towards three-minute songs for the simple reason that was about as much music as you could fit on those early vinyl records. The grooves on them would run out if you went on any longer. Fledgling stations built their broadcast schedules around songs that length and then sold ad slots to fit around them. Once that ad template got locked into place, DJs needed more songs that would fit in between them. Advertising was what kept the lights on in those broadcast houses, so the ads took priority. Songs were a secondary consideration; something to stop you tuning out between commercials.

Even after recording technology enabled you to make songs longer, the die was already cast. Audiences were primed for three-minute songs and radio needed reliable

* Actually, Jolley and Swain should shoulder some of it for creating such a seductive bass sound. Honestly, go and listen to Imagination and decide for yourself if that sound isn't worth airbrushing yourself out of history for.

space fillers, so if you wanted any airplay you had to play ball. Unless you had a very good excuse.

'Bohemian Rhapsody' is the classic example of one such excuse. Impossible to trim down but too good to ignore, radio made a rare exception. They made one for 'True' too.

Peter Powell played it on his Radio 1 show in the afternoon and enjoyed it so much that he played it again straight after. Audiences, thankfully, didn't revolt. 'True' went straight in at No. 1 when it was finally released in April and of all the people to knock off the top spot, we dislodged David Bowie.

We had been playing a gig in Nottingham that night which, by chance, Steve Strange had come up to see. It was wonderful to get to celebrate with him – the man who had given us our first proper gig as Spandau Ballet – but he wasn't the only person who got to share in our happiness.

Two comedians had been playing Nottingham that same night and were staying in our hotel. Which is why Spandau found themselves ringing in their very first chart-topping record in the company of Les Dawson and Jim Davidson.

The No. 1 couldn't have come at a better time because 5 May of that year was a landmark moment in pop music history. The 1,000th episode of *Top of the Pops* – and we would be headlining it.

They drafted in so many famous faces to mark the occasion, the show was an all-star cast – but the only one I got butterflies in my stomach to see was Cilla Black. After the show I plucked up the nerve to approach her in the studio and tell her that she had been my first big crush as a kid. I even relayed the story about how I had walked up to the TV when she was on and planted a little smooch on the screen.

It did not go down well. Cilla was horrified. She absolutely hated the story as it made her feel ancient and she left me in no doubt that I should have kept my mouth shut.

Ah, well. It didn't bother me too much. I had found another love through the TV screen on *Top of the Pops* – and she was waiting at home for me.

Mixed Metals

Here's a bit of Spandau trivia that has absolutely no bearing on anything else, but I've always found quite fun.

'True' regularly gets described as Spandau's signature hit. Maybe that's because it was No. 1 for so long. Maybe it's because it's the one that finally broke America. 'True' is the song that's cropped up on the soundtracks to films like *Sixteen Candles*, *The Wedding Singer*, *Charlie's Angels*. It's the one that cropped up on *The Simpsons* (twice). The one we played at Live Aid; the one that has been played at every wedding you've been to in the last 40 years.

That distinctive opening refrain is an exquisitely crafted earworm that can leave you singing it for days on end if you aren't careful, so I can see why it's the one people always remember.

But 'True' wasn't our biggest-selling single.

'True' was our first to go gold. But 'Gold' was our first to go platinum.

Wake-Up Call

Towards the end of 1983 Shirlie and I were getting some good stretches of quality time in together. One evening, we were round at George Michael's house. Unlike me and Shirl, who were now impressive young homeowners, George was still living at his mum and dad's. We're all hanging out, watching TV and having a few drinks – all very homely, all very nice. But when we go to leave, I forget to take my jacket.

The next morning I ask Shirl if she can drive me back to get it. She agrees and we head back to Radlett. Her white Ford Capri pulls up just outside the house and I knock on the door to ask for it. Yog answers and ushers me inside.

'While you're here,' he says, 'let me show you this new track I've been working on.'

George leads me up to his bedroom – the room where he had had Shirlie call me this time last year to set up our first date; the same date he would then crash – and sits me down to play me this tune: 'Wake Me Up Before You Go-Go'.

He'd got the title off Andrew. The two of them had been at Andrew's parents' house, staying up late playing music, but Andrew had to be up early the next morning, so left a note for his parents in the kitchen asking them to rouse him before they left the house. When he noticed he'd accidentally written 'Wake me up up' in the first line, he leaned in to his mistake and wrote 'go' twice at the end too.

Wake me up up
Before you go go

The track starts and George watches me as it plays. It's just a demo at this point, him singing over a bass line he was playing. My eyes get wide. I start nodding my head. 'Ah, George!' I say, full of beans. 'That's great. Really nice. Great track. Love it. *Love it*.'

Shirlie is still waiting outside, idling. When the song is over, I bundle my coat up over my arm, head out and pile back into the car as George waves us off.

'Everything OK?' Shirl asks, slipping the car into gear.

'Nope,' I reply. 'You're going to need to find something else to do, Shirl. Your career's over. What a pile of shite.'

1984
PARADE

'Purple Rain' | Miami Vice | *Torvill and Dean* | *MTV Video Music Awards* | *Apple Macintosh Goes on Sale* | *LA Summer Olympics* | Murder, She Wrote | *'What's Love Got to Do with It?'* | *Sarajevo Winter Olympics* | Threads | Teenage Mutant Ninja Turtles | Tetris | *Birkin Bag* | *Brighton Hotel Bombing* | Footloose | 'Like a Virgin' | *Tommy Cooper Collapses on Stage* | *Cirque du Soleil* | *Marvin Gaye Shot* | Stop Making Sense | Muppet Babies | *'99 Luftballons'* | The Unbearable Lightness of Being | Duck Hunt | *'I Know Him So Well'*

Making It Big

Once again, I was absolutely and completely wrong. 'Wake Me Up Before You Go-Go' was an absolutely mammoth record. Wham!'s first UK and US No. 1, it marked the beginning of an amazing year for them that – by anyone else's standards – contained enough to fill an entire career.

'Wake Me Up Before You Go-Go'. 'Careless Whisper'. 'Freedom'. 'Everything She Wants'. 'Last Christmas'. All released one after the other in 1984 and I honestly cannot think of a band who had a run of singles quite so hot. Forty years later and every last one of these tracks holds up impeccably.

In recent years, I've been touring the country with my Back to the 80s DJ sets. Like this book, these nights are a love letter to the decade. I play tracks that span every genre of the full ten years and encourage the crowd to dress in whatever 80s fashion they want. For some of them, that means going full New Romantic. Some go for the day-glo shell suits and sweatbands. There's always a few fellas who come looking like Don Johnson in *Miami Vice*. Others opt for the blue jean–black leather jacket ensemble, aiming for *Lethal Weapon* but often landing on *Lovejoy*.

But out of all the different looks I see out in the audience on those nights, there is one above all others that comes to the fore when the dress code is 80s. A baggy white T-shirt with a big black slogan on it.

CHOOSE LIFE. FEED THE WORLD. STAY ALIVE IN 85. I LOVE THE 80S.

From what I've told you so far about the scene I grew up in and the ostentatious, extravagant outfits we all swanned about in, you might think that a plain, shapeless T-shirt with a few words printed on it was the polar opposite of everything that the Blitz stood for. Choosing function over beauty, clarity over colour, comfort over style. Blandness like that must have made us sick to our stomachs, right?

Here's the twist, though. Those iconic 80s T-shirts were created by a Blitz Kid.

Katharine Hamnett was a little older than us, a graduate from St Martin's who had spent a few years travelling the major fashion capitals as a freelance designer before starting her own label in 1979 just as Billy's and the Blitz were getting going.

At that time I remember she was making these huge, brightly coloured shirts made from what I think was parachute material. They were lovely things. Very tactile – and definitely caught the wind if you were out when a breeze picked up. I had one in white myself. You'd wear it so that your chest was showing underneath and (although I never went for this myself) it really wouldn't have looked out of place to have a nice, chunky medallion rattling about down there. I remember George had a yellow Katharine Hamnett shirt that was a real favourite of his, which is likely why he was first in line when her signature style changed.

A few years later, Katharine's political activism came rushing to the fore and she started producing these statement shirts instead. 'CHOOSE LIFE' was her first. The stark simplicity of it harked back to the punk era, but the message was one of positivity. In many ways, it was the core of the New Romantic message just without the frills, whistles and bells.

This was the shirt that George and Andrew made famous in the 'Wake Me Up Before You Go-Go' video* – with Shirlie, Pepsi and the rest of the band all dressed in 'GO-GO' ones.

Curiously, the best remembered of the slogan T-shirts is probably the one that says 'FRANKIE SAY RELAX', which is the one shirt that Katharine Hamnett didn't actually create – but it came with her blessing.

Remember I mentioned a punk zine called *Sniffin' Glue*? The photocopied, black and white handbook for punks in the late 70s that self-destructed when it got too famous, encouraging readers to rip it off and replace it with their own version?

Sniffin' Glue was one of Katharine's major inspirations for those T-shirts – both in look and outlook. She had no problem with people taking the idea and stealing it. In fact, she actively encouraged it. Having come up through the same punk/post-punk/Blitz pipeline, this was the only creative culture she'd ever known.

---

* Roger Taylor also wore the 'CHOOSE LIFE' design in Queen's video for 'Hammer to Fall' later in the year.

So when Frankie Goes to Hollywood were causing huge controversy with 'Relax' in 1984 – a song the BBC had banned from the radio for its 'sexually suggestive lyrics'* – their label decided to capitalise on the controversy with a tie-in T-shirt.

What better way to shock your parents than by wearing a T-shirt that's all about delayed ejaculation?

This connection to those early punk ideals is key to understanding what happened next. Katharine's shift in style from bright-coloured parachute shirts to monochrome, but positive, political messaging marked a broader sea change in pop culture.

As both a former punk and former Blitz Kid herself, Katharine personifies it perfectly.

The punk era that our (slight) elders like Katharine had played an active role in shaping was all about saying fuck you to the Establishment. The monarchy, the government, the generation above. Set it all on fire. It all needed to go.

The New Romantic movement that I had played an active role in shaping (and Katharine helped style) existed as a reaction to that. A swinging back of the pendulum. Rather than wanting to destroy the Establishment, we preferred to avoid it completely and create an alternative world for ourselves instead.

In 1984 and 1985, these two ideologies would find common ground. The first major example of this occurred at the very end of 1984, when an ex-punk and an ex-Blitz

---

* This description always makes me laugh. 'John Wayne Is Big Leggy' by Haysi Fantayzee has sexually suggestive lyrics. 'Pull Up to the Bumper' by Grace Jones has sexually suggestive lyrics. 'Relax' is absolutely 100 per cent about sex. There's no suggestion about it!

Kid would join forces to create something that would permanently alter pop culture's power on the global stage. They would do it while wearing Katharine's T-shirts too.

But before that, at the start of the year, it was Katharine herself who gave a small preview of what was in store.

The Message

In March '84, Katharine was invited to an event in Downing Street. It was a reception for the fashion industry, which – thanks in part to the attention that the New Romantic style had earned Britain on the global catwalk – was thriving.

Her first instinct was to turn the invitation down. She wasn't alone in that feeling. All sorts of artists and activists considered Thatcher to be a physical embodiment of evil, the figurehead of a philosophy that made profit a priority above people. The idea of putting that to one side to enjoy nibbles and champers with Maggie the Milk Snatcher was abhorrent to every ounce of their being. Katharine wasn't keen on chumming about with Thatcher either, but she had a plan in mind.

It was a formal event to celebrate the best in British fashion, but Katharine turned up to No. 10 looking like she'd made the opposite of an effort. She had the air of someone whose alarm had gone off 20 seconds ago; someone who had rushed downstairs to let a plumber in. Her bobbed hair was all messy and distressed, and under her jacket she had on this huge, floppy white T-shirt, the type of thing most people would wear as a nightie or to re-grout the bathroom.

This was not high fashion. It was barely even fashion at all. But that was the point.

Someone at the door offered to take Katharine's jacket but she kept it on, clutching it closed across her chest until the time was right. As Maggie approached her with a hand outstretched and a photographer in tow, Katharine flung it open.

The first thing your eye is drawn to in that photo is the slogan on Katharine's top. Thatcher's eye is too. It was bold, it was clear and it was about eight inches from the prime minister's face. '58% DON'T WANT PERSHING'.

Pershing was the name of an American nuclear weapons system and America was drawing up plans in the 80s to stockpile its missiles in various tactical locations in Western Europe so they would be close enough to strike the Soviet Union should the Cold War start spicing up again.

The majority of Britons – understandably – didn't want the country to become a dumping ground for American cruise missiles, nor a tactical strike target for Soviet ones. That feeling would only intensify when the BBC's horrifying nuclear disaster movie *Threads* was released later in the year.

Katharine could have stayed home that day, designed another T-shirt, written another mission statement in the hope her message broke through. This way, she made sure that Thatcher couldn't ignore it.

This was the way things would work now. The Establishment we had deliberately tried to ignore would soon come crashing into us. Not because we couldn't avoid it any longer, but because it couldn't avoid us. We had captured the eyes, ears and hearts of a generation and that would grant us access to the levers of power, the like of which artists and musicians had never had before.

Christmas '84 would see it explode.

The Keycard Conundrum

Of all the technological advances rolled out in the 80s, one that didn't quite work out so well for me was the introduction of mag-stripe hotel keycards.

At the start of 1984, Spandau found themselves in Munich. Following the same formula that proved such a success with the *True* sessions, we decided we needed to escape the country again. Cast off the commitments of daily life, shut out the hundreds of bands that were popping up in the charts following the New Romantic playbook and hole ourselves away.

Steve Dagger's plan to have us do that at Compass Point in the Bahamas had been just the tonic we needed to kick us out of the second-album slump. Our new plan to lock ourselves away in a basement in Munich in the dead of winter, where the pavement above us was coated in snow and the last drops of sunlight died in the stairwell – well, it was a gear change.

We'd got the idea from Queen. We'd got to know them a little bit doing promo stuff around and about, and they had been working at this studio for the last few years. They had such an incredible sound at that point, recording songs like 'Another One Bites the Dust', 'Crazy Little Thing Called Love' and 'Hammer to Fall' in this same Munich bunker.

Musicland was the name of the studio. It had been responsible for Donna Summer's genre-bending electro-disco track 'I Feel Love' – the song that put Giorgio Moroder on the map and took synthesisers out of experimental art rock and put them slap bang in the middle of Top 40 radio.

But I cannot, for the life of me, understand how that place provided so much influence for so many artists. Led Zeppelin did *Presence* there. The Rolling Stones did *It's Only Rock 'n Roll* there. Marc Bolan & T. Rex did *Zinc Alloy and the Hidden Riders of Tomorrow* there. But the place was a fucking bunker. There are submarines crawling the ocean floor that had more character. Even ones that have been sunk.

I had been in basements before. Billy's had been a hotbed of creativity and inspiration, and it was as dingy as basements get. Musicland, though, I could not cope with.

Adding to the sense of claustrophobia was the fact that the hotel we were staying in, the Arabella, was directly above us. For two months our lives revolved around the staircases of the Arabella Hochhaus. Downstairs to the basement to work; upstairs to our rooms to sleep. So we were keen, whenever we got the chance, to escape the complex completely and get out to a bar or a club.

P1 ('Pee-Eines') was the one we could rely on most for a good night. One such night, we rolled back into the Arabella at around 3 a.m., feeling the effects of those big German beers. My hotel keycard in my pocket, I was quite keen for the loo, so as soon as we arrived I headed up to my room to answer nature's call. My keycard beeped, the door unlocked and I stumbled into the bathroom.

I don't know how long I'd been sat on the loo exactly when I first noticed the toiletries dotted around the bathroom sink, but I know how far I was through my business.

That wasn't my black leather toiletries bag. My after-shave was Aramis; I didn't wear Polo by Ralph Lauren. And wasn't Charlie a perfume for women?

As the realisation was trying to karate-kick its way through the drunken fog of my brain, I heard it. Someone snoring from the bedroom. Two people. A couple.

By this time, I'm sorry to say, it was too late. There's no way of sugar coating this, so I'll just tell you. I had done a poo. It was out. It was done. The bell could not be unrung. The toothpaste would not go back in the tube. So what did I do now?

Flush? I could. I should. But if I do, the noise means there's no way I'm getting out of here without getting busted. So do I just leave it and quietly sneak out?

I know there's a long, proud history of rock stars causing chaos in hotel rooms. Keith Richards throwing TVs out of windows. Keith Moon driving cars into pools. Billy Idol once had the Thai army call on him at a hotel in Bangkok and shoot him with tranquillisers to put an end to the three-week orgy he'd been staging in his room. But even he probably would have drawn the line at plopping in some strangers' loo and leaving it to soak overnight.

In the end, I left it. I had to. I had to walk away. The vision of it haunts me to this day and, in my quiet moments, I still think about the effect it must have had on that poor couple. Each thinking the other must have done it, leaving it there for their partner to deal with. Maybe they had an argument about it; a blazing row about their disgusting habits. Maybe they didn't – and maybe that's worse. My mystery log being a simmering resentment that bubbled away for years. A phantom turd that coloured every little thing they did from that morning onwards. All the while never knowing that it was actually the bass player from Spandau Ballet who'd done it.

Is there a point to this little story? Not really. But next time you arrive at a hotel and lug your heavy luggage up to the fifth floor only to find that flimsy keycard they gave you won't let you into your room, no matter which way round you try it, please do remember that the alternative could be so much worse.

Cabin Fever

Back in the bunker, things weren't going so well. Not for me, at least. The *Parade* sessions themselves were coming along nicely but being cooped up in that studio, in the cold German winter, miles from Shirlie – it was killing me.

The way a song is recorded, generally speaking, is that you get the drums and the bass down first. You lock in the rhythm section's tracks as a foundation and then you're free to experiment with whatever other instruments, effects and arrangements you want after that.

When you're doing an album, the process is the same – except you don't record it song by song, you do it instrument by instrument. Because of the delicate set-up involved in positioning mics for the drums, you don't want to have to dismantle that 12 times over the course of the recording. Instead, you have John get all his drum tracks down for every single track. Then he packs up his drum kit for good and I strap on my bass. My lines go down over each of his drum tracks and once that's all done, that was usually me done too.

At Compass Point, in the Bahamas, that meant from about day four I was free to spend weeks on end floating in the pool, drinking Mai Tais and getting myself nice and bronzed. It was bliss. Apart from his own flat, there was no place better for an unneeded bass player to find himself.

Musicland, on the other hand, was a nightmare. It was like sitting in a TV studio dressing room waiting to be called to set, but instead of waiting for half an hour I was waiting for six weeks.

The sole distraction down there was a pinball machine. I'm not anti-pinball, as a rule, but it's hardly the most nourishing thing for the soul. Six weeks of the sound of thumping bumpers is enough to drive anyone to despair.

And yet, I couldn't leave. Technically, I suppose I could have done. It wasn't like I was being held at gunpoint. I wasn't even under contract to put in a certain number of hours. If I wanted to walk out into the freezing Munich winter, then I was free to – but I still couldn't. I was too afraid of what it would do to the group dynamic.

At the Blitz and on stage we may have dabbled a bit with femininity – playing with colourful clothing, sparkly jewellery and make-up. However, there was no real hiding the fact that we were still – at heart, underneath it all – five North London lads. Lock us up in a studio for two months at a time and we became beasts.

A lot of what passed between us in those long, interminable sessions is what gets commonly brushed off as 'banter' nowadays. But then, like now, it was essentially us being arseholes to one another, behaviour that all too easily tipped over into bullying. Regrettably, most of this turned on Tony. When the five of us were together and got into one of those moods, it was Tony who bore the brunt of the stick.

It was never vicious. Never abusive or physical or completely out of control. It was just mean-spirited. Unnecessarily so. And relentless.

I know a lot of how men in their twenties communicate is wrapped up in piss-taking, ribbing, pranks and practical jokes. In many ways, I don't suppose we were that much different to any other group of blokes at that time who worked long hours together. It was just 'boys being boys'. Looking back now, though, I'm bitterly disappointed – in myself, definitely, but also at the rest of the band – at the way we treated Tony.

Maybe Tony doesn't care. Maybe he thinks we were all a bunch of pricks and is strong enough to rise above it all. I'm sure he is, but that still doesn't excuse the way he got treated in those sessions and grappling with it now as a grown man, I blush with shame at some of it.

What makes it especially disappointing for me is that Tony and I had actually grown a bit closer at Compass Point. What with him recently having married Leonie and me being in a relationship with Shirl, Tone became a much-needed source of companionship and strength while the rest of the band were off enjoying the single life.

He was someone who understood the weird juggling act that a coupled-up pop star has to perform. Splitting your time between two loves; spinning plates constantly so nothing crashes. So for me to turn on him seems just that little bit crueller too.

Part of it, I'm sure, was singer envy. It strikes every band at some point. Even though the spotlight was relatively well split across Spandau compared with some bands, attention always gravitates towards the singer. It's only natural. Not only are they the most visible, they're also the most vulnerable.

Singing is an unbearably exposing thing to do. Playing bass has its pressures, no doubt, but it doesn't require you to show your soul.

When I mentioned earlier that the rhythm section had the greatest responsibility in keeping the band on track, I stand by that – but it's a purely mechanical thing. Our mistakes can cause a song to collapse, but there's no emotional toll to be paid if that happens. I'd be embarrassed and beat myself up about it for days, for sure. In the end, though, it's only fingers and strings. It's not my voice. It's not my heart.

Tony always handled that role magnificently. He was a powerhouse. That voice of his set us apart from any number of the bands who played their instruments as well as we did. Leading a band is so much stress to carry on your back, so why we wanted to heap any more on him, I can't tell you. But I know that we did it and, what's more, I know that's why I didn't leave the bunker that day. Because I didn't want any of that banter to turn on me. The lightweight. The pin-up. The clothes horse. If I went home for the four weeks between my basslines and backing vocals, who knows what material they could workshop in my absence to start bullying me. The bassist. The baby brother. The one who could barely play his instrument anyway.

So even though I was miserable, I stayed put.

I don't see Tony much anymore and when I read in the papers that he will never do anything with the band again,

I can't blame him. I know the courage it takes to leave, because back then I didn't have it.

The Suitcase

When Spandau first started going out on the road, we had an official entourage of one: Alan Keys.

Alan was our earliest recruit that wasn't just a Blitz Kid we'd roped in to help out. He was a proper employee, placed in charge of our wardrobe. Everything else we could just about lug around ourselves but as our clothing was such a vital part of the band's appeal, it wasn't something we could afford to half-arse. Having a designated wardrobe technician to take care of all our outfits – for promo appearances, for photoshoots, for the stage – was essential.

At the beginning, that was all the help we really needed. Which was lucky because it was also the only help we could afford. After a few years, though, when the band started to get bigger, it became clear we needed some security.

For me, the turning point came in Liverpool. After a gig at the Empire in 1982, the band were all enjoying an aftershow drink in our dressing room when there was a tap at the window. We looked over to see a smiling fan waving at us, trying to get in. Under any other circumstance, we probably wouldn't have been quite so alarmed but our dressing room at the Empire was on the second floor and she had shimmied up a very flimsy drainpipe to say hello.

We immediately opened the window to pull her to safety only to find she had a mate in tow, hot on her tail. The two of them ended up being very sweet and were no threat to us at all, but there was no guarantee that every fan who was prepared to scale a building to seek us out would be so benign. It hadn't been so long ago that John Lennon was shot dead by an obsessed fan at the foot of his apartment building. Would-be assassins had been on the rise recently, a couple of others having taken pot shots at President Reagan and the Pope. It was a dangerous time to be famous.

By the time of the *True* tour, the crowds that formed outside our hotels were getting so large that we had a security team of five. Perhaps that was a little overcautious, but our entourage was also charged with some other, equally vital responsibilities.

For instance, there was The Suitcase.

The Suitcase was usually carried by Alf Weaver. As head minder, Alf was the one who kept the other four security staff up to speed and was therefore the one we could rely on for this very special task.

For this was no ordinary suitcase. This was Spandau's equivalent of the nuclear codes. Alf took our lives in his hands every time he took charge of The Suitcase. It was a serious task.

The case was standard size, but with a purpose-built interior featuring custom-cut foam inserts to securely transport some highly sensitive pieces of cargo. At all times, Alf would be carrying with him one bottle of Moët, one bottle of tequila, five shot glasses and five bibs.* This could be required at any hour of the day. If emergency struck and one of us started feeling a bit knackered, we would need our pick-me-up slammers, stat!

---

* The bibs were only for if we were in our stage clothes. We might have been big man-babies, but we weren't actual babies.

In those days booze was everywhere. Literally everywhere. If we weren't with Alf, then that meant we were either in our hotel rooms (where we would have a minibar) or we were on stage. And our on-stage solution to alcohol provision was, if I do say so myself, complete genius.

Drummers set up on something called a drum riser: a small stage upon a stage that allows them to still be seen when they're sat down at their kit. A booster seat for drummers, basically.

Usually, the drum riser doesn't need to be anything more than a foot high to work. Ours was six. Excessive probably, but the reason it had to be that big was because we kept a secret on-stage pub underneath it. It wasn't something the audience could see. The front and sides of it were all boarded up, so you could only access it from the back of the stage – but if you walked behind the drum riser you'd see it clearly: the Keeble Arms.

It was tiny, but it was filled to the brim with booze. Beers, wine, a fully loaded optics rack of spirits for easy one-handed pouring. There was even a dartboard in there. Not that we got any time to play during the show, but if any of us ever fancied a quick sharpener between songs, it was all there waiting, whenever we wanted it.

You can probably sense already that this wasn't a very healthy dependence we were fostering – but there's something very unique about the adrenaline rush of playing a concert that marries so well with drinking.

Adrenaline is hard to manage and something that, as a bass player, you have to be able to control. The rhythm section is there to keep the band in time. The adrenaline coursing through your veins pushes every fibre in your body forward ever faster, but while you're on stage you need to master it. You cannot let it disrupt your playing.

Keeping that spring coiled for a full two hours means that when the final chord is hit, you're fit to explode.

The adrenaline rush of coming off stage from a concert is one thing I've found impossible to replicate in later life, no matter what I've done. I've worked pretty extensively in entertainment now and there is nothing that compares to it.

Acting in a studio is a slow, unglamorous process. Late nights, early mornings, bursts of repetitive activity followed by hours of waiting. Alcohol just makes all of that harder.

Acting in a play gives you a connection with an audience that can be electrifying – but it's different. You're playing a character that you leave on the stage. When the curtain comes down on a play, I can't think of any actor who has responded by running back to their dressing room and pouring neat spirits straight down their throat (not unless things went really badly).

The closest thing I could compare it to anywhere else is sports. The football or F1, when winning teams start spraying champagne all around, greedily guzzling it from the bottle. I see that same voracious hunger in them. The sense of release is palpable. You can only win the FA Cup once a season, though. We were playing every night.

You step off stage on this incredible high and there's all these people wanting to see you. A different city's worth every night. Crate after crate of booze is laid out for you to host them – and we had a Spandau rule of throwing away the lids so that the drink had to get drunk. Every last drop.

My crunch point with drinking came a few years later, at some point in '86 or '87 (the detail is, predictably, a bit fuzzy). Somewhere on the *Through the Barricades* tour someone gave me one of those big biblical bottles of champagne. I can never remember which size is a Balthazar, or a Methuselah, or a Nebuchadnezzar, or whoever but it was one of those show-off ones and it was huge.

I know those things are made for sharing, but it was my gift and I fancied spoiling myself. So I did. So much so that I almost poisoned myself. I got as much of it down as I was physically able before I staggered into bed, but I just couldn't sleep. The rest of the bottle, from the other side of the room, was taunting me. It wouldn't leave me be. The idea that there was champagne in my room going unfinished, my brain wouldn't stop thinking about it. It wouldn't switch off, like it knew there was a job still to be done.

In the end, the only way to give myself some peace was to get out of bed and flush the rest of it down the toilet. I didn't care that I was sending it into the sewer. My brain wasn't mad that the champagne was being wasted. It just wanted the bottle empty. That was the rule in Spandau.

It was then I realised I probably needed to go a little easier on the sauce. I couldn't put my brain and body through that sort of argument again. It scared me quite how angry I was making myself over it.

But the hangovers weren't over quite yet.

Spandau Bubble

You can't avoid the news in the modern era. Scrolling through your phone, flicking through the telly, updates are everywhere. Everyone now isn't just up to speed on all the latest developments in international affairs, they're also up to speed on the fluffier stuff too. If a dog somewhere has taught itself to make a sandwich, then everyone and their nan will have heard about it in their WhatsApp groups before the day is out.

In the early 80s, though, travelling the world in a rock band, it was the easiest thing in the world to cut yourself off. No mobile phones, no social media. Sound check clashing with the *Six O'Clock News*.

As we weren't the type of band who smashed up TVs, we did have the option to watch news on tour. CNN had begun broadcasting in 1980: the world's first 24/7 rolling network news channel. At first, like MTV, you could only see that in America. Elsewhere, you got CNN International. I have some very fond memories of Bobbie Battista telling me all the most important headlines in my hotel room, but CNN International was really only a ten-minute loop that they packaged up to send out globally and it focused almost entirely on America anyway.

I suppose if I'd really wanted one, I could have got my hands on a newspaper. Any city that was cosmopolitan enough to make a Spandau gig viable would have been able to get an international edition or two. But when I woke up in my hotel room – a bellyful of booze still working its way through my system from the night before – I wasn't craving current affairs. I was craving coffee and carbs.

I'm not going to lie, it's a nice way to live. Selfish, sure. The height of it, really. But it wasn't sustainable.

I called it the Spandau Bubble – and I lived there for years.

Being in a band, thinking only of the next gig, the next single, the next TV appearance, it felt like there was never any time to keep up with what was happening back home. The strikes, the riots, the political crises. It was all so heavy. Dealing with it on a hangover, doubly so.

To give you an example I'm not especially proud of: when I heard that Argentina had invaded the Falklands and that Britain would be sending our armed forces out to fight, my first thought was 'Fuck! What's that going to do for our single?'

No thought for anyone whose lives were at risk. No immediate outpouring of sympathy for those who had loved ones sent out to war. Just concern for my chart position.

The Bubble never really burst, but what it did do towards the end of 1984 was start to change shape.

In October of that year, a news item was broadcast that would rock the world: Michael Buerk reporting for the BBC on the catastrophic famine in Ethiopia.

I missed it at the time. I don't know where I was or what I was doing instead, but I still saw that footage. It was that sort of broadcast. Like the Moon landings, or JFK in Dallas. You didn't have to catch it live. This footage would find you.

That report had a profound effect on everyone who saw it, but none so much as on Bob Geldof.

Band Aid

Gary had been shopping for antiques on the King's Road when he heard someone thumping on the window. He looked round, even though he expected it was someone wanting the attention of the owner, but it wasn't. It was for him.

Bob Geldof had been passing by chance and wanted to speak to Gary about an idea he'd had for a record. He'd seen this report on the BBC about a terrible famine in Ethiopia and his girlfriend, Paula Yates, had put this idea in his head of recording a Christmas song for charity. He felt he had to do something, so was asking around a bunch of musicians he knew to see if there was any mileage in it.

We were due to head out on tour the next day, our very first visit to Japan, so I think Gary's mind was a bit wrapped up in all of that. So he said the sorts of things you say to someone you've bumped into while shopping, giving Bob the old 'Yeah, sure. Sounds great. Give me a call a little closer to the time. I'll see what I can do' routine – and then went back to his antiques.

I don't remember hearing anything about it until Steve Dagger came into our dressing room one afternoon and told us we'd be flying back to London the next morning to go and record something at Sarm West Studios in Notting Hill. Trevor Horn's place.

We were backstage at a German TV show called *Thommy's Pop-Show*, waiting to promote 'Round and Round', the final single from *Parade*. By chance, we happened to be sharing the bill that night with Duran Duran.

Despite the rivalry that had been stoked up in *Smash Hits* between our two bands, it was actually pretty rare for us to cross paths, especially at this point. We'd been on world tours; they'd been on world tours. We'd been recording; they were starting up two new side-projects (Arcadia and Power Station). We were all busy, but we also always knew everything the other was doing. It was sort of like social media is today. Everything Duran Duran did got posted somewhere for us to see, so we felt like we never missed a single thing they did, even though the chances we actually got to hang out in real life were few.

The rivalry between our two bands was mostly a press invention, rather than a proper beef. We were always happy to play up to it, if only from a cynical marketing standpoint. The ongoing storyline was like a soap. It gave reporters an endlessly repeatable hook, and every time one of them wrote something about either of us, the other band would get a mention in passing.

In truth, though, we were all mates – and it turned out that no sooner had Geldof left my brother to his antiquing that afternoon, further up the King's Road he'd bumped into Simon Le Bon. He asked Simon if he fancied getting involved in a charity record too, dangling Gary's name as a bit of a carrot, and he bit.

When we heard that we weren't the only ones flying back to London to appear on this new Bob Geldof record, that the Duran boys were going too, the competition kicked off instantly.

It started as a drinking contest that night in Germany. While drinking we found out they had hired a private Learjet to fly them back to London the next morning. So what did we do? We hired a Learjet too. We weren't going to let those bouffant pretty-boy bastards upstage us. We would race them back! Round Two of this contest would take to the skies!

Waking up with stinking hangovers the next morning (testament to Spandau's great victory over those light-weights), we made our way to the airport and piled into our respective jets. Our pilots, keen on the idea of a race, gamely scorched their way across the clouds, radioing one another constantly from jet to jet to keep tabs on the other's co-ordinates to see who was winning.

In the spirit of good sportsmanship, Le Bon and le boys allowed us to share the emergency hair and make-up team they had called in to meet them at Heathrow. We all looked rougher than a sailor's palms the morning after the night before and were in no fit state to meet our public.

We had figured that when news trickled out that Spandau Ballet and Duran Duran were both due to touch down at the same airport at the same time, the arrivals hall would be flooded with screaming teenage fans. As a precaution we had called in extra security to contend with the heaving throngs, but it turned out we needn't have worried. There were about six kids there standing in arrivals, flanked on all sides by about a hundred police officers.

With hindsight, that was probably the moment where the penny should have dropped. It wasn't even close to starting, though.

The fans, it turned out, were all at Sarm West Studios – our final destination. And that gave us just the time we needed to really pull out all the stops.

Duran Duran might have got the jump on us with the private jet and the rapid-response make-over squad, but we were going to make a hell of an entrance where it counted. Spandau would roll up to the studio to take our place on this star-studded single in the biggest fuck-off Bentley we could find. The sort of thing the Queen would have turned up in if Geldof had called her in to play tambourine.

We would look like kings and steal every last bit of lime-light from those Brummie chancers.

If you've seen the Band Aid video, or recalled the original news reports from the time, you'll maybe remember how some of the other artists turned up that day. Paul Weller took the tube. Sting walked in with a folded newspaper tucked in his coat. Bananarama all clambered out of the back seat of a tiny two-door Golf GTI, spilling out like clowns from a clown car. Everyone else had just rocked up casually, ready to get to work.

Now here come Spandau Ballet, turning up to help the starving children of Ethiopia in a luxury car, having just raced Learjets across the Channel, swanning through Heathrow escorted by ten policemen per band member.

We thought we'd look awful because of our hangovers. We actually looked awful because of our hubris.

We had no clue what we had signed up to do. It was awful. And it was about to get worse. There were reporters and photographers and documentary makers buzzing about the place trying to get the story of this mysterious music project and someone made a beeline for us, asking us what we were doing there.

I'll spare my bandmate's blushes and not name him – if only because I dread to think what I'd have said if the microphone had been waved under my nose – but his response to the question 'Do you have any message for the people of Ethiopia?' was 'Yeah, I'd like to say hi and sorry that we haven't been able to get down there on tour this year, but we're hoping to fit it in soon.'

I owe whoever edited that Band Aid music video the coldest, crispest pint of their lives for not stitching us up and including any footage of that.

For the project, Bob had originally approached Trevor Horn to produce the song but Trevor was too busy to fit it in (and it was a good job too, because if Trevor had been the one trying to produce 30-plus artists, 'Do They Know It's Christmas?' probably wouldn't have been ready until the mid-90s.) However, Trevor offered Bob something else. He cleared 24 hours of studio time at his Sarm West Studios to use however he wanted. Given how in demand Trevor was at the time, that was no small offering – but the pressure was now on.

Production duties were handed instead to someone else.

Ultravox had recently appeared on Paula's show *The Tube*. While there, Bob had put the idea to Midge Ure and asked him to help write a song that would make the most money. Bob, an ex-punk. Midge, an ex-Blitz Kid. The time had come.

The resulting track hadn't won everyone over in the studio. I remember George Michael taking me to one side at some point in the day and telling me how much he hated it. He really didn't like it. Especially the lyrics. He thought they were far too heavy and that singing about famine on a pop record would be an instant downer. He thought a Christmas record should be happy – which I felt was a bit rich, seeing as his Christmas single, released that same year, was all about getting your heart broken by a lover on Christmas Day.

As it happened, though, Bob Geldof kind of agreed with him. I remember reading something in the paper after it came out where some journalist had said that it was crap. Bob, in his typically blunt fashion, said: 'I don't give a fuck. It's not about the record. It's not about the music. It's about making money.'

It's strange. On the one hand, 'I don't give a fuck … It's about making money' typifies a very specific attitude of the 80s. That things like art and integrity and intention don't matter. Money is the only measure that matters.

But when Bob says it he actually means the opposite. Flying in the face of the individualist, me-me-me attitude of the era, Bob – with Midge and Paula – had managed to turn the tide completely. They got dozens of the world's biggest popstars, each with their own gargantuan egos, to join forces in the middle of the busiest times of their careers to put this song together for free (a song not everyone liked) for the benefit of others.

That room stripped everyone of their ego, if only for a day. And it was interesting once I had been stripped of mine to hear what happened to Boy George. Jon Moss was the only member of Culture Club who was present in the room and people kept asking him, 'Where's George? When's he getting here?' Jon had no answer. He hadn't spoken to George; he figured he'd be making it under his own steam.

Geldof called him. The call had woken him up. Not because he was hungover. Because he was in New York. George, who didn't really know Bob all that well, didn't respond to the call all that well immediately. Getting harangued on the phone by a gruff Irish gobshite at any hour – let alone in the early hours – is hard, and George wasn't hugely keen on flying across the Atlantic at short notice to come and do Bob a favour. But when Bob listed off the people he knew that were all there and working – Sting, Bono, Duran, us, Midge, Bananarama, Marilyn … That was enough for him. All the Blitz Kids were there and Boy George would be damned if he would let any of us steal his spotlight while he had breath in his body. So he hopped on a Concorde and joined in.

And like the rest of us, within minutes of entering that room, his ego floated away. (The moment was when he said he could do with a drink and Geldof told him, in that stern way of his, 'There's a fuckin' pub around the corner.')

I remember hearing that the idea was to raise about £70,000. That was the shot. The Band Aid project wouldn't have been in vain if we pulled in 70 grand. Within weeks it had raised £8,000,000. I'm astonished every time I think of that. Even in the Spandau Bubble, I knew things were tough in the UK. I knew many people were struggling, striking and scrimping. So to see this record inspire such generosity, with ordinary people helping strangers in even more dire need, was immensely humbling.

For a culture that was increasingly obsessed with material gain, that was no small order.

It continues to raise money for the Band Aid Trust – and the lyrics still come in for a pasting each year too, so maybe George was right (as usual).

It's strange to hear it now. Like 'True' or 'Gold', it's one of those songs that became so big that it doesn't really bring back any specific memories. I've heard them so many times now, in so many situations, that they've detached themselves from me and exist now in the ether. It doesn't make me sad. I don't feel as if I've lost anything. It's nice to hear those songs and enjoy them the way that other people do.

It's another of those instances where the barriers between the band and audience fall. We all enjoy the same experience; we all have the same memory.

To date, 'Do They Know It's Christmas?' has sold nearly 4 million copies in the UK. It must have been a massive pain in the arse for the British Phonographic Industry when it did its first million too because they had to make up a platinum disc for each of the artists involved in it. No doubt someone's Christmas was ruined having to frame up dozens of plaques right at the busiest time of the year. If it's any consolation to whoever did mine: the one festive decoration I insist upon hanging in the Kemp home every Christmas? My Band Aid disc.

'Last Christmas'

One thing that has been interesting in this digital era is seeing how popular a lot of those 80s classics still are. Never is that more clear than at Christmas.

Ever since digital streams started counting towards chart positions in 2014, the December Top 40 has been absolutely dominated by the same handful of tracks each year. 'Do They Know It's Christmas?' is one of them, getting streamed millions and millions of times over the holidays, raising yet more revenue for the Band Aid Trust – which it's amazing to think is still generating funds nearly 40 years on.

'Fairytale of New York' regularly re-enters the chart and claims the nation's favourite polls a lot too.

The one I feel is destined to live on longest is 'Last Christmas' by Wham!

That song has always held a very special place in Shirl's and my hearts, for obvious reasons, but before I get too sentimental about it, I want to tell you about the first time I saw that song in concert.

It was the first time I'd ever seen Wham! live at Wembley. At this point in the decade the tanning craze was really starting to kick off. What had been a non-existent fad in 1980 when Steve Norman and I were out in the Saint-Tropez sun roasting ourselves to a crisp was now becoming a national pastime. Tanning salons and solariums popped up in high streets all around the country throughout the 80s as people wanted to get that sun-kissed look year round.

The tan was a sign of internationalism, of travel, of wealth – a lot of what the 80s held so dear – so naturally all of the bands were getting stuck right into it around this time. We'd only just weaned ourselves off all that white foundation, before we were bouncing in and out of sunbeds to keep our golden tans topped up (a godsend through those long stints that we had to spend in subterranean German studios).

I was always so jealous of George's gorgeous Greek skin, but he loved a sunbed as much as any of us. More so. So much so, in fact, that I thought he'd folded tanning into Wham!'s live shows.

As the show was reaching the finale, in the quiet between songs, the big lights in the arena went down, leaving just a gentle wash of buzzing off-blue. In this half-light, one of the stagehands wheels this huge contraption on from the wings. A rack of glowing cylinders, tubes hanging down in this big long line, sending a blinding blue glare out into the audience.

For a moment, I genuinely thought it was a sunbed. It made sense to me. We had a fully functioning pub built into our staging and George loved to tan at least as much as we loved to drink. Maybe this was some gimmick for 'Club Tropicana'? (They'd already played it, but maybe this was a reprise?)

I felt like such an idiot when George introduced the next song as 'Last Christmas'.

It wasn't a tanning bed. It was tubular bells.

It's a poignant listen for us now, having lost George on Christmas Day. What makes it especially hard is that he loved Christmas so much. It's the time of year when a generous soul like Yog's thrived. Finding perfectly pitched presents, lavishing you with hampers, hosting a Boxing Day party for all his closest friends and family. We had been all but ready to go to that party when we got the call.

As you'll know, 'Last Christmas' finally made it to No. 1 36 years after it was first released. The song had always been denied the top spot (which George gave away gladly) because of Band Aid. Wham! donated their royalties from 'Last Christmas' to the Ethiopian famine too – which meant that both the No. 1 and No. 2 records in Christmas '84 were helping feed those in desperate need halfway around the world.

It's testament to the timelessness of George's talent that the song could still top the charts with ease in 2021 and not sound out of place. I wish so dearly that he could have been around to see it happen. Not just because he deserved it but because I would love to have shown him – just once – that he was wrong.

See, Yog? You don't need to make a Christmas song happy.

1985

LIVE AID

Back to the Future | *Sinclair C5* | *New Coke* | *'We Are the World'* | EastEnders | *McVitie's Hobnobs* | *Mikhail Gorbachev* | *Casio SK-1* | A View to a Kill | Love in the Time of Cholera | *Brixton Riots II* | Brothers in Arms | Nick Kamen's Boxer Shorts | Desperately Seeking Susan | *Comic Relief* | *Paul Hardcastle* | *Windows 1.0* | The Color Purple | *Dolmio* | *Wreck of the Titanic Located* | *Vodafone* | The Man Who Mistook His Wife for a Hat | *'Axel F'* | The Breakfast Club

Saxophones

Fucking saxophones.

If you couldn't avoid the sound of a synthesiser in the early 80s, then in the mid-80s the sound that was everywhere was the saxophone. Soulful sax like Sade's 'Smooth Operator' and 'Your Love Is King'. Frantic sax like 'The Heat Is On' by Glenn Frey. Plaintiff and wailing sax like 'Careless Whisper'.

Yet in 1985, I would have been happy to take a hammer to every last sax in the world and dump the mangled, twisted metal into the Thames. Except I couldn't even do that, because the only river near me was the Liffey in Dublin. Why? Because of the fucking saxophone.

It wasn't the saxophone's fault. And I loved our saxophone player too. The reason I was so mad had nothing to do with either of them. Not really. It was just hard not to vent. I was homesick and I couldn't go home. Stranded in Dublin – and would be for most of the year.

If we'd been stranded in Auckland, arrested for crimes against Elvis, it might not have been so bad. If we'd got stuck in LA, keeping vigil besides Steve Norman's hospital bed, things might have been different. A bit more distance from home could have helped me adapt my mindset.

Being a stone's throw from home in Dublin, though, it just made it feel as if I was banged up in a holding cell. Close enough to smell my mum's Sunday dinners, but far enough away that I couldn't pop over for one. Agony.

Legally, I suppose I could have gone home. But also legally, it wasn't recommended.

Let me backtrack a bit ...

Exile

In terms of Spandau, in 1985 the band was at the height of its commercial power. 'True' and 'Gold' had been absolutely massive singles. The *True* album was still selling well, as was our follow-up, *Parade*. We had lined up a huge world tour to promote the album, and that was going to be keeping us busy through the year – which was great, as we needed something to do.

Because this was the year we were all going to become exiles.

I hadn't really been keeping too close an eye on my income over the years. I knew things were going well for the band financially, but because so many of the experiences I'd been having in the last five years weren't ever reaching my pocket there was no need for me to keep tabs on anything. Every flight I took was paid for. Every hotel was expensed. On tour you get something called 'per diems', which is a chunk of petty cash to sort out your daily sundries – essentially pocket money for grown-ups.

You could have a decent time on it, but it was never so much that you'd consider squirrelling it away as savings. You burned through it, knowing there'd be another brown envelope coming soon enough.

Throw in the bottle of champagne and the bottle of Jack Daniels that were laid out for each of us backstage after the show every night and there wasn't very much I actually needed cash for.

The whole thing was such a whirlwind, taking me from dole-drawing former print apprentice to world-famous rock star, that whatever wage I was earning from the band was good by me. I'd been able to move out from my parents' place. I'd got my flat with Shirlie. If I ever went out with Chris Sullivan I could get my round in without any risk of the tongue-lashing he used to give me if he caught me shirking.

Everything was such a dream, I hadn't really stopped to think about the pounds and pennies. I was out of step with the rest of the decade, though, where yuppie culture was really starting to take hold. Where a person's worth was their net worth and vice versa. Money ruled in 1985 and I hadn't the first clue how to master it.

Under Thatcher at that time, the top tax rate was 60 per cent. After agents' fees and the like were deducted, I was making about 20p in the pound. It was therefore recommended that we take what was called a 'tax year'. It was something a lot of the big bands were doing and it required us to register ourselves as being nom-domiciled for the duration of the financial year.

This isn't quite as drastic as it might sound. We were at a stage in our career where Spandau could head out on a worldwide tour in support of whatever album it was we had out (at this point: *Parade*). By the time we'd hit all the major cities across all the continents where we could feasibly draw a crowd, we were looking at being away for the best part of a year anyway.

So we'd declare ourselves non-doms, head off on tour and work our arses off on the road to make every penny count.

That was the plan, at least – and it started off well. Our first major stop was Down Under, to complete the Australasian leg of the 'World Parade' tour.

I have incredibly fond memories of Australia. Every time we've played there it's been like a little slice of paradise. The venues, the vineyards, there's a real magical quality to those big Australian gigs. In fact, playing out there for the first time was one of the moments where the enormity of Spandau Ballet really hit me square between the eyes.

The day we took our first flight from Heathrow to Sydney, I remember all of the bands' families, aunts, uncles, cousins coming down to the airport to wave us off.

At this point we'd been flying constantly for a while. Airports and aviation were not novelties to us anymore. Our families were used to us being away for long stretches of time. Yet the idea of a flight to the opposite side of the globe – a land where night is day, where summer is winter and where the local fauna is on the dangerous side – had everybody acting like we were high seas explorers about to set sail on a maiden voyage for king and country.

When we finally did arrive in Sydney 24 hours later, there was an army of Spandau fans there to greet us in the airport concourse. I knew we had fans in Australia. I'd been told our sales figures and knew we'd sent videos out to the TV channels there. But it wasn't until I was greeted into this new country – a place I'd never set foot in – by all these screaming fans, who all knew my name, that I realised quite how big this band was.

It's the strangest feeling knowing that your face is stuck on a bedroom wall on the other side of the world. That a kid you've never met, and are likely never going to meet, treats you the same way I treated Generation X. They have your 7-inch records sitting in pride of place on their record player. They've listened to tapes of your radio appearances so often that they've worn them out. It's wild to be someone else's Billy Idol.

That this could be happening in countries dotted all across the globe? That the sun was never setting on Spandau? The human mind just isn't made to process that properly.

New Zealand was a little bit trickier for us. For some reason I genuinely can't remember, we had to cancel a gig there. Unfortunate, but inevitable. The one thing I do remember is being told that it would be wise to keep a low profile while we were out that way. No causing any drama that might disappoint fans any further.

Anyhow, completely unrelatedly, Tony decided he'd take this unexpected time off as an opportunity to catch up with a few friends who also happened to be in Auckland at the time: Queen.

Tony and Freddie met up in Freddie's hotel bar, where the two of them enjoyed a few quiet drinks. Then they enjoyed a few louder ones. Then, once they'd polished off a full bottle of vodka and were getting stuck in to some port, Freddie was struck with an idea. Tony should join them on stage that night! Darling, it would be a riot! For one night only: 'A Night at the Opera' becomes 'A Night at the Ballet'!

Pissed beyond belief, Freddie called Brian May and told him Tony was going to join them on stage to sing 'Jailhouse Rock'. A song, it turned out, neither Tony nor Freddie could remember the words to come the time.

I don't know how anyone could forget the words to 'Jailhouse Rock' – much less two of the world's most famous frontmen – but the pair of them just ended up garbling out a bunch of nonsense. Apparently at one point Tony segued into 'Tutti Frutti' by Little Richard. Whether it was intentional or not, I'm not sure even he could tell you.

The rest of Queen (all sober) managed to keep the show on the rails but, needless to say, when the papers hit news-stands the next morning, our low profile was blown.

Leaving New Zealand with our tail between our legs, we headed off to California for gigs in San Francisco, Irvine and Los Angeles. Sadly, LA was where the wheels came off.

Or, to be precise, the tendons.

Injury Time

Steve Norman is such a gifted musician; one of the most natural I have ever met. You could leave him in a room with a bunch of paperclips, a few pipe cleaners and some Sellotape and somehow he'd be able to get a tune out of them. He *was* music. It flowed out of him like water. Whatever instrument you handed him, that was just a way to start it pouring.

At some point after we'd recorded the *Diamond* album – which had had brass arrangements by the excellent

Beggar & Co – Steve started introducing his own saxophone to rehearsals. He'd been on guitar, keys and percussion up until that point, but from 'True' onwards, he made his stand-out contributions to the band on the sax.

The effect of that on the Spandau sound was incalculable. The portability of the instrument meant Steve could get much more involved in our live shows again too. Rather than being cooped up in bongo corner at the back of the stage, he could move around the stage and be dynamic like the early days.

This added an enormous sense of fun to the show and Steve loved it too, playing up to it like a real sax god. But that night in LA, disaster struck. Throwing himself fully into one solo, Steve dived forward right to the front of the stage, kneesliding up to the lights, when POP! His tendon snapped.

Suffering an injury on stage is such a discombobulating experience, so I knew how Steve felt. Something similar had happened to me in Tokyo.

Japanese crowds have a reputation for being very polite and respectful. They're especially attentive if you ever try to talk between songs, offering an eerily reverential silence, even if all you're saying is, 'This one's off the new album …' It might be the language barrier, it might be the culture, but they instinctively treat these off-the-cuff comments as if they're as much a part of your art as the music.

But don't let any of that fool you. They also know how to get crazy.

I had also been giving it the old rock god treatment at the front of the stage that night, walking right to the lip to be as close to the crowd as I could. They were screaming and throwing bunches of carnations onto the stage. As I turned back towards the boys to rejoin the band, a hand shot out of the crowd and grabbed my leather trousers. My other foot had come down on a bunch of carnations, squishing them into slippery mulch underfoot. As I tried to wrestle myself free from the fan's grasp, I skidded on the flowers, completely lost my balance and came down hard on the stage.

When a bass player hits the deck with his volume up high, he really makes his presence felt. This awful, low booming explosion rang out around the arena. Slowly, I managed to get myself upright and reassured the crowd I was OK as the guys played on, but I could tell something wasn't right. The crowd had their white-gloved hands up in front of their mouths. The band were looking at me oddly.

It was my arm. Owing to an old injury I had sustained (and refused to get the recommended surgery for) my shoulder had a tendency to pop out from time to time. Usually it was something I could manage myself. This time, though, it left me looking like a Ken doll that had been mauled by a wolf. You'd have needed a degree in applied mathematics to have any hope of figuring out what angle that arm was sticking out at.

One of our roadies, Nicky, put an end to the one-man horror show I was performing by running on stage and wrenching my shoulder back into its socket again; a temporary measure before I could get some proper emergency treatment after the show from the ever-reliable Dr Jack Daniels.*

Unfortunately for us, Steve's busted knee would need much more specialised attention. He needed surgery, which

* I saw a real doctor in the end, don't worry …

meant cancelling shows, and – right then – there was no telling how quickly he would recover.

Again, we found ourselves in the position where we had to seriously consider whether or not we could replace a member of the band. Steve's sax was an essential component of our sound. We couldn't just muddle on without it. Imagine the crowd's disappointment at that pivotal moment in 'True' when Steve comes bursting in with that solo and all they got was silence. What were we going to do? Have Tony do it on kazoo?

We had a massive tour mapped out. Hundreds of thousands of fans had bought tickets to see us. All of us.

We were a gang, and gangs stick together. The tour dates would be pulled and we would play again when all five of us were fit enough to put on the best show we could. We weren't in the business of short-changing anyone.

Our only problem now was that with our world tour cancelled, we'd have to pack our bags and head for home. But we couldn't go home. We had no home. We were exiles.

China

When people speak of a worldwide tour, they never actually mean the whole world. You travel that distance, definitely. Every year you have an album out, you'll do what amounts to more than a full loop of the planet between flying to Japan, Australia, the USA and all around Europe.

Nowadays, bands have plenty of other stops en route too. South Korea is a huge market. There's so many venues popping up in South America. Playing out in Dubai and the Middle East has opened right up in recent years but, in the 1980s, there were some places that you just couldn't go.

South Africa under apartheid, for example, was not a place bands booked. The Soviet Union started to let a few big Western acts in towards the end of the decade – your Billy Joels, your Bowies, Eltons and Ozzys – but getting behind the Iron Curtain to play was not easy.*

Most impenetrable of all, though, was China. This massive country might as well have been a blank space on the map for a Western band. So when Shirlie called to tell me that one of Wham!'s managers, Simon Napier-Bell, had secured them a ten-day trip to China where they would play two gigs, I couldn't believe what I was hearing.

China? No one plays China. No one sells records there. Why were they trying to break it?

The point had never been for Wham! to break China, though. It was to break America.

This was the sort of maverick management move that would have turned Dagger green with envy. From a marketing standpoint, it was genius. George had been quite clear with Simon that he wasn't prepared to wait the usual three or four years it took to conquer America. They needed a smart shortcut. And what would cause a bigger splash in the States than a Western band who made their way to China?

Culturally, it was an unprecedented move. Nothing like this had been seen before. After years of being closed off to

---

* Spandau were once offered a gig in Bulgaria around this time, but we were offered payment in tractors and other agricultural machinery, so politely declined the offer.

foreigners, China was slowly beginning to emerge from its Cultural Revolution and cast its sights out to the wider world – but, even still, it took Simon 18 months to make the arrangements with Chinese officials. For two gigs.

George always said those China gigs were the hardest he'd ever played in his life and it's not hard to see why. For instance, the band had brought a breakdancer along as a support act, figuring they'd send him on first to whip the crowd up a bit. The breakdancer (called Trevor) went out and tried his level best to spark a mood, giving the audience a demonstration of how to body pop, but his efforts were instantly undermined by the big booming voice that came over the Tannoy instructing the local audience that dancing was forbidden and police officers were patrolling the floor.

Consequently, Wham! arrived on stage to a stone-cold crowd.

The band didn't have much luck getting a reaction out of the audience either. It wasn't that the Chinese people weren't enjoying the music, it was more that they didn't have the first idea how to respond to it. When George asked the audience to put their hands in the air and clap along, they thought he was asking for a round of applause. So they politely obliged – and clapped completely out of time with the beat of 'Club Tropicana'.

Security, who were clearly concerned that such an outrageous display of Western decadence would kickstart a riot in the Workers' Gymnasium, cracked down on anyone attempting to stand up and dance.

Still, however much of a struggle the show was, it got the desired results. Wham! were everywhere in the Western media, with double-page spreads detailing their historic trip. Even Chinese state media were pleased with it, calling the show a 'sensation' in its characteristically understated way.

Footage of the trip would become the 1986 documentary *Foreign Skies: Wham! in China* – the premiere of which took place at Wembley Arena, moments before Wham!'s last ever show: The Final. It made for an incredible end to an incredible career, but it had been a hell of a slog to make it.

Behind the scenes, that trip hadn't been the glorious voyage of adventure it seemed to the outside world. The culture clash really took its toll on the band. George and Andrew were followed and filmed every step of the way, either by media or minders, never getting a moment's peace. Shirlie and Pepsi found themselves completely sidelined, isolated and kept at a distance from the rest of the band. The band's trumpet player, Raul, suffered a horrifying mental breakdown on one of the flights between cities, stabbing himself in the stomach mid-flight, causing horror and panic to everyone on board (including Shirlie, who was sat next to him as he mumbled demonic mutterings throughout).

What Wham!'s trip to China did on the geopolitical stage was momentous. It was a huge part of this wider cultural shift where the actions of what had started in our little London clubland clique were now having serious global ramifications. But this came at a cost. We were kids who had grown up wanting to be popstars, putting on our mum's make-up, singing into hairbrushes and playing dress-up in the clubs. Now we were out in the world making actual history. It was amazing to see this unfold in front of us, but it was so far beyond the scope of anything we'd signed up for. We were completely unprepared to be so powerful.

Personally, that trip was totally devastating for Shirlie. The effect it had on her has lasted for 40 years and continues to this day. She helped change the world, but it also changed her too.

If there's been one tangible benefit for our family, though, it's Iris. One day in China, the band were taken to a food market. Shirlie has always been an animal lover; a real soft touch with our furry friends. Seeing the way that animals were treated there, visions of dogs and cats being wheeled around the market, getting butchered and boiled, blasé as anything, had a profound effect on her.

As a result, Shirlie is now a patron of the Rushton Dog Rescue, an organisation who go out to China to save dogs from the barbaric treatment they suffer at the hands of the meat industry there. Iris is one of their rescues. A miniature poodle who was pulled from the wagon, she is now my little cheerleader, yapping along at me constantly to keep me going. And although she upstages me constantly on *Gogglebox*, our family wouldn't be complete without her.

A reminder that, even in the very worst of circumstances, there is always love to be found.

Sound Check

Back in Dublin, alone in my flat, I looked out of the window in despair. The five of us had all taken flats in the same apartment complex. Staring out into the gardens now I could see Tony and Steve out there, smoking pipes. *Pipes*.

What had we become? This year was supposed to be our year. We were a band at the peak of our powers. Young, good-looking men who had been riding high on a hell of a wave. Five years of hard graft, about to pay out in the most spectacular experience of our lives – and now we were all confined to what felt like a retirement home where our only excitement was getting some air in the garden and puffing away on a pipe. Safe to say, I hadn't ever had a daydream about this.

As I sat moping, though, plans were afoot elsewhere that would once again change the career of Spandau. Right in the middle of 1985 we would be offered a lifeline of sorts. A reason to return home for the UK – if only for a weekend. We had booked a gig. One that would turn out to be the biggest of our lives. The biggest of anybody's lives. In fact, it would be the single biggest rock concert in history.

Live Aid.

Convinced there was more that bands could do to raise awareness and money for the plight of the people of Ethiopia, where famine was still raging across the country, Bob Geldof and Midge Ure drew up plans to stage a massive stadium show for the Band Aid charity.

It had been easy to get acts on board. The unexpected runaway success of 'Do They Know It's Christmas?' at the end of '84 meant everyone wanted to take part this time. So many acts wanted to play that the concert became a network of shows, with flagship events taking place simultaneously in London and Philadelphia, alongside a series of connected satellite gigs around the globe.

I knew the gig would all be for a great cause, but even if the only promise was that we'd get out of these flats and in front of a crowd again, I'd have walked from Dublin to Wembley on my hands to play it. I couldn't wait.

Part of what had got me so excited was that I had just been to see the biggest concert of my life so far: Bruce Springsteen at Slane Castle.

Whatever else had been happening in the charts, whatever fashions and cultures were cropping up in the clubs and magazines, Bruce Springsteen was about the biggest star in the world. As much as British bands had been dominating MTV and shifting records by the pallet, The Boss absolutely eclipsed it all – and his *Born in the USA* tour was Bruce in his imperial phase.

I was absolutely floored by the sound, size and scope of it. Seeing him play a gigantic venue like Slane Castle was just what I needed to blow the cobwebs away. When I watched him play that night in Ireland it seemed to be about the biggest thing I could imagine. Oh, how little I knew.

The funny thing was that, a month after that gig, I would be playing on Bruce's stage myself at Wembley. Bruce wouldn't be on it at the time, sadly, but it was definitely his stage.

Bob Geldof had tried his hardest to get Springsteen to play Live Aid. I think there was even talk that the event might take place the week before, on 6 July, to time with Springsteen's last night in London. He had sold out three consecutive nights at Wembley Stadium. For most bands, the biggest place you could hope to play was Wembley Arena.

To give you some sense of the difference in size between these two venues, at the end of our *True* tour we played six consecutive nights in Wembley Arena. With 12,500 people present each night, that made a total of 75,000 across that week.

Bruce played to that many people each night in Wembley Stadium – and did three nights back to back. Nearly a quarter of a million people over the course of a long weekend. And that was just the UK. The full world tour was humongous.

He would have been a mammoth fish for Geldof to land but, unfortunately, it wasn't to be. Still, The Boss didn't let us down completely. Even though he couldn't play, he did leave Live Aid a little something. His stage. The stage Springsteen played those landmark Wembley gigs on was the one that we would all get to use for Live Aid.

We arrived back in London first thing in the morning on the 12th and were taken straight to a helipad in Battersea. From there we piled into a helicopter and were flown over to Wembley.

I hadn't seen much music in stadiums before, but I was used to stadiums themselves. As an Arsenal fan, I had plenty of memories of going up to Highbury and getting crunched in shoulder-to-shoulder with about 50,000 other football fans. One of my earliest was the Fairs Cup semi-final: Arsenal vs Ajax. I remember it like it was yesterday. It's hard to forget the sensation of being swept up in it all. Every time one of our players attacked the goal, the entire crowd would rush forward and you'd get moved down a dozen steps before the crowd would start ebbing back. It was a Mexican wave, but instead of going side to side, it would happen front to back.

For that reason, it was a little bit unsettling to look out onto the stadium that day, before the crowds filed in. Football stadiums were tied up in my mind with hooliganism. Fighting at matches was absolutely rife in the 80s, with people turning up to games just to beat the shit out of each other. The ominous crackle of violence breaking out hung over all the big games in that era and spilled out onto the streets most match days.

I suppose we were lucky that Duran Duran were playing the JFK Stadium in Philadelphia because if there'd been a Spandaus v Duranies face-off at Wembley that afternoon, the event could have become a humanitarian catastrophe of its own. Mullets yanked. Earrings ripped out. People garrotted with their own skinny ties. Carnage.

However, any fears of Blitz on Rum Runner violence were quickly alleviated when we watched Status Quo pick up their instruments and kick off a sound-check rendition of 'Rockin' All Over the World'. There wasn't going to be any tribalism here. Live Aid was going to be about the unifying power of music. Not just here in Wembley Stadium. All around the world.

Genuinely, in all my memories of the Spandau days, I cannot think of a time when I was happier in the band than in that sound check – and we weren't even the ones playing. After a brutally lonely few months, to be there in the wings of Wembley, our arms wrapped around each other, beers in hands as we bounced around yelling 'A-here we go, a-here we go, a-here we gooooo' along with the Quo – I could have cried.

I was back in Britain. We were about to play the biggest gig of our lives.

And best of all, I was going to get to see Shirlie.

13 July 1985

Getting in a helicopter first thing after a Friday night when I'd finally found my rock-star feet again was not ideal – but my hangover hit uncharted heights when I looked up and saw who our pilot was.

Noel Edmonds.

Thankfully, this was in the days before Noel had become one of TV's premier pranksters, otherwise a pack of wild horses could not have dragged me onto that thing. It was bad enough having a celebrity in charge of the chopper,* but if he'd been in his *House Party* era, hungover hallucinations of Mr Blobby sitting up front as his co-pilot would have sent me over the edge.

The choppers were scheduled to land at a nearby cricket ground, about 400 yards away from the stadium. However, there'd been a bit of a diary clash. As well as Live Aid, there was also the final of some cricket tournament due to be held the same day, which the cricket lot refused to cancel. They wouldn't budge and the helicopters couldn't land anywhere else nearby that was useful, so a compromise was struck. Every 40 minutes or so the umpire would have to blow a whistle and send all the players off to the edge of the field to give the helis somewhere to land.

I've always wondered what it must have been like for spectators watching the match that day. This loud rock gig

---

* It was all above board. Noel owned his own helicopter company and was laying on air transfers for the stars as his contribution to the day.

blasting out just over the way, providing a much more dramatic soundtrack than cricket crowds are used to, while play gets stopped at regular intervals so Elton John and Bono can scurry across the boundary.

Having been in Wembley Stadium the day before and getting a sense of the scale of the place, we weren't too fazed as we waited backstage to go on. We were just anxious to get playing.

Spandau were scheduled to play after Ultravox: our longtime label mates and band of our Blitz Kid comrade, Midge Ure. Their set finished with their signature song, the one that had proved so influential in shaping the entire MTV era. 'Vienna'.

We couldn't have asked for a more perfect lead-in.

Our set kicked off with 'Only When You Leave', a track from *Parade* that had done well in the charts the year before – a No. 3 hit in May '84. The response was immediate and immense, 70,000 people singing along, clapping their hands. The vibration of that is like nothing else I've ever known. It's not just the thrumming of pent-up adrenaline I'm talking about. It's a physical thing. Acoustic. That many bodies dancing about, singing your words back at you at the top of their lungs. It's something you feel. Not just in your soul, but in your actual skin and bones. It pushes you back like a gale.

As I would often do when Tony started pacing from wing to wing, making sure everyone in the crowd got a few bars of his attention, I wandered into the middle of the stage to fill the space. Wembley Stadium. A kid who once stuffed his face into his mother's behind when he saw someone he knew from school now playing bass for a stadium audience. How had this happened?

The roar of applause as that first song ended was deafening. Not because we had been especially fantastic, but because the crowd was ten times the size of our usual one. The heat of it, the energy. I had no idea we could command this kind of crowd.

And then we made our fatal mistake. Gary uttered the words that no crowd likes to hear, but rock bands never seem to learn.

'This next song ... is a new one.'

We were lucky not to have set off a tornado, making two billion people around the world sigh simultaneously like that. It could have blown the Earth off its axis.

It was such a stupid schoolboy error to try and debut a new track at Live Aid. Bob had specifically warned all the acts not to piss about with new stuff, to get out and play the hits. Such was our young rock-star arrogance we thought that rule wouldn't apply to us.

It wasn't even as if we were trying to plug anything either. Our next album was still such a long way off, there was no release planned. We'd only really started knocking a few ideas into shape in rehearsals in Dublin and that song we played, 'Virgin',* didn't even end up being released as a single. It was an album track.

We played an unreleased album track. At Live Aid. What were we thinking?

I don't know what possessed us to do it. Ego, obviously – but beyond that, nothing. The thing is, audiences just don't know what to do with themselves when you play new material. They don't know when to clap. They don't know any words to sing. They just have to stand there and

---

* It was so new at that stage, Gary introduced it as 'We Are Virgin'.

absorb it. Endure it. It's always a bit of an indulgence to do this even in your own full-length concert. But in a three-song set at a benefit gig?

When I think about what Queen did with their set later that night, I flush crimson with embarrassment. It was a masterclass in giving an audience what they want. Such was their commitment to keeping the audience on side, they didn't even play their big hits in full. Why do a second verse of 'We Will Rock You' when you can strike up into 'We Are the Champions'?

The amount they crammed into that 21 minutes. There's many reasons why Queen were the subject of an Academy Award-winning biopic while Spandau Ballet's Live Aid set is yet to be given the same treatment, but it was clear as they played that we were all witnessing history.

My only criticism of Queen's set? I'd have loved it if they could have got Tony out to do 'Jailhouse Rock'. Or 'Tutti Frutti'. His pick.

We redeemed ourselves with our final song, 'True'. Playing with the sun overhead, beaming down over what felt like all two billion people there in front of us, I was once again struck by how essential audiences are. From our first showcase in Halligan's Rehearsal Room, to here at Wembley Stadium, I'm not going to insult your intelligence by pretending that playing to 20 mates in a sweatbox on Holloway Road is in any way comparable to playing Live Aid. It categorically isn't. But the underlying truth of it is that both of these gigs depended entirely on the audience.

There is just no match for the sound of 70,000 people swaying and singing. We might have had the amps, but the audience had the power. In that sense, our only job was to give the audience the prompt to unleash it. All they needed to hear was that opening synth chord, those opening flicks of guitar and they were away. Slowly, blissfully singing, 'I know this … much is …'

I wish I could give you more backstage gossip from the wings of Wembley Stadium that day but I'm afraid the truth is that I'd double-booked myself. Tempting as the prospect of standing around making small talk about the latest Fairlight synthesiser was, I had somewhere else I needed to be.

My flat.

Shirlie and I hotfooted it out of there and headed back to Highbury to watch most of the rest of the afternoon from bed. I'm not sure about this, but I reckon I might be the only person in the world who can count himself as one of the two billion people who watched it at home on telly and as one of the two hundred who played it.

Phil Collins can have his Concorde story, playing the same gig across two continents. I know where I'd have rather been.

The Encore

I don't know if I was actually the only person to experience Live Aid both on stage and at home on the telly, but one of the truly remarkable things about that show is how much of a shared memory it is for everyone who was alive that day.

What's great is because nobody can lay claim to the whole of a show that big, it means it belongs to everyone. If you were at Wembley, you can brag about catching that historic leg of the gig, but you missed the Beach Boys,

Madonna, Led Zeppelin, Duran Duran, Mick Jagger, Tina Turner and Bob Dylan in Philadelphia. If you were at JFK, you saw some phenomenal names – but you missed just as many in London.

If you were watching on TV, you missed out on the feeling in the stadium, but you got to see so much of the rest of it. It was an unbelievable feat of satellite technology to link it all up – and it is mad to think that it really only could have happened in a relatively tiny window of history too. At the point where satellite broadcasting was just good enough to pull together a global simulcast seamlessly, but hadn't developed to a stage where everyone has 200 channels all fighting for the audience's attention.

Everybody has their own individual memories of that day, but there is also a huge collective pool of them to enjoy too. It sometimes was the smallest things. This year, I was scrolling through Instagram for five minutes on 13 July and someone had posted a few snaps from that day including one of me and Shirl backstage. It's a surreal feeling to know that some of your most personal, best-cherished moments also belong to others. It's not bad. I feel honoured that people are reminded of me on that day and choose to share it.

Anyhow, I couldn't lay about in bed watching Live Aid on telly all evening. I was due back on stage for the finale.

After a blissful few hours snuggled up with Shirlie watching the show on our telly, I headed back to Wembley. The journey from Highbury to the stadium wasn't far, so I was back in plenty of time to catch a few of the final acts.

I got an incredible view of Paul McCartney singing the night's penultimate number, 'Let It Be'. I was so close I could see the handwritten lyrics he had sitting on his piano.

I've never been much of one for memorabilia as a rule. I've been to all sorts of fancy places – from five-star hotels to celebrities' houses, celebrated studios to the coolest nightclubs in history, but I've never really felt compelled to swipe a little souvenir.*

I'm just not a natural collector. Most of the things I amassed from my own time in the band I've either given away, donated to charity or lost track of – save for a few prized possessions.

It was maybe a bit impulsive of me. A Spandau fan once came up to me to ask me if I'd sign something. I told her of course and she reached into her bag to pull it out. It took me a second to realise what I was looking at, but once she'd shaken it loose I could see it was the stunningly crafted frilly shirt I'd worn in our video for 'The Freeze'.

She had won it in a competition. I had offered it up as a prize for one of the magazines back in the day (*Smash Hits*, I think it was) and hadn't thought any more of it. But I was so overcome in the moment that I offered to buy it from her right there and then. The way I was feeling when I set eyes on it again, she probably could have taken me for thousands. I'm sure the moment would have passed, though – and I hope it's bringing her more joy than it would for me.

---

* The one exception: I was once invited to Buckingham Palace and my daughter Harley Moon and I spent a fair chunk of the event scouring the grounds for some corgi poo. I thought it would make a good paperweight if we got some of the Queen's own dog dirt cast in Perspex. And the beauty of the plan was that if we got caught by any guards trying to steal it, we could just claim to be cleaning up. A foolproof scheme. Sadly, the grounds were immaculate. Not a turd to be seen.

Anyhow, that all said, when I saw McCartney's handwritten lyrics sitting up on that stand from across the stage at Live Aid, my inner magpie took hold.

I'm having them, I thought. The second McCartney's fingers leave those keys, I'm swooping in.

Alas, in all the commotion of the full cast coming on stage for an all-star sing-along of 'Do They Know It's Christmas?' I missed my chance. As I dived to grab them, some beefy bloke from the stage crew got in front of me and whipped them away out of sight.

I suppose I'm still left with the priceless memory of getting to sing in the finale of Live Aid. But those lyrics would have looked great on my fridge.

The Morning After

There's a slight coda to my Live Aid experience, a mystery that has gone unsolved until now.

The next morning, I woke to find reporters gathered outside the front of my flat. I'm happy to say I've generally had a pretty good relationship with the tabloids over the years, but I knew this sort of sight was not good. Reporters don't do the rounds in packs like this if all they want to say is, 'Well done last night, Mart! We were wondering if we could get a picture of you looking cool for the history books?'

Immediately my mind started racing, trying to figure out what I'd done to attract the attention of Fleet Street's finest. I'd left the after-show party early. I hadn't been the one who'd said 'fuck' on telly.

The cameras hadn't caught me trying to pinch McCartney's lyrics, had they?

I chucked on some trousers and went down to see what they wanted – but it wasn't me they were wanting to talk to. It was Shirlie.

They'd heard a rumour from backstage at the arena yesterday. A witness saying they'd seen Shirl getting up to a bit of no good in the toilets. Snorting cocaine. With Princess Diana.

'You what?' I said, bursting out laughing. 'Shirlie and Diana?'

I have since made a vow to Shirlie. In front of witnesses, I promised to love, honour and obey her. So if my wife tells me that she didn't rack out lines with the Princess of Wales that day, then I am duty bound to believe her.

But even if I wasn't, I'd still be inclined to take her word for it. The two of us were inseparable that day. We'd spent half the concert here, watching it on the telly at the foot of our bed. The only time I wasn't glued to Shirl's side was the 15 minutes I was on stage. I mean, I know the crowd was disappointed that we chose to play new material, but I don't reckon it was enough to turn Diana to drugs.

I can't pretend that the backstage area of Live Aid wasn't awash with coke. It was the mid-80s, we were all rock stars and Status Quo had been invited. Of course there was cocaine. It's entirely possible that someone saw two blondes indulging in a cheeky rail or two in the toilets.

The story never ended up running, though, so I assume the reporters had no other leads. To this day I have never been able to figure out exactly which two blondes that source must have seen. If I had to guess, my money would have been on Rick Parfitt and his reflection – but, sadly, with Rick and Diana both gone now, we may never get an answer.

The Instigator

It's been a while since you've mentioned Blitz Kids, Martin. Is everything alright? Blink twice if you need help.

OK, OK. I warned you I would get a bit like that, but there was one conspicuous Blitz Kid absence in the Live Aid line-up, given what a household name he had become. Where, you might ask, was Boy George in all this?

George was more involved in Live Aid than people tend to realise. Not in the organising of the event (his spiralling heroin addiction meant he wasn't much use to anyone on that front) but in the inspiration for it. George was the one who actually put the suggestion in front of Bob Geldof in the first place.

It happened in December '84, when Culture Club played a string of gigs at Wembley Arena to round off their year. Spandau had put in a few dates there at the start of the month, so we knew how ambitious it was to sell a run at a venue that big. Dagger reliably informed me that Culture Club were struggling to sell it, especially in the run-up to Christmas, so they had devised a little festive gimmick. At their last gig (22 December) Boy George would stage a mini-Band Aid reunion as an encore, inviting a few friends and guest vocalists to join him on stage.

'Do They Know It's Christmas?' was riding high in the charts and well on its way to becoming the fastest- and biggest-selling single of not just the year, but all time.

Paul Young, George Michael, our Tony, Marilyn and Elton John all turned up to join Culture Club for what was supposed to be a one-off live rendition, but Boy George was so bowled over by the response it got in the arena, he mentioned to Bob that a charity concert could be a feasible next step for Band Aid.

Bob gave an interview in early '85 saying he'd be happy to help out if it was something George was seriously pursuing. As George has since freely admitted he was 'otherwise chemically engaged' for most of 1985, the idea was left floating in limbo – so Bob and Midge picked it up, dusted it down and put on what became Live Aid.

Bob got his knighthood for all this the following year and, while it is completely deserved, I feel as though I have a duty to remind people that, without the cloakroom attendant from the Blitz, rock history might never have been made that day.

1986

BARRICADES

QuickSnap Camera | 'Freddie Starr Ate My Hamster!' | Gary Lineker's Golden Boot | Bombay Sapphire | Challenger Disaster | M25 Completed | GCSEs Start | Hands Across America | OutRun | Top Gun | Goal of the Century | Dirty Den Serves Angie Divorce Papers | iThree Amigos! | The Phantom of the Opera | Wham! The Final | Mike Tyson Youngest Heavyweight Champion | Mexico 86 World Cup | Chernobyl | Marcos Flees Manila | Dockers | Inheritance Tax | Edinburgh Commonwealth Games | Watchmen | Licensed to Ill | The Legend of Zelda | Ferris Bueller's Day Off | Archers Peach Schnapps

The Dark Arts

Of course, youth culture can never just be left alone. There's always a generation of pearl-clutching parents who are shocked – *shocked* – at what kids these days are getting up to, and the 1980s was no exception.

America was leading the charge on the crackdown. A number of songs by artists in the mid-80s had caused concerned parents to have kittens because of their strong sexual content. A list of songs that parents took particular objection to, known as the 'Filthy Fifteen', was drawn up, including 'Darling Nikki' by Prince, 'Dress You Up' by Madonna and 'Let Me Put My Love into You' by AC/DC (OK, that one wasn't subtle).

For the very first time in history, pop music was alluding to the existence of sex. Before 1984, rock'n'roll had strictly been about chaste, wholesome fun – but then Prince decided to invent orgasms and everybody had to suffer.

All the outrage led to the Parents Music Resource Center (PMRC) being established: the political committee that introduced those helpful little 'Explicit Advisory Content' stickers, so that impressionable young kids could more easily spot which albums contained filth and depravity at a glance.

I'm sorry to report that Spandau never quite made the cut* but Def Leppard did. Their song 'High 'n' Dry (Saturday Night)' was censured as one of the 'Filthy Fifteen' for encouraging drug and alcohol use.

The PMRC was the formal part of the movement, but these things always spill out into weird, fanatical wings. Over the course of the 80s, there was also growing cultural panic that children were being lured into the arms of the Devil (in part by bands including backwards messages from Lucifer himself on their albums), a contagion that became known as the 'Satanic Panic'.

I would love to say that nobody had anything to fear from Spandau Ballet on this front, but I'm afraid that wouldn't be the whole truth. I have, in my time, dabbled in the dark arts.

Like a lot of the people I was hanging around with in the 80s, I developed a fascination with ouija boards. I don't know if they work. I don't know if there are spirits trapped between this world and the next, trying to communicate with us via the medium of upturned tumblers. I like to think I have always kept – and will continue to keep – an open mind about the ways of the world.

And I would love an explanation for what happened in Steve Strange's flat that night.

It was while he was living off the King's Road in Chelsea. It was me, Gary, Steve Strange, Billy Idol and Billy Idol's

---

* No one ever played our partially nudey 'Paint It Down' video, so no one ever got scandalised enough to care …

girlfriend at the time, Wendy. Dressed in the wildest New Romantic clothes, really at the height of our flamboyance,* the five of us gathered round the table to commune with the other side.

Placing our fingers on top of the glass in the centre of the board, we called out to the room, 'Spirit, if you can hear us, tell us your name.'

I don't know if you've ever sat at an ouija board, but at a certain point the glass starts to feel heavy. I'm not saying it's a spirit, but there's definitely an aura that you create in the room, and I always remember a point where it feels like there's some sort of suction acting on the underside of the glass, sticking it to the table.

'Spirits, is there anybody there?'

The weight of it just changes and before long you find your fingers being drawn around by the glass as it begins to move about the table. Now, I'm a sensible man. I was a sensible kid too. It sounds mad, but it used to happen. The glass would move.

'Spirit, do you have a message?'

To start with, it would move randomly. It wasn't one person shoving it about; it's more of a joint energy. A feeling takes hold. The movement becomes more natural. The directions become clearer. But we still couldn't make head or tail out of what this spooky bastard was trying to say.

'Spirit! Speak to us!'

All of a sudden, the glass lurched. To D. To O. To N. To T. Then across to M and O. Then to V and E.

D-O-N-T-M-O-V-E.

---

* Billy always kept his signature leather gloves on, but even he looked more like a pirate than a punk at this point.

Don't. Move.

Obviously, we do. All of us jump up, screaming in each other's faces, our lace frills flapping as we bolt for the door, directly disobeying the spirit's strict instruction. And as we do, I swear to you, this velvet curtain of Steve's – this heavy, heavy velvet curtain hanging by his window that doesn't look like it's moved as much as an inch in 30 years – comes flying out from the wall.

I wish I knew who it was that frightened the life out of us all that day, but I haven't dared call on them again. I like my own soft furnishings too much to risk it.

Stranger Coincidences

Ready for a Blitz theory that stretches the outer limits of credulity? One that will really have you wanting to pat me on the knee and call for the nurses?

I reckon I can trace a line from *Stranger Things* – the popular Netflix show in which the citizens of Hawkins, Indiana spend the entirety of the 80s being terrorised by a series of terrifying supernatural beasts – back to the Blitz.

Full disclosure: I haven't been able to check any of the details of this with the Duffer brothers, who created the series. They may well have an alternative explanation for all this but, for what it's worth, here's my two cents.

First of all, what is the name of the handsome hero in *Stranger Things* that everyone is supposed to root for? Steve Harrington.

What was the birth name of Blitz founder Steve Strange? Steve Harrington.

Two Steve Harringtons: one Strange, the other Stranger.

Not convinced? Fine. How about this?

The fourth series of *Stranger Things* inspired a brand new generation of viewers to discover Kate Bush for the first time. Specifically, her song 'Running Up That Hill'. Its distinctive riff gets used throughout the series, both as a motif in the score and as a piece of music in the actual world of the show itself – playing a pivotal part in the storyline of Max.

That riff, that standout sound, is played on a very important synthesiser. The connoisseur's choice: the Fairlight CMI.

When I first saw a Fairlight in action, it was like being shown alien technology. Part piano keyboard, part computer keyboard and part black-and-green screen, the music it made sounded like it was being beamed from outer space. Celestial, almost. Like being bathed in starlight. The single press of a key could turn one note into a full electro-symphony, as though the planets themselves were singing.

The Fairlight came with a couple of tripwires, though. Not only was it eye-wateringly expensive, but it was such a sophisticated bit of kit that only a handful of engineers actually knew how to program it.

The prog-rock lot all went crazy for them. Peter Gabriel, Alan Parsons, Pink Floyd. Naturally Trevor Horn used one. And, starting with her 1980 album *Never for Ever*, so did Kate Bush.

Never for Ever was the first commercially released album to feature the Fairlight CMI. You can hear it throughout the album, but the breaking glass and cocking rifle samples on 'Babooshka' are some of the best-known early examples of its use.

By the time she recorded her 1985 album *Hounds of Love*, Kate had learned the ropes and was producing and engineering songs like 'Running Up That Hill' herself. But the person who initially programmed the Fairlight for her at the start?

Richard Burgess: producer of the first two Spandau Ballet albums and one of the regular faces you could find scuffing up a WWII-themed wine bar in Covent Garden in 1980 when he wasn't working with Kate on *Never for Ever*.

A Blitz Kid.

The Letter

On account of being lodged deep inside the Spandau Bubble throughout most of '84, I hadn't been alert to many of the details of the miners' strike when it was happening. To my shame, I had to be filled in on it all at the Band Aid sessions by George Michael.

When I heard that the print workers' union had gone on strike in '86, though, that news got through to me – and it gave me a moment's pause.

My dad had been a printer. I had been a printer too, I suppose. A printer's apprentice, at least. Printing was the track my life was set on before the Blitz went and changed everything. It was going to be my career.

It wasn't one I'd chosen. Dad got me that apprenticeship and had stuck his neck out quite a bit to get it. I had no technical experience to speak of. I'd only worked Saturday jobs and other small-fry gigs. Shifts in a fruit and veg shop with Gary on Essex Road. Handing out free copies of *Miss London* magazine to commuters coming out of Aldwych tube station. All of them paid jobs, but nothing I could rely on long term. I could barely even rely on them short term. I was forever short of cash. My primary expertise was in nursing a single, slowly flattening pint for a full evening.

The apprenticeship was a good scheme, more than a kid in my position probably deserved. I'd left school with two O Levels and nothing much in mind but daydreams. To be handed an opportunity to learn a proper craft and be paid while doing it was far beyond anything I'd have been motivated to seek out for myself.

If all Dad had wanted was to get me working and bringing in money, he could have easily circled a bunch of assorted ads in the classifieds and made me apply to them all. Knowing that he had enough faith in me to recommend me was touching. Following in the family trade was a working-class tradition and I wanted to do my old man proud.

Try as I might, though, I hated that job. I was training to become a compositor, which – I'm told – was actually one of the more respected jobs in the field. They could have fooled me.

They roasted me constantly. Old fellas who'd been working the plates for 20, 30 years. Lifers who had moulded generations of spotty little twerps like me, brought them in close under their wing, then teased them endlessly with the same crap pranks.

Every morning, I'd make the tea and deliver it to everyone before being given my assignments for the day. There'd always be something. Go and ask such-and-such for a long weight. Nip out to the hardware shop and find me a left-handed screwdriver. I knew I could always squeeze an hour out of an obvious wind-up like that, taking myself away for a bit of peace and quiet wherever I could find it (which is not that easy in a print shop).

Being the office whipping boy wasn't something I much fancied as a future, but unless I got lucky and became a rock star – what else could I do?

Where would I be now, I wonder, if Dagger had never insisted that Gary recruit me? If Steve Strange had taken one look at my outfit that first fateful Tuesday at the Blitz and cast me from his door? What if we'd played our first showcase at Halligan's that Saturday morning and everyone there just stood and stared? There were so many points where it could have gone wrong.

The apprenticeship lasted four years. If I'd completed it, I'd have likely taken up my first proper position sometime around the *True* sessions. Instead, I sat by a studio poolside in the Bahamas, humming that catchy vocal riff on my sun lounger.

By the end of '85 in an alternative timeline, I'd have had a good few years under my belt as a fully trained compositor. It would have been me putting in orders for chicken lip sandwiches and sending some poor pipsqueak apprentice off to fetch them for me. I'd have earned my stripes. My feet would have been under the table.

But then what? In January '86, the print workers' union voted to go on strike. As a result, Rupert Murdoch summarily fired thousands of workers and drafted in scab labour to take their place. A bitter stand-off between the printers, the police and the press would be drawn out for the entire year. Violence broke out along picket lines. Over a thousand arrests were made. Thatcher's legislation would tightly hamstring the unions and the police took every opportunity to enforce her rules as rigidly as they could.

Meanwhile, as all this happened in the forefront, technology was shifting around in the background. The craft of hot-metal printing I had been learning wasn't the future-proof vocation I'd figured it to be in 1978. New, less labour-intensive types of printing were being rolled out. Even if the union triumphed against Murdoch, how long could they realistically fight that tide?

The print industry wasn't pop culture. This wave of emergent technology wasn't opening up exciting possibilities for press operators and their families. It was ruining livelihoods, communities. Working people were putting their bodies, their health, their lives on the line for the right to a fair day's pay and they were getting ground into dust.

I think of my father, a printer all his life. He had always been so supportive of me and Gary and the choices we made. Even the smallest ones. Even the time I threw on that brown crimplene dress of mine and headed out to the pub with a face full of slap, a single dangling earring and a barnet full of hairspray. I must have looked like a pantomime dame fallen on hard times. Striding out into the street in all that would have definitely given the neighbours something to talk about.

As I passed Dad in the living room on my way out the door, he called out after me.

'Martin!'

A pause.

'Have you got your keys?'

When I told him about the band, about the sort of reception we'd been getting and the bright, endless future that the Blitz Kids had got all mapped out I'm not sure he understood anywhere close to a fraction of what I was telling him. He understood where it was all leading, though. He knew what I was going to ask him next.

I needed to leave my apprenticeship. He'd put himself out to get it for me and I appreciated that more than anything. I realised giving up a trade in the middle of massive economic uncertainty to chase some far-off fantasy of being a bass player in my brother's band was insane. I knew we could fail. Our band could come to nothing and I'd be stranded; unable to simply start again from square one. I'd just have to hobble on.

But I had no choice. I had to do it. It might only have been the promise of something, but I'd never wanted anything as much as I'd wanted to be in this band. I had to make it work.

So he wrote me a letter.

Dear George
I want to ask you if Martin can leave his apprenticeship position in your print shop. I know the hours of training and hard work you have put into Martin over the last year, but I feel I have to give him a chance in life.
   Martin wants to leave to become a pop star.
   Thanks for understanding,
   Frank Kemp

I've thought a lot over the years about the moment my life was truly transformed. Was it the moment we signed our deal that day at Chrysalis? The time we first played *Top of the Pops*? The morning Dagger called with the news that

'True' was No. 1, and I nearly lost my kneecaps to the John Keeble Room Service Express?

No. It was then. The day my father wrote that letter.

My ticket to the world.

Behind the Scenes

The 1980s was an incredible decade for Hollywood. I know, because as the end of our year abroad drew to a close, we passed the time hosting regular movie nights with Def Leppard and Frankie Goes to Hollywood.

So many classics came out in that era. Big popcorn blockbusters like *Raiders of the Lost Ark*, *Top Gun*, *Die Hard*, *Terminator*. Massive family favourites like *ET*, *Ghostbusters*, *Back to the Future*, *The Karate Kid*. Beloved romcoms like *Pretty Woman*, *Dirty Dancing*, *Splash*. All those coming-of-age comedies that stuck a load of Second Invasion bands on their soundtracks.

They were some cracking years for cinema, but you ask anyone in the music industry what the best film to come out of the 1980s was, and you'll get one answer: *Spinal Tap*.

If you've never seen this comedy masterpiece, *This Is Spinal Tap* is a rock'n'roll mockumentary profiling a fictional English heavy metal band. Largely improvised by its stars Christopher Guest, Michael McKean and Harry Shearer (and its director Rob Reiner, who also gave us *Stand by Me*, *The Princess Bride* and *When Harry Met Sally*) the film could easily be a straight-shot doc it nails band life so perfectly.

There's a famous story about Liam and Noel Gallagher from Oasis going to see a Spinal Tap gig once in Carnegie

Hall. The Gallaghers had both seen the film and loved it, but when Guest, McKean and Shearer all came on stage in different costumes, playing the part of their own support act (a traditional folk trio called the Folksmen), Liam couldn't get his head round it.

When Noel explained to him that they were all actors, that the whole thing was a deadpan comedy routine, Liam said, 'Nah, I'm not 'avin' that' and stormed out – never watched the film again.

He definitely wasn't the first musician to be duped by it either because when I first saw *This Is Spinal Tap* in that flat in Dublin, I was watching it with Joe Elliott and a few of the other guys from Def Leppard and it was well over halfway before they twigged it was a spoof.

The thing is, if you've ever been in a band, you'll know how true it all rings. The famous scene where the lead guitarist, Nigel Tufnel, is showing off his custom amp that goes all the way up to 11 ('Well, it's … one louder'), that is something I swear producers had said to me before *Spinal Tap*. I've definitely seen musicians get every bit as precious as Nigel when people get too close to their instruments, giving their own rendition of the 'Don't point! Don't even look at it!' dialogue.

The bit about the backstage riders felt like it had been written to skewer me personally.

A rider – if you don't know – is the catering and hospitality requests you make of a venue when you play a gig. The hot meals, the hummus, the bottles of mineral water, wine and whisky. The bowl of M&Ms with all the brown ones taken out. That stuff.

A lot gets made of bands having excessive riders but the truth of it is that you send all that paperwork off a long time in advance of the actual gig, so you can't really predict what you're going to be in the mood for on any given night. As such, you tend to ask for a range of solid basics. In theory, this should create a much-needed shred of consistency out on the road. In practice, you end up like Spinal Tap, obsessing over the regional discrepancies.

When I saw Nigel Tufnel complaining about the haphazard olives on his charcuterie board, some of them having 'little guys' in them (pimento peppers), others not ('I mean … it's a complete catastrophe!'), I've known that feeling.*

One moment I lived almost beat for beat is the 'Hello Cleveland' scene, where the band get lost in the maze of corridors coming out of their dressing room and are late reaching the stage. I'm close to breaking into a cold sweat, just thinking of it now.

We were playing in Belgium and had stepped off stage briefly before the encore. Now, it's important for you to know that I am not a smoker. Never was in the 80s, never have been since. I absolutely hate it. So what possessed me to take a drag on this joint that one of the crew passed me that night as I walked by them in the wings, I'll never know but it absolutely knocked me for six.

I was stoned out of my skull within seconds and must have wandered off somewhere because before I knew it I could hear the audience erupting into cheers – my cue that John was taking up his place at the drums again.

I could only have taken a few steps away from the stage door, at a maximum, but suddenly I had no idea where I

---

* There were cities – and I won't name names – where my aftershow cheese board just wasn't up to scratch. I never let it affect my performance, though. I rose above it. I'm a professional.

was. Nowhere led back to the stage. I started running down the corridor hoping it would lead me somewhere I recognised, but all of it looked the same. It was like some endless nightmare where I was running constantly and the same bit of background kept whizzing by over and over and over again, like a *Scooby-Doo* cartoon.

What I had failed to realise was that the theatre was circular. I was pelting round and round the perimeter of it like a hamster in a wheel. I have no idea how many laps of that building I must have done before I finally tumbled out into the lobby.

How much you want to rely on my recollection of this, given the effect the dope had had on me, is up to you. But in my mind, I have a clear memory of walking up to the door of the auditorium, behind the crowd, and looking through a little porthole window at the rest of the band on stage, hearing my brother ask into the mic, 'Where's Martin? Has my brother gone?'

My guardian angel came in the form of Alan Keys, who must have been tailing me. Slapping a hand on my shoulder he momentarily brought me back to my senses. He ushered me through the corridors and back onto the stage to everyone's bemusement – the band and audience alike.

Why do I enjoy watching these moments I have lived being made fun of in fictional form? I don't know. That's the genius of *Spinal Tap*. A pitch-perfect parody of the rock'n'roll life, made with only the punchlines.

Cruel Summer

Ever since we shared a bedroom as kids back in our house on Rotherfield Street, Gary has always played his songs to me first. As his brother, I'm the closest thing he has to himself that isn't actually him. I get the soft launch. If he's happy with my response, the band gets to hear it. After that, the world.

I remember him debuting an acoustic version of 'True' for me early on. I could tell it was a personal one for him, though he didn't ever tell me what the lyrics were about. I'd only learn much later he had written it grappling with his unrequited feelings for Clare Grogan of Altered Images. He wasn't alone. *Gregory's Girl* had made an entire generation of boys (and plenty of girls too, I'm sure) fall in love with Clare, so it's no wonder that song struck such a chord with the public.

I remember the night he played 'Through the Barricades' for me the first time so clearly. It was while we were in Dublin. Gary called me up to the flat he and John were sharing to hear it. I assume John had heard this one being written, because he had a massive smile on his face the second Gary plucked that first note.

If you got him to play it for you today, I don't think it would sound any different to what I heard that afternoon. The song was all but finished right from the start. You could have knocked me down with a toothpick when it was over. It was magnificent.

He didn't need to tell me what that song was about. I knew when I heard the title.

The story isn't really mine to tell, but Thomas 'Kidso'

Reilly had been part of our road crew in the spring of '83 – the dates we had been playing when 'True' topped the charts. His merchandise company, Bravado, was doing Spandau's merch and he was the one who sold it all to fans after the show. With 'True' at No. 1, he was a busy boy that spring.

His older brother was Jim Reilly, the drummer from Stiff Little Fingers. Thomas was Jim's kid brother, so 'Kidso' was what they called him. Kidso had made a real career for himself touring with all sorts of bands. Depeche Mode. Altered Images. The Jam. Our fellow Blitz Kids, Bananarama.

He was acting as their road manager when it happened in the summer of '83. Kidso had gone home to Belfast for a couple of days, using his time off to pay a visit to his mum. He'd caught up with a few friends while he was back and they all went out to kick a ball about in a nearby field in the early evening sun.

With dinnertime approaching, and a night out on the town planned for later, the boys decided they would head home, grab a bite to eat then get themselves ready to meet up again for drinks.

According to reports, British soldiers on patrol stopped them on their way home and began to search them. They were wearing T-shirts and shorts, carrying nothing more threatening than a football. There was no obvious reason to stop them, much less search them, but the soldiers still did so. The search became aggressive. An argument started. Kidso, sick of being harassed for no good reason, had had enough. He turned to leave.

As he walked away, his T-shirt in his hand, one of the soldiers raised his rifle, took aim and fired.

Kidso was shot dead. A single bullet in the back. Twenty-two years old.

News of his death was a gut punch to us all. Kidso and I were roughly the same age. Both younger siblings who idolised our big brothers. Both given golden opportunities by them to make a living in this incredible industry. Now he was gone. Murdered.

The news hit Gary hardest of all. I knew he had been close to Kidso. It had been Clare Grogan who first introduced the two of them and Gary had taken a real shine to him. After a gig we played at the King's Hall in Belfast in December '84, Gary met up with Jim and Jim took him to visit Kidso's grave.

It had taken years for Gary to figure out what he wanted to say with 'Through the Barricades'. Then one night it just happened. The song woke him at 2 a.m., arriving fully formed.

To this day, I still think it is the best song he's written and I think he does too. Tony has said as much in interviews too.

It's the oddest thing in retrospect. That a song we all loved so much, a song about the futility of division, would be the thing to break us up.

The Bishop

It looked like Batman was coming up our stairs.

I must have been seven when the bishop came to visit our house on Rotherfield Street. He had come to see Gary. Using the second-hand acoustic guitar he'd been given for Christmas, Gary had written a song; one that he'd been asked to perform in school assembly. It was called 'When Jesus Rode to Jericho on the Way to the Cross' and it went down very well with everyone. Particularly with a special guest that had been invited to attend: the Bishop of Stepney, the Right Reverend Trevor Huddleston.

Now he was paying us a house call.

I will never forget looking over the banisters as he made his way up to our floor. He must have been six foot five, a giant gold cross on, a flash of silver hair, flowing purple robes that looked like they filled the entire staircase. I'd only ever seen superheroes dress like this.

Sat in our living room, the bishop told us he had brought a gift for Gary. He reached into his bag and pulled out a box. It was a tape recorder.

'Whatever songs you write,' he said, handing it across, 'I want you to record them on this and send them to me.'

A tape recorder? For us? He really was a superhero!

This was the stuff of dreams. A tape recorder was so expensive in those days, I hadn't even dared to imagine what it must be like to own one. This wasn't the sort of thing we could cheekily nudge onto the Christmas list in the hopes that Santa would see to it. This was a serious luxury.

The recorder was only part of the present, though. The equipment itself was obviously hugely important – to Gary and to all of us – but it was the show of encouragement that was the real gift. Gary can't have been much older than nine. The Bishop of Stepney had heard one song of his and was now offering to be a casual mentor. This was a mind-blowing pat on the back.

I also got something out of it too. Beyond just nicking it and using it to record stuff off the radio. It taught me a foundational lesson.

As well as being a printer, my dad was an amazing painter. He only ever did it as a hobby, painting for himself, but his work filled our little flat. I loved it all. Up until the moment the bishop came for tea, however, it had never dawned on me that other people could value someone else's art. That strangers could see and appreciate something you'd made – and appreciate it enough to want to give you a tape recorder.

I don't know how long Gary went on sending tapes to the bishop – if His Grace got early demos of singles like 'Round and Round' and 'How Many Lies?' – but I know the two of them stayed in touch.

In June 1986, the bishop called Gary to invite him to play as part of a free one-day concert on Clapham Common. The Festival of Freedom in Namibia and South Africa: Artists Against Apartheid.

It was a very impressive line-up. Big Audio Dynamite. Billy Bragg. The Communards. Roddy Frame from Aztec Camera. Sting. The Blitz was well represented too with Boy George and Sade playing sets in support of the cause, as well as – according to the posters – Gary Kemp.

Not Gary Kemp of Spandau Ballet. Not Spandau Ballet. Gary Kemp. Of Gary Kemp.

Gary had been playing the odd gig without us recently as part of his involvement in Red Wedge: a collective of musicians and artists who were organising concerts, rallies and media appearances in support of the Labour Party to drive out Thatcher's government in the upcoming 1987 election.

Band Aid and Live Aid showed what pop music's collect-ive power could achieve. *Wham! in China* had shown that it didn't just have to be about fundraising either. Diplomacy through pop culture was possible too.

Gary wanted to be part of that, to keep pushing for change. Before '86 he didn't have much to contribute, though. Now he had a song that could happily sit along-side the folk-punk protest of Billy Bragg or the social commentary synth-pop of Heaven 17's '(We Don't Need This) Fascist Groove Thang'.

He had 'Through the Barricades'.

As part of both Red Wedge and Artists Against Apartheid, Gary played 'Through the Barricades' solo, under his own name, three times before he would have to give it up to Tony.

That was tough for him. However personal the writing of 'True' had been, trying to distil his complicated, unre-quited feelings for Clare Grogan into pop lyrics, that was nothing compared with what went into 'Through the Barricades'.

'True' was a young man's crush. 'Through the Barricades' was a young man's life. They were worlds apart.

Tony does a magnificent job with the song. As apprehen-sive as Gary was about letting someone else become the voice of it, I know he thinks so too. Spandau Ballet didn't break up because disaster struck that song. It was nothing but success for us.

But as I'd quietly feared for years would happen, padding around that Munich bunker playing my 800th game of pinball, Gary was starting to see there was a life for his songs outside of Spandau. Trevor Horn had told him he didn't need John on his records. Jolley and Swain had showed him he didn't need me on his records. Now he was starting to wonder if he even really needed Tony on them either.

And once that rift appeared, it was only a matter of time.

1987

ALL CHANGE

Dirty Dancing | *Roland TB-303 Bass Squelch* | *Nike Air Max* | *Rick Astley* | The Simpsons *Debut on* The Tracey Ullman Show | *Red Bull* | *Black Monday* | Going for Gold | *Thatcher's Third Term* | *It's a Sin* | *Spandau Prison Demolished* | *Amiga 500* | La Bamba | *Space Raiders* | *First Rugby World Cup* | *'Jack Your Body'* | *Kidnap of Terry Waite* | *'Mr Gorbachev, Tear Down This Wall!'* | Street Fighter | *'China in Your Hand'* | *M|A|R|R|S* | The Tommyknockers | *Drunk Oliver Reed on* Aspel & Company | Trump: The Art of the Deal

A New Band

I read somewhere once that you replace every single cell in your body every seven years. A full head-to-toe overhaul. It's a gradual change, imperceptible to the eye. An eye itself that is constantly changing. Moment by moment, bit by bit, the process never stops. Quietly, continually, you regenerate – until before you know it there's nothing left of the person you once were.

The person I started 1987 as was not the same person who started 1980. Physically. Mentally. Creatively. I was different. We were all different.

Our European tour for *Through the Barricades* was our biggest ever. Especially in southern Europe, we seemed to be on fire. Suddenly we were stars the size of Michael Jackson in places like Italy, Portugal and Spain. In Madrid we played what must have been the largest Spandau Ballet gig of our career, at Casa de Campo, a gigantic public park in the heart of the city, five times the size of Central Park in New York, nearly seven times the size of Hyde Park in London. We played to 120,000 people that night – among them, the King of Spain.

The numbers were fantastical. Fever dreams. Shows that were going pound for pound with the Springsteen one I'd seen back in Slane Castle. The thing I could barely comprehend two years ago was now my bread and butter.

We were one of the biggest bands in the world, but we were no longer the same. Every last cell of us had changed.

A New Sound

When you write music, you write it for the space in which it will be played. Your choice of instruments, arrangements, melody and harmonies – all of them are tailored to suit the venue. It's been that way throughout history whether it was Bach composing cantatas for church, Verdi writing arias for an opera house or Benny Goodman arranging his big band for a ballroom.

The symphony is built for the symphony hall, not the other way around.

It's exactly the same with pop music, and you can trace the trajectory of a band's success through their sound.

Take Spandau. In the early days, when we were playing 200-capacity rooms, we were a tight classic rock band with a monophonic synth. We wrote the power-pop songs for those small venues, because that's what plays well in them. Drums, bass, guitars and a single synth line were all we used on *Journeys to Glory* because that set-up perfectly filled the grungy, smoky Blitz gigs we were playing.

When we moved to the proscenium-arch venues for the *Diamond* album – 2,000-seater theatres like the Hammersmith Odeon or Newcastle City Hall – the sound had built up a bit. We had the excellent Beggar & Co do brass arrangements. Steve Norman cracked out his bongos and conga drums. In the Blitz, there had barely been space for one drum kit, let alone three. In the spacious Palace Theatre, Manchester, though, why not?

By the time Steve had picked up his sax for songs like 'Gold' and 'True', we were playing 6,000-seater arenas where those killer solos could bounce freely around the cavernous walls. It became part of our core sound. Synths had become polyphonic too, meaning you now could play chords and create bigger clouds of sound. In the Blitz, too much of that would have swamped the rest of the band. But in the NEC in Birmingham or the Royal Highland Exhibition Hall in Edinburgh, you could set up a whole rack of these synths. Hire a sixth member to come and play them for you too. You've got the budget. You've got the space.

By 1987, we were playing stadiums with capacities anywhere between 12,000 and 120,000. You need a big sound to play a big place. Our early Yamaha CS-10 synth would have sounded as thin and weedy as one of those musical birthday cards in a space like that. You need some serious heft to shift the sheer amount of air in there. So our songs started to sound like Bon Jovi. Proper anthem stadium rock.

To a degree, our hands were tied. Playing a stadium is a weirdly delicate thing. I'm sure you can picture that classic music documentary cliché of a singer stepping out onto an empty black and white stage for the sound check, the sound of each footstep echoing. The lights flick on, the buzz of the electrics is all you can hear as the singer looks out over a venue that will soon be filled with screaming fans. There's a little squeak of feedback as they put their lips to the mic and say, 'Check!' and then their voice ricochets around the stadium, '… check … check … check … check'.

That echo is no joke. The actual physical distance between the stage and the seats at the back is often so big there's a delay in the sound getting to them. The fans down the front hear your song half a second before those at the back. It creates amazing natural reverb, but that's something you have to account for – not just in your playing, but in the original writing.

Fast, complicated riffs and intricate melodies turn to mud in a massive arena. The tiny details you obsess over get lost. Big, chunky chords left to ring out and long, belted vocals, on the other hand, suit the stadium and sound unbeatable.

There's a thought that when bands reach a certain stage in their career, their sound gets a bit pompous. Things feel overblown, a little flabby. Critics will say it's laziness – and maybe it is with some bands – but the demands of creating a successful stadium show are tough. You need to keep building and building and building these shows, creating ever greater spectacles. Partly that's a creative thing – you want to make the most expansive show you can. But on a far more practical level, it's because you need to entice the same fans to return each year (as well as a load of new ones to fill all those extra stadium seats).

While the change in sound makes total sense for the fans who come to see these concerts, for the fans who listen at home to the records, it can sound jarring. The difference between *Journeys to Glory* and *Through the Barricades* is stark. We sounded like a completely different band – but that's because we were.

Everything was changing. Everything had changed.

A New Scene

We hadn't been writing for the clubs since 'Chant No. 1'. We knew that. We'd made a conscious decision to cleave ourselves from the scene and had long since made our peace with that decision. Our club passes rescinded, Spandau were now a stadium act.

The sound coming out of the underground now was hip-hop and rap. 1987 was a landmark year for the genre. NWA formed – the band that gave us Dr Dre and Ice Cube. Public Enemy, Ice-T, Eric B. & Rakim all released their debut albums, while the Beastie Boys were tearing up the *Billboard* chart with '(You Gotta) Fight for Your Right (to Party!)'.

The acts that Chris Sullivan had been inviting to play the Wag in those early days were now breaking out everywhere, and he was continuing to give early gigs to so many new acts there who are now household names: Kool Moe Dee, De La Soul, Queen Latifah.

Jon Baker – our old pal Mole from Axiom – had moved into music promotion and production too, arranging UK tours for Doug E. Fresh and Slick Rick, while his label Gee Street Records signed Jungle Brothers, Stereo MCs and P.M. Dawn.

While all that music sounded a million miles apart from what Spandau created, it came from similar roots.

A lot of the rap records released in the late 80s used the exact same synthesisers and drum machines we had been using at the start of the decade, yet this new breed of producers was getting a completely different sound from them. Machines like the Roland TR-808 and the Linn

LM-1 had been used to give our records and club nights a flavour of the futurist art scenes of Europe. Now they were telling the stories of young black kids in South Central LA and the Bronx.

Sampling also became huge, something the Fairlight first introduced to recording studios. The Fairlight gave producers the capability to digitally encode sounds and then drop them into a song with the press of a button. Kate Bush famously sampled the sound of breaking glass on her song 'Babooshka' in 1980 – using a Fairlight that was programmed by Spandau's earliest producer, Richard Burgess.

The records hip-hop DJs were using on their turntables to sample and scratch were often 12-inch mixes. Though this had been happening since the early 70s in the disco and funk scenes, Spandau had been one of the first pop-rock bands to create these remixes for our own singles. We had done it for the nightclubs – creating extended versions with instrumental breaks and slow-building percussion to let people enjoy the groove longer on the dancefloor – but this also made them perfect for sampling.

Spandau had dabbled with some early hip-hop ourselves in '81. Quite a few of the post-punk, new-wave bands were at the time. If I hadn't been pissing about on those piano-key stairs in Bond's that night in New York, I'd have seen Debbie Harry doing her rap about a guitar-eating man from Mars in the second half of 'Rapture'. Gary had a few bars of rap in 'Chant No. 1' – a nod to the scene.

Although 'Chant No. 1' was probably our most obvious nightclub groove, it was 'True' that ended up being our first experience of sampling. 'Set Adrift on Memory Bliss' by P.M. Dawn came out in 1991. It was a monumental record;

the first single by a black rap act to top the *Billboard* Hot 100. Though I can't lay claim to any of its success (not least because it's the one song I didn't actually play on), that 'True' sample sounded so good in a new context.

What was so brilliant about it was that it was a continuation of the club culture we'd known. The next natural step. Sampling had hints of that same *Sniffin' Glue* ideology, letting the next wave of creators plunder its ideas for all they were worth. Of Rusty and the Visage demos. Of Steve Strange and fashion. Of Katharine Hamnett and the 'FRANKIE SAY RELAX' T-shirts. You take the bits you like, then make the product you wanted. The Walkman effect.

Mixtapes were also a huge part of the rap and hip-hop scene. Not the musical love-letters we'd send our girlfriends and boyfriends, but as demo tapes. Hip-hop artists used mixtapes to make a name for themselves by recording their sets, compiling their best tracks onto cassettes then passing them out around gigs to spread the word. Like CVs, but cool.

Fundamentally, this was all technology we were familiar with. If only purely technically, we knew how this new group of artists were creating their sound. If Spandau wanted to make a rap record, it wasn't mechanical know-how holding us back. It was something else. A new culture, a new scene. Something we couldn't hope to try and keep pace with.

Not that we needed to. As I say, at this stage we were selling tickets in the sorts of volumes we had never dared imagine. Out on the road, we were living the full rock-star fantasy. We just weren't selling records in anything like the same number anymore.

1982 to 1984 had seen us turn from an Underground Act into a Mainstream Act. Live Aid in '85 had cemented our place as an Establishment Act. But the release of a Greatest Hits album had taken us one step further.

We were now entering Heritage Act territory. Our shut-up-and-play-the-hits era. The full stop of the Spandau journey was heaving into view.

Touring

If you ever get the chance to be famous anywhere, I can really recommend Italy. It's a fabulous life. The food, the wine, the culture, the community – and Italian crowds are some of the best in the world.

I've never known exactly why we became so huge in Italy around '86/'87. The *Parade* album went over well there but, for some reason, *Through the Barricades* took us into another galaxy. My guess is Tony's voice, which sounded so incredible in those gorgeous Italian venues, is the secret sauce. That dramatic baritone turned perfectly to pop. The passion of theatre against a beat you can dance to.

I don't think Tony's voice was wasted on our records at all but, as a vocalist, he was leagues above most 80s pop singers. Punk kicking down all the barriers to entry meant even people with actively horrible singing voices could front bands. I didn't mind that. Anyone whoever heard me in a Defects rehearsal underneath that dry cleaners will know it suited me just fine. I genuinely love that punk allowed people to express themselves however they wanted – regardless of talent – but it did sometimes mean that expert craftsmen didn't always get their dues.

Italians take their singing seriously, though, and they loved Tony. I'm not kidding when I say their crowds are some of the best. Compare it with a place like Belgium* – where even your biggest fans will sit with their arms crossed, leaning back in their chairs, inspecting every inch of you like a line manager sizing you up for your annual performance review – and the difference is crazy.

In Italy, you only need to step out onto the stage and they're already out of their seats. They have no inhibitions. None. They'll dance, they'll sing, they'll basically do your job for you.

I remember once looking out onto the crowd one night in Naples and noticing that the wheelchair section down at the front of the auditorium was huge. Unusually so. Multiple times the size you'd expect from any other venue of this size.

Obviously it's great that the city of Naples made its venue so wheelchair friendly. In the 80s, there was nowhere near as much consideration given to such matters as there is today – and it's not like continental Europe, with its ancient buildings, was originally built with accessibility in mind.

I knew I shouldn't be distracted by it, but I couldn't stop thinking about it. So I asked one of the local crew, 'What is all that at the front? Why so many wheelchairs?'

He told me it was the Mafia. They were all kneecapping victims of the Camorra. Maybe it was classic Neapolitan humour that went over my head and he was just pulling

---

* At least we had fans in Belgium. The toughest nut to crack was always France. Other bands will tell you the same: if you weren't Johnny Hallyday back then, France wasn't interested.

my leg – but I'm telling you, I didn't see anything like that many wheelchairs up north.

Even if the Mafia had set about most of them, it didn't dampen their spirit one jot. They were always amazing, amazing audiences.

Concerts were still a huge bright spot in our lives. Whatever else was going on with our record sales, our home lives and the uneasy feeling that was starting to bubble with Gary's newly developed taste for solo sets, getting out there in front of the largest, most appreciative crowds of our careers was still every bit as fun as it ever had been.

The days could be a grind – hungover in a strange city, or hungover in transit to another strange city – but one person I have to thank for getting me through them was John Martin, our tour manager. He had more than enough on his plate getting the five of us where we needed to be and when, but he used to do the loveliest thing for us each day. John compiled a daily digest of tour stories. A typed Spandau newsletter that would get posted under our doors each morning.

I don't know whether he stayed up all night to compile it, or whether he was up with the lark to make his final edits, but he documented everything. Where we'd been playing and when. Who was last to leave the after-party. Who'd fallen down what stairs. Recipes for cocktails that the crew had created using the local liquors. How many of those cocktails you could safely drink before you fell down the stairs. Helpful, informative, news you can use.

That wasn't the only thing that was keeping me sane out on the road, though. Thanks to a new invention, I was getting plenty of post stuffed under my hotel room door.

Communication

For all the money that got blown at the height of my rock'n'roll career, most of it I reckon I could make a decent pitch for.

The after-show champagne? It's thirsty business under those hot stage lights. We all deserved a little drink after a hard night's work.

The after-show cheese board? I liked a quick cheese sandwich before I hopped in my pre-party shower and I needed to line my stomach if I was going to drink all that champagne.

Renting the entire corridor of a hotel to throw parties with total strangers in every city we went? Being on tour is lonely. We needed company and you can't put a price on the memories we made for the people who joined us for those parties. The 80s wasn't all just about me, me, me.

The figure that I dread to try to tot up, though? My phone bill.

Nowadays, with Wi-Fi and FaceTime and WhatsApp, you can connect with loved ones wherever you are in the world. You can see their faces, talk for hours if you want. If the time zones make it difficult you can leave a voice note for them to pick up when they wake. Modern technology allows for us to be a constant part of one another's lives.

On tour in the early days, things were not so easy – and they definitely weren't so cheap.

I would go down to reception at the hotel we were staying in for a night and find that I'd racked up a bill for £600 making long-distance calls to Shirlie when I'd rolled in drunk from a club. The lines, I have to say, were usually really good. Impressively clear. Whether they were worth the small fortune I sunk on them every other day, I couldn't say. I have deliberately tried not to think about how much I spent on phone calls in the Spandau years.

The other option at our disposal was a bit cheaper: the classic postcard. Wherever I went on tour, I would send Shirlie a postcard. It was never the most reliable method, as anyone who has ever sent a holiday postcard will know. Even if you don't mistakenly post it in a brightly coloured foreign bin, the chances are still high that you end up arriving home before it does.

Postcards also had one other major drawback. In our early days, Shirl was still living at her mum and dad's house so any messages I jotted on the back of a card would be read by them first. They could easily have been read by an unscrupulous postie too – and I definitely didn't want to risk Shirlie reading our red-hot correspondence on the front page of the *News of the World*.

It might not be such a bad thing that I was forced to curb my wilder passions, though. Shirlie has saved all of the postcards I sent her (all the ones that arrived, at any rate) and they're a nice document of our relationship. It probably wouldn't make for such a romantic keepsake if I'd written every last thing I was thinking, drunk in my hotel room, thousands of miles away from her. Not something you can safely hand down to the kids.

We got to talk more privately on the phone, but at the sorts of prices the hotels charged back then it wasn't much different from dialling one of those specialist lines you found flyers for in all the Soho-style neighbourhoods.

However, communications were about to enter a brand new era. 1987 saw the launch of the very first Nokia phone. This thing was yet to have Snake, but the Cityman 900 would allow you to make and take phone calls anywhere with a device the shape and size of a house brick.

This was a real step forward from the sort of mobile phones that had started to emerge earlier in the decade. Dagger – a man who was forever needing to make a call – had one of the very earliest ones. It was this huge unit that looked like a VHS recorder he had to strap over his shoulder and carry under his arm. To me, it didn't look much different from the sort of thing radio operators would have been lugging about on their backs during the Second World War, but I wasn't complaining. I wasn't the sucker who had to haul it about. I just got to make the odd call on it from the tour bus.

The real breakthrough for me was the fax machine. Those things were a miracle. No longer would I have to calculate complicated postage fees with foreign currency. No longer would I have to cross my fingers that my postcards to Shirlie would arrive before the next ice age dawned. And, best of all, I would no longer have to cram my deepest, most intimate thoughts into half a side of A5, where the world and its wife could take a butcher's at it.

Now I could write my fiancée a proper love letter and send it instantly across the world to wherever she was. Even better, she could get faxes to my hotels wherever I was as well. With the regular post, you could never have reliably synchronised something like that. We knew our tour schedules but you'd often only be staying in places for one night. Arranging for the concierge to send our messages on to the next hotel would only have started a global game of cat and mouse, our love letters chasing one another around the world.

With the fax came this entirely new feeling. A sensation I had never experienced before. The excitement of arriving back at your hotel room to find an envelope that had been slipped under your door. When the novelty of travel was beginning to pale, the emotion wrapped up in receiving these missives from home could be overwhelming.

For a real feeling of home, though, you couldn't beat the care packages. These were much more old-fashioned, proper parcels sent through the post – but they did have one hi-tech element.

Care packages got sent less when we were on tour and more when we were off recording, staying in the one place for a month or two and having a lot of down time. These home comforts were an absolute lifeline when I was losing the will to live in that Munich bunker, or in my Dublin flat, or wherever it was that I was sitting around waiting for my life to get started again.

As well as our Tetley teabags, our tins of baked beans, our copies of *Smash Hits*, *The Face*, *Billboard* and *Record Mirror*, there was one very special luxury in there for the five of us. Something we would gather round to enjoy as a whole band. VHS tapes of the latest *EastEnders* episodes.

Before video-on-demand streaming, this was really your only option if you wanted to keep up with your shows from back home while you were away. Getting VHS tapes mailed to you around the world was an extravagance, I admit, but I can make a pretty good pitch for justifying that expense too.

It was all essential research, part of my decade-plus plan to learn everything I could about Albert Square before infiltrating it myself as Steve Owen, causing all sorts of dark and deadly havoc in the borough of Walford and then meeting my own end in an explosive, high-octane car chase.

All money well spent, I'm sure you'll agree.

A New Station

As I said, the effect that MTV had on us, on Duran Duran, on all the bands of the so-called Second British Invasion, was immeasurable. Had that channel launched even a year later, giving the Americans half a chance to up their game, it's entirely possible we would have never broken the States.

MTV drove so much business on the other side of the pond that record companies thought nothing of signing off six-figure budgets for music videos, because they knew the promotion it would bring was worth every last penny. That channel was such a crucial element in so many major decisions in the music industry in the 80s that it's easy to forget that, up until 1987, it wasn't actually broadcast in Britain.

It seems crazy in hindsight that MTV Europe didn't launch until this late in the decade, especially as we had been so instrumental in the network's success. But after what felt like months of it being trailed, with Dire Straits namechecking MTV in their song 'Money for Nothing', it finally arrived on these shores.

Spandau hadn't been scrimping on our music videos in the meantime. At our most extravagant we were spending in excess of a quarter of a million on a four-minute video. The sort of price tags that made the budget of 'Muscle

Bound' look like back-of-the-sofa spare change.

For the first half of the decade, we'd worked regularly with Russell Mulcahy, who by now was working with bands like Queen on 'It's a Kind of Magic', Def Leppard on 'Pour Some Sugar on Me' and Go West on 'Call Me'.

From the *Parade* album on, though, we forged a closer relationship with Dominic Anciano and Ray Burdis, who ran the production company Fugitive Films.

The producers behind many of our videos, it was Dom and Ray who had also been the ones looking to make a movie about the Kray twins. They had been hitting up against quite a few roadblocks, though – including the fact that Roger Daltrey of the Who had optioned the rights to a book on the Krays and was working on a script. It didn't stop rumours continuing to appear in the press about Dom and Ray's efforts, however, especially the whispers about me and Gary being considered for the parts.

Dom and Ray must have been watching over those videos with a hell of a hawk's eye to have seen any potential in me, though, because I was barely ever in them.

I know it's not the first time I've griped about my lack of visibility in Spandau videos. If you think I sound a bit sensitive about it, you might be right. I probably am, but I reckon you would be too if you'd flown out to New Orleans to shoot a video for your new single only to find that your storyline doesn't involve you sitting peacefully on a porch by the water's edge, playing guitar like Gary. Or staging an exciting mini-jailbreak in the middle of a Mardi Gras parade like Steve and John got to. Instead, you're the one who gets strapped to a floating log in the middle of a swamp where a fucking great big alligator makes an unrequested cameo and starts circling you.

I imagine you, like me, would be especially peeved if after taking your life in your hands for the good of that shoot you find the final edit of your scene lasts for all of two seconds and – because the camera is concentrating on the (admittedly very attractive) model – the only visible part of you is your bouffant hair and a tiny glimpse of one knee.

It's the sort of incident that tends to rankle. A bit.

Not every video was as death-defying as the one for 'I'll Fly for You'. Shooting 'Highly Strung' in Hong Kong was a real highlight for me.*

Although I'd loved our time in Japan – even after the gig with the dislocated shoulder – I was left a little bit flat by my experience. Perhaps the visions I had of Japan in my head had been clouded by too many martial arts movies in my youth (and too many sake bombs dropped in sushi restaurants in my young manhood), but I was surprised by how much American culture Tokyo seemed to be emulating.

It was almost as if our national styles had all shifted like the top row of a Rubik's cube; each rotating one step around the globe. Americans wanted to look like Brits. Londoners were increasingly fascinated by Japanese style (with street-fashion features in *i-D*, David Claridge's Great Wall club and Boy George's geisha era), while all the kids in Tokyo seemed to want nothing but blue-jean Americana.

Hong Kong, though, had been like stepping back into a bygone era, a place every bit as decorative as my dreams.

---

* I also got some decent screen time in that one, chasing my love interest through the streets of the city, so maybe I am just a simple camera hog at heart …

But while we were finally making videos that were every bit as expensive and international as Duran Duran's, it was becoming harder and harder for us to get them played on MTV. It wasn't wasted cash, as another station had started that was loving the latter-day Spandau sound: VH1.

The Radio 2 to MTV's Radio 1, VH1 was a sister channel targeted at courting an older audience, the 18–35s who liked their pop culture a little softer, a little smoother, dare I say a little safer. This was where we got our plays now. MTV was now the preserve of hip-hop, dance and a much more glossy pop sound.

The Factory

The pivot point for pop had come in 1985 with Dead or Alive's 'You Spin Me Round (Like a Record)'. That song is a juggernaut. Nearly 40 years after its release, I promise you, you can still fill a dancefloor anywhere in the world with that record within 15 seconds.

It was Dead or Alive's only No. 1, but the producers behind it were only just getting started. Mike Stock, Matt Aitken and Pete Waterman would take the sound of this record – the hi-NRG beat that was booming in the gay clubs – and use it to build a gigantic pop factory that would come to take over the charts for the rest of the decade.

Their next success came with a bunch of Blitz Kids. 'You Spin Me Round' had caught the ear of Siobhan, Keren and Sara of Bananarama, who had been busy working with Jolley and Swain on their third album. When the girls presented Jolley and Swain with the idea of covering 'Venus' by Shocking Blue as a dance track, the boys balked a bit.

Siobhan took it to Stock Aitken Waterman instead, hoping to replicate the same feel as Dead or Alive. Sure enough, 'Venus' went top 10 in the UK and was a *Billboard* No. 1 in the States – one of Bananarama's biggest, best-remembered hits.

1987 was a banner year for SAW. It got going right from the off too, as one of their most enduring contributions to the pop canon was recorded on New Year's Day. A song by the studio's tea-boy, Rick Astley.

'Never Gonna Give You Up' was the biggest-selling single of the year* and has to be one of the best-known pop songs of all time now, especially after it effectively became the theme tune for the internet. That song has been a staple of memes for well over a decade and every link you click online now contains at least a trace chance of getting you Rickrolled.

Students of soap-opera history will recall that 1987 was the year Charlene and Scott got married on *Neighbours* (although the lag in broadcast meant that British audiences wouldn't see it until later). Charlene and Scott – or rather Kylie Minogue and Jason Donovan – would both go on to have massive pop careers under the wing of SAW, who were responsible for 'I Should Be So Lucky', 'Especially for You', 'Too Many Broken Hearts' and countless others.

'Respectable' for Mel and Kim. 'Toy Boy' for Sinitta. 'The Harder I Try' for Brother Beyond. Songs for Samantha Fox, Debbie Harry, Donna Summer, Hazell Dean and the England football team.

* BLITZ KID ALERT: Mike Stock said his inspiration for the production of 'Never Gonna Give You Up' was the song 'Trapped' by Colonel Abrams – produced by Richard Burgess.

Not to mention 'Living Legend' for Roland Rat.

The power of SAW even made it to my front door. After Wham! split up and George went solo, Shirlie and Pepsi teamed up to make an album of their own in '87. During that time SAW got them in to try out some songs.

The way their production line worked was that they'd churn out backing track after backing track and then bring in different vocalists to try them all on, like a fashion fitting. Pepsi and Shirlie worked on a couple of tracks with them. 'Who's Gonna Catch You?' eventually ended up going to Mel and Kim.

All of this led to their production house becoming unofficially known as the 'Hit Factory'. Again, it was all being achieved with the same machines we had used* but producing another totally different sound.

The way that Band Aid had summed up and capped off the first five years of the decade with 'Do They Know It's Christmas?' in '84, Stock Aitken Waterman would cap off the second in Christmas '89 with Band Aid II: a re-recorded version of the same song featuring all the pop acts who had made it big by the end of the 80s: Kylie, Jason, Bros, Cathy Dennis, Wet Wet Wet, Lisa Stansfield, Technotronic and – the only vocalists to span both – Keren and Sara from Bananarama.

As for us? Bananarama had proved that the shift from Blitz to Hit Factory was possible. So did Sigue Sigue Sputnik and Roland Rat – but for Spandau, sadly, the moment had passed.

---

* SAW would even jokingly credit drum production to the mysterious engineer 'A. Linn'.

The Beach

Gary and I had gone for a walk on the beach in Poole. We were down visiting Mum and Dad in the house we'd managed to buy them there. Our way of saying thank you for all they'd done for us. It had been nice, our family all together under the one roof again, like we had been in 1980 – but it was also nice to get a bit of fresh air too.

As the two of us made our way along the shore, the salt wind whipping at our faces, he dropped the bomb. He didn't want to make another Spandau record.

I knew this day was coming. I think I'd known for years. Although I hoped he'd see sense and that this was just some passing malaise, I knew Gary was done. For him, Spandau was over. It had been since he wrote 'Through the Barricades'.

Through the Barricades had struggled. The song had been a hit, but the rest of the album struggled. Had the whole album tanked, perhaps Gary would have given up completely. Hung up his boots and called it a day. But the fact that the one song he hadn't wanted to give up to Tony was the same one that had broken through showed him he was still capable of writing hit records. He just couldn't do it for the band anymore. He wanted to make his own album.

'I don't see why I have to write all these songs and then give them away.'

The position of sole songwriter was one Gary had ended up with by default rather than him taking. In their early days as the Makers, he and Steve had shared songwriting duties, but as soon as the deal was signed with Chrysalis, Steve had a crisis of confidence and stopped.

Spandau's successes didn't encourage him to start up again; if anything, they made him more apprehensive to meddle with the winning formula. I suppose the reason he wrote one song for our final album was that the downward trajectory we were on meant it was now or never. That, or he felt confident he could finish us off for good.

I pleaded with Gary for hours that day, imploring him to reconsider. To make another album. We couldn't destroy this thing we'd built. That was never the plan. We were supposed to keep working to make the future better, not undo the things we'd made.

That was what I said, but in my heart I also knew I was scared to think what a future for me outside of the band would look like. With Gary threatening to pack it all up and head out alone, I wouldn't just lose my band, I could lose my brother too.

1988
SUMMER OF LOVE

Die Hard | *Bros* | *Football Inflatables* | *Seoul Olympics* | *George H.W. Bush Elected* | A Brief History of Time | *Lockerbie Disaster* | *'I Think We're Alone Now'* | *'Doctorin' the Tardis'* | *First World AIDS Day* | *Calgary Winter Olympics* | The Satanic Verses | *Edwina Currie's Egg Scandal* | *Red Nose Day* | Celine Dion Wins Eurovision | *'Heaven Is a Place on Earth'* | *'Sweet Child o' Mine'* | Who Framed Roger Rabbit | Cocktail | Straight Outta Compton | *Radio 1 Big FM Switch On*

Ibiza

Those trusty synthesisers that gave our post-punk power-pop a futuristic edge – which had since been repurposed by the East and West Coast hip-hop scenes and the Stock Aitken Waterman pop powerhouse – were now serving yet another purpose. They were being used to create electronic psychedelic soundscapes for people to dance and trip to for hour after hour in hot, sweaty raves.

The dawn of acid house arrived in '88 and everyone's eyes were turning towards Ibiza clubs.

This one was a particularly weird one for me to swallow because at the start of the decade it had been Spandau setting the agenda out in Ibiza: we were the first British band to play Ku Club.

Ku Club, better known as Privilege now, was one of the earliest superclubs in the world, hosting up to 10,000 party people a night. It also was given a roof at some point along the line, but back in 1981 when we played it was like an extremely early stadium gig – playing the stage that spans a giant swimming pool right in the centre of the club.

If you've never been to Ibiza, the island has two sides to it: San Antonio and Old Ibiza Town. Nowadays, people tend to move freely from one half to the other, but back when we first went in '81 it was a very different vibe. San Antonio was the side where all the beered-up Brits abroad would go, all package holiday hotels, full English breakfasts and cold Carling. A hotbed of sunstroke, shagging and drunken scrapping.

Old Ibiza Town on the other side was a much more refined affair, where the international jet set went to enjoy champagne, seafood and – in 1981 – Spandau Ballet.

That's not to say that the Old Town was entirely devoid of danger. It just posed some very particular ones. For instance, I was nearly gored by a bull when I was there. I still have no idea what it was doing in the club, who the hell thought it was a good idea to set it loose or why it took such an interest in me. Surely it wasn't my dashing red tunic?*

After we left the stage and were enjoying a few drinks at the bar, this hysteria gripped the crowd. Suddenly all these people start screaming, throwing their hands in the air and diving into the pool. I can't lie, I'd hoped this was the sort of response we'd have got for our set, but no. They were saving all that for when livestock was released into the crowd.

---

* OK, I admit it probably wasn't the smartest choice of clothing in which to face down a full-grown bull. I can see that now. To be fair to myself, though, I hadn't anticipated coming face to face with a live bull at the after-party when picking my outfit, so I think I can be forgiven.

As people peeled off into the pool like in an old Hollywood musical, I came face to face with the hulking great beast, but I couldn't follow everyone else into the pool. My mascara would run.

In a career that has seen quite a few close calls with death, this, without question, would have been the single stupidest way to have bowed out. Pierced on the horns of a bull in a superclub, dressed as Will Scarlet, trying not to let my hair get wet.

Our little clique continued to play to the Ibiza scene throughout the early 80s. Ibiza had also been where Shirlie, George and the rest of Wham! went to shoot the video for 'Club Tropicana', which is a fantastic time capsule of that era – a video postcard that made British pop look so global, gorgeous and bronzed.

Now in the second half of the decade, the island had become the heart of the European dance scene, playing a new type of electronic music grown out of the clubs of the American Midwest. DJs like Derrick May and Juan Atkins in Detroit, and Frankie Knuckles and Marshall Jefferson in Chicago were developing yet more new sounds out of the same kit.

As much as all that tech had been essential in creating Spandau's early sound, what it did for us was accentuate our songs. Ours were guitar songs rearranged for synths to sound modern and exciting. With these new waves of dance music coming up in the late 80s, what we were hearing was a type of music that was driven purely by this tech. Music that couldn't really have existed at any earlier point in human history. That blend of samples, synths and relentless driving beats was absolutely right on the bleeding edge of invention.

The future just kept coming.

Spandau might not have been able to make the jump to acid house, but it doesn't mean that the Blitz Kids went completely unrepresented in this bold new frontier. Far from it. Bob Elms, Sade, Leigh Bowery and others were all regular faces at the growing acid club night Shoom that Danny Rampling had started in late '87 in (where else?) a basement.

And in 1988, one of the most commercially successful songs from the genre would make it to No. 1 in the UK charts. 'Theme from S'Express' by S'Express: the dance act headed up by Shoom DJ, former Billy's regular and bona fide Blitz Kid Mark Moore.

Summer of Love

To most, the Second Summer of Love in 1988 meant heading out to the Haçienda, chucking back an E and pranging out to acid house until the sunrise.

MDMA, which had been taking a back seat to cocaine for so many years, was finally ready to make its move on youth culture – and the effects were transformational. You didn't even need to take ecstasy to feel them. They were present in everything you consumed in those years.

In music, the middle was pulled straight out and a focus on beats, bass and top lines was everything. In fashion, you no longer dressed like a silken peacock for a big night out; you dressed in whatever light, breathable cotton would let you dance for hours on end without dehydrating.

Yellow smiley faces were slapped over every wall, billboard and shop window in the country. Even football, which had been blighted by hooliganism for so long, felt the benefits of it when all the usual thugs and maniacs that had terrorised the terraces for so long started dropping Es on a Saturday afternoon and enjoying much more blissed-out matches.

Any fear that the decline of the New Romantic movement would help usher in a return to punk's nihilistic outlook was totally dashed in 1988. Pop culture was now an endless procession of light and love, grinning and gurning.

We could have done with a few of those good vibes ourselves during rehearsals for *Heart Like a Sky*. Generating a bit of love with one another as we ground our way through those sessions – however artificial or chemical – might have made the whole thing more pleasurable.

For all we were struggling in Spandau, though, I did still manage to enjoy my very own Summer of Love. Just not the same one as everyone else.

Shirl and I had been together for five years at this point and I felt like I had always been the one saying, 'It's not the right time to get married. It's not the right time to start a family.' I know now that there's never a right time. The right time doesn't exist, until it does.

She was always the one to push things forward. It was during a trip she had taken to Dublin to see me that we'd taken a trip down Grafton Street and passed a jewellery shop* together. She saw a ring in the window and mentioned that she liked it, so we went in and I got it for her. I didn't really ask her to marry me; she hadn't really

---

* I think it's still there now, near the Phil Lynott statue.

asked me to ask her either. It was clear that that's what we were doing, though, bypassing the whole question-and-answer portion of the process and just skipping to us being engaged.

I thought taking the plunge might help get me through those dark days in Dublin, toss a bit of light down at the end of the tunnel, but it didn't really. I still missed Shirlie terribly every moment we were apart. Now instead of pining for my girlfriend, I found myself pining for my fiancée, which, somehow, made it worse.

When I returned from Dublin, I hadn't been in a rush to be married. Our lives were still so busy, so weird. She had Wham! I had Spandau. Then she had Pepsi & Shirlie. I had more Spandau. We never got anything like the time we wanted to spend together and, knowing that the engagement hadn't helped ease my heartache, marriage only risked making it tougher as I'd then be pining for my wife.

But, as with every other last thing in my life, things were changing. Everyone I knew was growing up. My friends, my brother.

One of the big moments had come a few years previously: the wedding of our friends Bob Geldof and Paula Yates. Sorry, Sir Bob Geldof. I've never got used to hobnobbing with a knight. The idea that my mate Paula – the one who had crashed Nixon's suite with me in Paris; who had got Sting to take his trousers off on telly – had married a knight? Typically Paula, but still. Signs that you're now cultural royalty don't come much stronger than that.

There's a photo of some of the guests that day – 14 of us – all posing for the camera. Bob and Paula sit centre, with Paula dressed in the most stunning scarlet satin wedding dress, with a train that pools out eight feet in front of her.

To Paula's right is Midge Ure, his kilt every bit as red as her dress.

Lining up along the back are various members of Spandau and Duran, with Steve Norman putting in an especially scene-stealing turn looking like The Greatest Showman in his crimson top hat and tails. George Michael is wedged in between me and Gary, and Aled Jones is there too – who can't have been that long out of nappies.

But the one that melts my mind, sat to Bob's left, is David Bowie, reclining majestically in an old oak chair.

Professionally, I cannot believe that Bowie was once the man I woke up to every morning, Gary's posters of him looming large over me in our bedroom.

Personally, I had actually been trying to keep a low profile around Bowie that day. It was only the second time I'd met him in person and I hadn't really coated myself in glory the first time. In fact, I was lucky not to have coated myself (and him) in sick.

It happened right at the start of Spandau and was – as is the case with so much of those early years – thanks to Steve Strange. Steve had been invited to a party at Tony Visconti's studio in Soho and asked me along as his arm candy. The night, if memory serves, was an album playback – but what that album was, I couldn't tell you. It might even have been one of Bowie's own playbacks but, as an underemployed, unsigned musician, I was only interested in two things: what my own band was doing, and getting tanked up on the free food and drink.

Even accounting for my teenage arrogance, though, I knew that being in Tony Visconti's studio was a big deal. This was hallowed ground. T. Rex, Thin Lizzy and Bowie himself had all recorded here – and seeing actual David

Bowie across the room was utterly surreal. I knew I couldn't pass up the chance to meet him, to shake the man's hand – if only so I could tell my brother and really make him jealous. It took a lot of free studio wine to build up my courage enough to make my way across the room and brave it.

How much I'd had that night, I couldn't tell you exactly. At parties like that, someone was forever refreshing your glass, which makes it hard to know – in measures or millilitres – just how much you've had. All I can tell you is, whatever it was, it was about a glass and a half too much.

As I cut across the room with my arm outstretched and David Bowie reached out his hand to take mine, the weight of it all suddenly hit me, sloshing around the inside of my eyes and making the room swim. The next thing I know I'm headed towards the floor in a knot of my own making in the corner of the studio and looking up at that famous snaggletoothed smile of Bowie's, laughing.

Cringesome as it might have been, there was one positive to come out of that incident. Had it not been for me humiliating myself in front of one of my idols so early on in my career, I may have learned too late about the perils of making an introduction on free-event wine. If I'd learned that lesson in the foyer bar of Yakety Yak on opening night and made my way over to Shirlie with a skinful sloshing about inside me, there's no telling where my life might have ended up.

The Best Man

My brother was newly married too. It had happened in a flash. He had married Sadie Frost, a model he'd first met on the set of our video for 'Gold'. 'Gold' had been part Bond, part Indiana Jones, and Sadie played a sort of nymph character, painted head to toe in gold body paint. It was a fairly pivotal role as she held the final piece of a mosaic that Tony had spent the whole song trying to complete.

More recently, she'd also appeared in our video for 'Fight for Ourselves'. In it, Sadie plays a fan who manages to sneak into one of our gigs, shifts into an animated parallel dimension (no doubt heavily inspired by a-ha's groundbreaking 'Take on Me' video), where she briefly drags Steve Norman into her monochrome world for a kiss.

Gary had bumped into Sadie again by chance at a bar. Sadie had been crying and Gary moved over to comfort her. They became close. They became closer. Then they moved in together.

From a purely selfish standpoint, this all worked out very well for me. It wasn't because I was still feeling like an outsider in the band (and in the wider music industry) for being in a long-term relationship. By now, all of us were shifting into this stage of life. The band were all partnered up and by the end of '88, me, Gary and John would all join Tony as married men. Steve would follow soon after in 1990.

My reason for being glad about Gary's relationship with Sadie was something else. He had started writing songs again. Whatever creative blockage he had suffered at the end of the *Barricades* sessions was swiftly smashed to pieces by Sadie. The *Heart Like a Sky* album came thundering out of him. Songs like 'Be Free with Your Love'. 'Crashed into Love'. 'Big Feeling'. The pattern was clear.*

All my fears of the band coming to an end, of Gary shutting up shop. Maybe they had been unfounded?

I was Gary's best man. As I stood by my brother's side that morning, I thought about all the ways in which we had stood shoulder to shoulder through so much of our lives. Sharing our first bedroom in Rotherfield Street. Sharing the bus ride together from Islington to the Blitz. Sharing a microphone stand as we belted out backing vocals in videos and venues all over the world. Sharing the cover of the 100th issue of *Smash Hits*. Sharing the roles of Ronnie and Reggie Kray – which we had recently started researching in earnest as things on that front were picking up steam.

Now we were sharing this moment too. My big brother was getting married and my two families – both biological and band – were united to celebrate.

Dagger, ever hot on the admin, was managing people perfectly. He was laying on coaches, moving everyone about from spot to spot, keeping things ticking over. I, less hot on it, quickly became flustered as various family members insisted on turning to me with their problems. I swear I spent most of Gary's big day trying to placate

---

* Funnily enough, the most apt title on *Heart Like a Sky* was probably 'Motivator', which was exactly what Sadie had been for Gary. However, it was the one song in Spandau history that Gary didn't write. Clearly Steve Norman could tell which way the wind was blowing too.

people about place settings. Everyone seemed utterly hell-bent on being the ones who got to sit closest to the cake, to the point where aunts were falling out with uncles, cousins were butting heads, even Mum and Dad were getting snippy.

I mean, it was a nice cake. As puddings go, it was up there as one of the best I've seen. But I still don't think it was worth the colossal amount of bickering I had to deal with. Perhaps that's what decided it for me. The Great Cake War of '88.

I knew that when I got married, I didn't want any of that hassle. Don't mistake me, I love weddings. They're wonderful, joyous occasions – and I love getting people together at the drop of a hat. The idea of having a wedding myself, though? It just left me shrugging.

It wasn't that I didn't love Shirlie. I loved her more than anything. I couldn't have been prouder to be the man she loved either. I'd tell anyone who was prepared to listen. I think it was growing up in a band, growing up in entertainment that had caused it. It does something to you. Shirlie felt it too.

Weddings – at their best – are a celebration of the couple. A day where they are the centre of attention, the focus of all the love and joy in the room. To be that focus is an absolutely sensational feeling. The best in the world. I know because it was my day job. I spent night after night enjoying that very feeling on tour.

I have been in so many rooms where people have made a beeline through the crowd to shake my hand. To tell me how great I was, how good I looked, how pleased they were for all my success. And I loved it. Every second of it. If you think I'm about to pretend otherwise and tell you it got boring after a while, I'm sorry. It didn't. Not a bit of it. Every little tickle of your ego is great. Even when people weren't being particularly sincere, it's never not nice to hear a compliment.

But that was the thing. All my family, all my friends, they had been celebrating with me all the time. They had been there when we got our first chart placement. They had been there when we pressed our first album. They had come to the airport to wave us off to Sydney. I had my pick of days that I could point to where I had been made to feel like I was the most special man in the world.

I didn't need another one.

Not to mention that the notion of putting on a wedding for the two of us came with unbelievable pressure. Two members of two of the biggest bands of the 80s getting married to one another. The guest list would be filled with the most debauched maniacs in the music industry, all mixing with our families.

If we were expected to make our wedding the most special day of our lives, what on earth could we do? Shirlie and I had both played Wembley Stadium. How would we top that for prized memories?

Could you imagine if my grandkids were to ask me, 50 years later, if the day I'd married grandma was the most special of my life and I started umm-ing and ahh-ing, and saying things to them like, 'Well, what you have to understand is … I played Live Aid.'

I hadn't even stayed at Live Aid. I turned down the chance to hang out with Freddie Mercury and Elton John and David Bowie and Paul McCartney on that most legendary of days. I took myself away from the biggest stars in the world, at the biggest rock concert in history, because the only person I really wanted to be with that day, truly and honestly, was Shirlie.

And I would do it again in a heartbeat.

So we did it again. We took ourselves away.

St Lucia

Once again, it was left to Shirlie to pose the question. Not to me, but to the receptionist at our hotel.

'Excuse me,' she asked, popping down to the front desk. 'Do you do weddings?'

We'd been in St Lucia for a week, enjoying some much needed rest and relaxation, when the mood took Shirlie. We'd heard a lot about this place. Pepsi, Shirl's bandmate, had been telling her for years about the beautiful Caribbean island her parents were from. Gary had been here earlier in the year too. It was on a beach in St Lucia that he'd proposed to Sadie, writing 'Marry Me' in the sand before the sea swallowed it up.

Little did I know that Shirlie had also found out St Lucia was a place you could just turn up and get married. Very little fuss. Very little paperwork. Just the hotel receptionist running her finger down the diary and saying, '14 November? I think that's our next available spot.'

Shirlie had brought along an outfit for the occasion. Not a wedding dress exactly, but not not a wedding dress either. It was more a wedding mini-skirt – paired with a white lace off-the-shoulder Bardot top, white cowboy stilettos and a white bow for her hair. She'd snuck it all into her suitcase, just on the off-chance that something might happen, so she wouldn't be completely unprepared.

If I'm making this sound like an ambush, it really wasn't. Shirlie had always been very straightforward with me about what she wanted and I was completely honest with her in return. I knew she wanted to get married. Not for the big fairy-tale wedding. The idea of that left her as conflicted as it left me, dreading the many and varied ways that George, Andrew and Pepsi would no doubt find to upstage our first dance.

What Shirlie wanted was the security. The stability. Between us, our love wasn't in question, but to most of society at the time it constantly was. Family, friends, the media. Everybody would feel so comfortable asking us what was going on, what was wrong, why weren't we married yet. An underlying assumption that there must have been a problem somehow. Unless she became Mrs Martin Kemp, she knew that whispers would always be following her.

She also knew that I wasn't against getting married. It was never that I had grand objections to the institution of marriage. I confess I didn't especially see the point of it; a piece of paper could never tell me how much I loved Shirlie better than my own heart could. That said, I couldn't come up with a good reason not to get married either. I had definitely thought about it and I had no issues with making a commitment. I suppose I had just got by coasting for so long – and had done so well on it – that I was never moved by any great urge to alter anything.

As I said before, I'd been waiting for the right time, never realising that you have to make it the right time.

The quintessential lesson of the 80s – and it had taken me almost the entire decade to apply it to my own life.

A wedding in St Lucia would be the perfect solution. The two of us, thousands of miles from our lives back home, finally becoming a family – ready to announce ourselves to the world when we returned.

The one nod to tradition we observed that day was that Shirlie and I wouldn't see each other before the big moment. We took separate rooms to get ourselves ready. Shirlie in the outfit she'd sneaked in in her suitcase. Me in a dark navy jacket with brass buttons and white trousers, looking like a ship's captain.

The ceremony took place on a clifftop, overlooking the sea. We couldn't arrange a white limousine or a four-horse carriage to wind its way up the beaten track to the summit, so instead my bride was brought to me in the back of a pick-up truck.

In that moment, I knew we'd made the right decision. I don't imagine getting hauled halfway up a mountainside in the back of a Jeep is anyone's first choice of wedding transportation. It definitely wasn't Shirlie's, but if we'd had concrete ideas of how we wanted our wedding day to go then having to hitch a ride with a local gardener, sitting among his tools and jerry cans of tractor fuel on her way to the altar could have easily ruined her day.

As it was, nothing could have ruined that day. All I needed was right in front of me, tugging the hem of her miniskirt down as she clambered from off the flatbed.

She was here. The girl in white from *Top of the Pops*. The one who had captured my heart in half a bar. The one who had left me hanging on the telephone for almost a month. The one who had brought George Michael on our first date.

Now we were finally alone. Together. In paradise.

Well, not exactly alone. The truck driver was there. And the officiant. And two of the hotel staff who'd graciously joined us to act as witnesses. But it was all we needed.

The ceremony was short. Suspiciously short, looking back on it. I'm sure it was all above board, but it really wasn't much more than, 'Martin, do you love Shirlie? Shirlie, do you love Martin? Yes? Then that's it. You're married. There you go.' That was all we needed.

At dinner that night, sat in St Lucia's finest restaurant, I was struck once again by how perfect everything was. A warm, island night with a breeze blowing in over the beach. Chilled champagne and a fabulous lobster dinner. A table overlooking the bay that was crawling with beetle-like bugs. The place was practically alive with them; the carpet, a shimmering sea of black.

I'd first seen one scurry its way up a guy's jacket and disappear down the back of his neck. Then I felt one crawling up my leg. I remember watching wide-eyed as some poor woman with this huge, hairsprayed beehive had them crawling around her barnet like they were scouting out a new nest. Her hair was so rigidly set that she clearly couldn't feel them moving around up there because the screaming didn't start until one of them fell onto her table.

Don't get me wrong. Bugs aren't my idea of a good time. Especially at a restaurant. I can't think of much that can kill the mood quicker than a bug – but my mood that night was unkillable.

The screaming didn't faze the staff. This was the Caribbean. Nothing fazed them. They simply moved us to a new table and treated us to a big slice of banana pie to ease our troubles. And as we tucked in, I thought how lucky we were not to be dealing with friends and family all finding bugs in their starters and their suit pockets.

This really was bliss.

The Next Generation

14 November 1988 wasn't just the day Shirlie and I became man and wife. With equal measures of luck and effort, it was also the night our daughter was conceived.

I won't go into the details here. There are plenty of other books, magazines and movies that can explain the process much better than I can.

I mention it only because this was the final piece of the puzzle. I had worried for so long about what I would do if I was no longer a red-hot rock star, blazing a trail around the world. But now that I could see that day looming on the horizon, I looked at where I was.

Shirlie and I were no longer boyfriend and girlfriend. We were man and wife.

Spandau Ballet were no longer the hottest new sound. We were a heritage act.

And in nine months' time, I would no longer be a kid. I would have a kid.

The next generation was on its way. In 40 weeks, she would be here. Things would change so profoundly that I would become a stranger to myself. My life would both expand to meet its greatest challenge yet and contract to focus in on the tiniest, loveliest little bundle I've ever met. My baby, Harley Moon.

However I was going to be able to shape the world now, it would no longer be for me. It would be for her.

Strike Two

I didn't know what to say. Neither did the rest of the band. There wasn't anything *to* say. Gary wasn't asking us. He was telling us.

I recalled what he had said to me on the beach that day: that he didn't want to make another Spandau album. He was wrong. He'd made one. And he'd made the whole thing himself.

When Gary called us in for the rehearsal sessions for *Heart Like a Sky*, we thought it would be much the same sort of set-up we'd seen for all the others. Instead, he presented us with fully recorded demos for every song. He'd programmed the drums the way he wanted them on a drum machine. The bass lines had been put on tape with a synth. The vocal phrasing and melody was all there for Tony to parrot. Gary had done it all and was now handing us out our parts.

This was not the way we were used to working. Gary used to play us a bare bones version of a track in rehearsal and we'd all join in. He'd give John direction on how the drums should sound, but John would figure out exactly what beats to hit and how. Although I had my limitations as a bass player, I knew how to pick out good phrases and flourishes. I played along and Gary would let me know what worked, what didn't.

Gary handed Tony a melody, but there was always room for adjustments. Not anymore.

Technology had given him the tools he needed to replace us. He no longer wanted a band. He wanted session musicians – and that was a very different job. One I wasn't sure

I wanted, and one that Tony and John and Steve definitely didn't.

Sad as I had felt in '86 on seeing the news about the printers' strike, I also felt safe. As if my gamble had paid off. Leaving the printshop to become a pop star was a million to one shot, and it had meant I hadn't needed to be there on the picket line, facing down police brutality to protect my job, as cheaper, more efficient technology rendered me and my future career obsolete.

What had it actually bought me? Two years? Maybe I could squeeze one more out of this? Machines could do my job better now. They already had been for years. That wasn't even me playing on 'True'! It was a synth! How could I not have seen I was on borrowed time?

What made all of this worse is that I knew I had a safety net. Gary and I had been working with Dom and Ray on this Krays movie. Things were moving. It was still slow going and nothing was guaranteed but the wheels were in motion.

If I was getting sidelined from Spandau by a robot, at least I still had our film up my sleeve. CGI wasn't good enough yet to have Gary play both Kray brothers (and Tom Hardy was only 11 at the time), so there was no way he could replace me in that.

The rumours had all been in the press, so they hadn't passed the rest of the band by. They knew the Kemps were all set with their little side hustle, so if they were being shut out of Spandau, what would that leave them with? A solid back catalogue of songs that had filled some of the best venues in the world – but how long would that last?

Like MTV found, there's only so long you can put on the same night's programming.

The Blitz Kids had stopped playing dress-up a long time ago. We would finally need to grow up.

1989

THE FALL

Game Boy | *Magnum Ice Creams* | *Polly Pocket* | Weekend at Bernie's | *Sky TV* | *'Pump Up the Jam'* | Road House | *Tiananmen Square* | Exxon Valdez *Spill* | *'Like a Prayer'* | *Band Aid II* | The Remains of the Day | *Madchester* | Seinfeld | *Hillsborough Disaster* | *Jive Bunny and the Mastermixers* | *Tim Berners-Lee Proposes the World Wide Web* | *'Ride on Time'* | *Huggies Pull-Ups* | Bill & Ted's Excellent Adventure | *Desert Orchid* | *Guildford Four Freed* | *'Eternal Flame'* | Dead Poets Society | A Prayer for Owen Meany

The Argument

It was never about the jeans. They might have been what started it. They were definitely what Gary and Tony were screaming about – but we all knew the jeans were not the problem. It was everything but the jeans.

It's funny. After all the wild outfits we'd worn over the years – the doublets, the tabards, the leather and lace – it was now a pair of jeans we were at each other's throats over. The jeans were Tony's. He'd turned up to the set of our video shoot for 'Raw' in them and Gary hit the roof.

'Are they from fucking Marks and Spencer?'

Music videos had started out as a bit of fun. A bonus project you got to do as a band with a bit of money. Then they became essential as the MTV boom continued. Budgets rocketed and videos became a way to travel the world, to make full-scale spectaculars. To play at being a movie star.

By the end of the 80s, for a Spandau Ballet on the descent, they had become a treadmill. With no chart positions to speak of and all of MTV's excitement reserved for rap and techno, our promos had become little more than a contractual obligation needing to be honoured. A chore to be completed. No amount of budget or bright ideas could turn the tide. We just needed to shoot, wrap and get out of there.

Why Gary would even give two squirts of piss about a pair of jeans at that stage – M&S or otherwise – I can never be sure. To Tony, though, this was just another example of Gary being a domineering, dogmatic dictator.

The arguments had been growing. In volume, in frequency, in severity. Rehearsals, recording, touring – they had all become fraught and miserable. I only had to think of the band to give myself a knot in my stomach, an ache in my chest.

My role in the band had become so small, I barely knew why I was bothering to turn up. When I'd first got hints of this feeling in Musicland in Munich, I hadn't wanted to leave because I was afraid the band might start ragging on me, making jokes at my expense. What I wouldn't give for a joke now, though. I'd happily be the punchline of any gag if it gave any of us a chuckle. Anything would be better than all this yelling.

Now it was all just so bitter.

Yet, away from the band, I was happier than I'd ever been. I had married the love of my life. The baby we'd been trying so long for would soon be here. And now the lifeline I had needed to forge a career for myself if the band imploded had come. The Krays film was greenlit.

After years of development hell, things were finally clicking into gear. A script. A shooting schedule. Co-stars. It had been nearly four years since I'd read that snippet in the *Sun* about Gary and me being considered for the roles of

Ronnie and Reggie. I'd always known never to put much stock in what you read about yourself in the papers, but this had come to pass. The film was happening – and that was causing much more tension in the band than Tony's jeans.

Though it always went unspoken, we could feel the rest of the band really starting to resent the movie. They knew our heads were elsewhere. Being micromanaged is bad enough at the best of times, but when it's not even the micromanager's primary focus, it must be especially galling.

Any simmering resentment they might have felt towards me – Gary's baby brother who had got himself into the band, taking that early cover of *The Face*, getting extra attention because the two of us are brothers – started to bubble up. The Kemp boys, sticking together.

I've since read Tony said that these were the unhappiest times of his life and I don't doubt it. As far as he could see, all his work in Spandau – and Steve's and John's – was going towards making me and Gary movie stars. And what was he getting in return? Snippy sartorial advice.

'They're not fucking Marks and Spencer. They're fucking GAP.'

That was the afternoon I knew for certain it wasn't worth asking Gary about doing another album. It was never going to happen and, what was more, I wasn't sure even I wanted it either.

This was done. It was over.

Buzz

If ever I mourn for the days of those massive tours, yearning for that irreplaceable rush of adrenaline you get from having 10,000 fans scream your name, there's one person I think about. Someone who experienced a genuinely irreplaceable rush of adrenaline.

Buzz Aldrin.

If anyone knows what it is to have enjoyed the single most exhilarating experience humankind has ever known and then having to make your peace with the fact that nothing you do for the rest of your life can ever hope to come close to matching it – it's a man who has walked on the Moon.

I met Buzz once. I got to talk to him for about half an hour on the set of a TV show. I mean no disrespect to anyone involved in the production of said show when I tell you what it was, but it was an absolutely absurd place to bump into an Apollo 11 astronaut.

Al Murray's Happy Hour was a Saturday-night comedy chat show on ITV in the late 2000s where Al Murray (performing as his Pub Landlord character) did the usual three guests on a sofa format with a musical act to throw to.

I was one of the guests on an episode where Buzz was the headliner. Some technical hitch with the cameras halted recording in the studio at some point, which left us sitting at a loose end for a while. Naturally, the only person anyone wanted to hear talk was Buzz, so – leaning over Jodie Kidd, who was sat between us – I listened raptly as he told me the story of how he saved the Apollo 11 mission from catastrophe with a felt-tip pen.

In getting on and off the lunar module with a cumbersome life-support backpack strapped to his spacesuit, Buzz accidentally bumped into a few things and damaged a circuit breaker. This damage was preventing them from being able to lift off and return to the orbiting command module so, of all things, he jammed a pen into a hole in the control panel to push the two broken parts back together long enough to reconnect the circuit and take off.

He had flown into space, safely touched down on the surface of the Moon, furthered the knowledge of all mankind forevermore – and in the end it was a felt-tip pen that stood between him and Neil Armstrong dying on that pioneering mission and him returning safely to appear on *Al Murray's Happy Hour*.

It's always good to be kept humble when you start drifting off into egomaniacal territory. Rock stars are often so coddled they can lose a sense of perspective about their problems, so it's good to be kept grounded from time to time – especially by someone whose problems were literally astronomical.

The show ended each week with the host and the musical guest performing a cover of a Queen song together, which meant my meeting with Buzz Aldrin ended sat in the studio half-light watching Al Murray sing a duet of 'Radio Ga Ga' with Sophie Ellis-Bextor.

It was one of the most bizarre yet life-changing evenings of my life. My only problem now is that I'll never get the same rush from doing a chat show ever again.

Chain Reaction

I'm sure you've heard of the 'butterfly effect'. It's the theory that under the right (or wrong) conditions, a butterfly can trigger a tornado. Not through direct cause and effect, but by starting a chain reaction.

Here's a bizarre example of mine that I still find mind-blowing.

In August 1981, Gary and I appeared on the cover of *NME* next to the headline 'Soul Boys of the Western World'. That would go on to be the title of a documentary made about Spandau Ballet in 2014 – but that wasn't the extent of that cover's effect on the world of cinema.

The two of us were styled for that shoot in Zoot suits. It wasn't as audacious or New Romantic as some of the other shots we'd done for magazines around that time. This one was focused more on classic tailoring, shot in simple black and white.

This was the cover that caught the eye of Dominic Anciano and Ray Burdis, *The Krays* producers. It was that particular picture that made them think there was maybe something in the idea of casting the brothers from Spandau Ballet in their project. They wore a quality-cut suit well. They didn't rely on flashy colours and combos. They looked good together.

That *NME* shoot helped shape their entire conception of how *The Krays* might look. But the butterfly was only getting warmed up.

A few years later, Gary was working out in Hollywood. His career after *The Krays* went from strength to strength.

He'd shot *The Bodyguard* with Kevin Costner and Whitney Houston not long after and was now starting work on *Killing Zoe*, a crime thriller that Quentin Tarantino had a hand in producing.

Tarantino had seen *The Krays* when it came out and told Gary he had been a big fan. Gary was flattered, but figured it was just something Tarantino was saying for the sake of being nice. Not a bit of it. Tarantino is a huge movie buff and has endless enthusiasm to talk about cinema – so the two of them got stuck right into it.

Over the course of their conversation Tarantino let slip that he'd given out copies of our *Krays* film to everyone he'd worked with on his first movie. The style of those Kray twins, man! That violence! That was what he had wanted to achieve with his project, so he told his entire crew that *The Krays* was the look to shoot for, the template for his protagonists.

That look was hugely successful. In fact, it became a defining image of 90s cinema – plastered on billboards and bedroom walls absolutely everywhere.

Not *The Krays*, but what Tarantino did with it.

Reservoir Dogs.

Sparring Partners

'What I want you to do is get on the floor and go back to when you were two.'

When Gary and I realised we needed help, this was not what I'd had in mind.

Charles Verrall was the husband of our old drama teacher, Anna Scher. We had come back to Anna's theatre school to get ourselves some refresher lessons as it had been a long time since we'd done any acting.

'Actually, Martin, I want you to be two. Gary, you be four.'

As kids, we'd been pretty prolific. By the age of 15, I had something like 30 credits on my CV of various films and TV shows I'd acted in. Since setting off on our Spandau adventure, though, the most acting either of us had done was in our music videos – and they weren't exactly the most demanding roles.

I could give wistful, lovelorn looks at models quite well. I could pout for the camera and stomp about like Mick Jagger until the cows came home. Flicking through *The Krays* script, though, those moments were few and far between, so I felt I could do with some professional guidance.

'Begin.'

The instruction felt ridiculous. We weren't playing the Krays as babies. Ronnie and Reggie were London's most terrifying thugs; hard bastards whose whispered names drained faces. They were not little kids who rolled around on the floor of a children's theatre school. Still, we were determined to make these roles the best they could be. We had come here for advice – so down we went.

I pictured myself on the floor of our house in Rotherfield Street. In my mind, the rug was actually the one we had in the 70s – so my timing was a bit out – but I imagined being two. I was driving a little Dinky toy car with one hand, a Corgi car with the other. I was tracing those 70s swirls like they were the streets for the cars, trying to keep them from crashing. Gary came over to join me. He wanted to play.

I looked into Gary's eyes. He looked into mine. Slowly,

it all began to peel away. The baggage of the last ten years. The arguments. The barked orders. The feelings of inadequacy. The endless times that Steve, John and Tony had come moaning to me about my brother's tyranny. The devastating secret my brother had lumbered me with about wanting to break up the band.

The last few years, since he dropped that bombshell on the beach, had been so tough. Fighting in the studio. Fighting out of the studio. Touring with a whacking black thundercloud over us because everyone was miserable and away from their wives and our songs were barely crawling into the Top 100 anymore because we were writing music for stadiums we were now struggling to fill and starting to book back into some of the proscenium-arch shows again except they weren't even our songs anyway because Gary had taken control of everything and made it quite clear he knew what was best for all of us because it had always been his band and now he wanted to take it away from all of us and I …

I blinked. It was gone. Reset. I was two. He was four.

Gary wanted to play with me. I was his baby brother and the baggage I carried was a toy car in each hand. He wanted us to play together. I wanted nothing else in the whole wide world.

In a crowded field, that theatre exercise was the single most bizarre thing we did to prepare for our roles as the Krays. It was also the single most important, and nowhere did that feel more the case than in the ring.

There's a scene in the Krays where the two of us fight in a fairground boxing ring. Gary (Ronnie) knocks out the fair's prize fighter and the crowd is asked if anyone else would like to take Ronnie on. I (Reggie) step up.

The two of us glove up, face down, and then duke it out as hard as we can. Long after the bell rings, calling an end to the round, the brothers continue to batter each other, bloodied and bleary-eyed, until our mother is brought in to break us up.

I absolutely hated filming it. Getting punched in the face, even when playing a part, is not fun. The scene left me with almighty migraines* and having to shoot it again and again and again was a very particular type of torture.

But when I think how much worse that scene could have been – if all those lingering resentments had been left to fester and we hadn't had that moment of connection on the floor at Anna Scher's – I don't know where it could have left me and Gary.

As it was, when we broke away from that fight, my skull feeling as though Thor had given it a good going over with his hammer, thunder and lightning brewing behind my eyes, Gary said something to me I will never forget.

'What do you think, Mart? Am I doing it right?'

I had heard that first question a hundred thousand times in the last ten years. Gary had always played me his songs and asked for my opinion. That second question, though? Was he doing it right? I couldn't remember the last time he'd asked me that. In the band he had always valued my feedback, but never needed my reassurance. Now, for the first time in over a decade, he was asking for it.

And for the first time in over a decade, I felt as though I could answer. After years of feeling like I had been riding

---

* I would later discover these migraines were likely the result of two blossoming brain tumours that would lay me low for years in the 90s.

on his coattails, getting to join his ready-made band, being taught the bass by him, handed all of these world-famous songs to play, I would never have known how to answer, what to contribute. Acting was something that was in us both from the start, though. It was a world I knew. A world that was part of me. He wanted my opinion and I now had a worthwhile one to give.

'Yeah, Gary. You're doing great.'

The Firm

If the 'Chant No. 1' video that we shot in Le Beat Route was a Who's Who of the Blitz Kids, then that boxing scene in *The Krays* is the same thing, but for the Firm. The spectators who were cheering me and Gary on as we jabbed and parried were all the Krays' old associates. A real rogues' gallery – in the strictest sense of the term.

Though meeting the crème de la crème of East London's criminal class had never been high on my bucket list, I have to say they were all incredibly helpful and generous with their time. We were lucky to have made that film at a time when all the people who knew Reggie and Ronnie personally were all still with us, so could give us an insight into the roles.

As it turned out, we probably would have had a harder time not getting their insight. I'm telling you, you don't know critics until you've worked in front of retired London gangsters.

Every one of them, those big hard bastards, would have pages and pages of feedback for us. 'Mart, if you're gunna play Reggie, you gotta do it like this.' 'That ain't how Reg talked. Nah, nah, nah.' 'Not like that, no. You're gettin' him all wrong. 'Ere. Look.'

One old bruiser came up to me one day and told me, 'Mart, every time Reggie spoke, he sniffed,' before giving me a sinus-shredding demonstration of one – in case I'd never heard of sniffing before. I told him thanks, really helpful, always glad to take notes on board, etcetera. Then as Gary and I are acting out this scene, the cameras rolling, the crew all in place, I see this same guy bouncing up and down behind the camera on his tiptoes, trying to catch my eye and throwing his head back miming a sniff like the biggest ham who ever worked in this town.

It was relentless – and they were not the sort of people who were used to hearing 'no'.

That all said, the twins' older brother Charlie was a great help. He was around a lot of the time and gave us so many tips for that boxing scene. He was also the one who introduced us to Auntie May, the woman who mostly brought the twins up. We went to her flat just off of Hoxton, right by where my nan used to live. As we drove up close to her place we were pulled over by the police, who asked what we were doing. When we told them we had come to pay a visit to Auntie May, they escorted us the rest of the way.

Sat in her front room, she brought out these photo albums. Those huge ones that people used to have back in the day; thick, cardboard pages with cellophane flaps on them, front and back. Made the albums thicker than door-steps and you'd only get a few photos on per page, but they made for fascinating browsing. Not least because in almost every other picture there were all these missing people.

It wasn't just chunks missing; a 3×5 trimmed down so she could squeeze more of them on the page. These were intricately edited. The outline of a human shape that had once been there but was now just an inverse silhouette against an intact background. Like a giant white jelly baby standing in the shot.

The effect wasn't actually a million miles away from the one we'd used in our video for 'Fight for Ourselves', the one where Sadie Frost and her mate enter an alternative dimension and sneak onto our stage to dance as white shadows.

When we'd finished looking through them, I couldn't help but ask, 'What was with all the missing people, May?'

'Queen's evidence, luvvie. They're the ones who turned against my boys.'

Sure enough, as these former associates had each made their appearances in the Old Bailey one by one, Auntie May had been sat with a set of scissors, patiently and precisely snipping them out of history.

So, no pressure to do right by her boys then.

The Interview

One of the reasons Roger Daltrey had struggled to get his *Krays* film off the ground was because there was a lot of opposition to the entire notion of one even existing. The reason Ronnie and Reggie had been handed down such huge sentences was because the state wanted to make examples of them. It wasn't just that the crimes they had committed had been serious, it's that they had glamorised the whole world of organised crime. They had made the gangster life seem appealing. Their sentences were a way of sending out a warning shot to anyone who thought of following in their footsteps.

The prospect of putting the Krays on the silver screen, the idea that there could (or should) be any interest in making movie stars of these violent criminals, caused a fair amount of uproar. Questions were even raised in the House of Commons about it. Is there any way to make a film about the Krays that wouldn't on some level humanise them? Turn them from monsters into men, perhaps paving the way for some sort of public rehabilitation?

That was the fear, at least, and I can't honestly say it was an ungrounded one. When Gary and I went to meet Ronnie ahead of the shoot, he was definitely magnetic.

There's not much glamour in Broadmoor. High-security facilities – prisons, psychiatric hospitals – are generally pretty unsettling places, but Broadmoor was truly daunting. Like a haunted castle. So Ronnie definitely stood out.

As we stepped into the hall, a small man sat at a table in an elegant blue suit, brilliantly shined shoes and a monogrammed shirt rose and waved us over.

Because Broadmoor is a hospital rather than a prison, our meeting didn't happen behind any sort of glass partition. This happened in the hospital dining hall, right out in the open, at one point with Peter Sutcliffe, the Yorkshire Ripper, milling around.

Walking towards Ronnie, I thought about shaking his hand. Would I do it? Would he offer? I had heard and read so much about Ronnie and Reggie; I knew what those hands had done. Ordinarily, I'd have done everything I could to avoid an ethical quandary like this – but we had travelled to Broadmoor specifically to see him, effectively to get his blessing to make the film. Could I really spurn him in those first crucial seconds, especially if he was being nothing but civil to me? Men like the Krays attach a lot of importance to respect and manners. Shaking his hand, though, was that some sort of endorsement? Would that make us friends?

It's an odd position to be in as an actor. You have to divorce your personal assessment of someone and replace it with a professional one. I wasn't playing Ronnie in the film, Gary was, but the shot was still the same for Reggie.

You can't approach a role with the mindset that this character is an irredeemable villain. Not if you want to be convincing. You have to find some shared humanity with them. Find the bits that resonate, the common threads, and build from there. Actors play killers and criminals and creeps all the time – but we were really jumping in at the deep end with having this as our first role.

I took Ronnie's hand in the end. It was an unremarkable handshake. No ice-cold sensations; no vice-like grip on his part, to send a message. He could have been a mortgage broker for all that the handshake told me about him, but it still did nothing to ease the tension.

'Hello, boys. Sit down, sit down.'

I couldn't believe I had cleared the handshake hurdle only to run smack bang into one I hadn't even considered. His voice! It was so high. Not quite like he'd been sucking helium, but still not what you'd expect from a terrifying king of the underworld. It caught me so off-guard I almost burst out laughing. If I was worried how he'd react to me fumbling a handshake, I dread to think what he would have done if I'd let out a titter on hearing him speak. It wasn't too many pages into my research around the Krays before I learned that these were not the sort of men who cared to be laughed at.

Ronnie was older now, years past his prime, but I didn't much fancy my chances if he'd felt the urge to throw me over a table or two.

Whenever I meet someone new, I never assume that they know our music, but I figured it would be especially hard for Ronnie, given his situation. He didn't, but he had done a bit of reading up on us and had come to one important conclusion. 'I hadn't heard of you – but when I heard you were playing the two of us I saw your pictures and I was most pleased because you're both very good-looking.'

I learned later that Ronnie wasn't totally out of touch with the modern pop scene, though. He was a big fan of Kylie Minogue and apparently even once called up a tabloid news desk to ask them to send him a copy of one of her singles. That Stock Aitken Waterman sound really was all-consuming. It had broken into Broadmoor.

It didn't take much to get him talking. Without so much as asking a question, Ronnie began laying all his cards out on the table, telling us everything. He was utterly forth-right about the things he'd done: the violence, the killings, the terror he'd wrought across the city.

Despite all that, it was strange to learn how much Gary and I had in common with the Krays. When he described the houses they came of age in in East London, they sounded like our old place on Rotherfield Street. The spider-infested outhouse. The Anderson air-raid shelter in the backyard. The levelled-out bomb sites all around our neighbourhoods.

Their years as shapers of the London club scene in the 60s were familiar to us too. Working-class boys enjoying celebrity status around town in the nightspots of the city.

Parties where they would be rubbing shoulders with the biggest stars of the day: Judy Garland, Diana Dors, Frank Sinatra.

It didn't seem that dissimilar to the parties in the 80s where we had rubbed shoulders with Mick Jagger, Grace Jones, the Prince and Princess of Wales.

Reggie Kray, who I play in the film, once wrote: 'I seem to have walked a double path most of my life. Perhaps an extra step in one of those directions might have seen me celebrated rather than notorious.'

It's a sobering thought. My nan was from round their way. The Krays used to come to the pub on our street, the Duke of Clarence. The lives we ended up leading worked out quite differently, but they hadn't started that way and didn't diverge nearly as far as we first thought.

It truly was the case of a step here and a step there. It's great to be able to tap into that common ground when you're playing a character – and it's probably why I felt like we played those roles so well – but it's quite a thought to be left with.

We had a bill to settle before leaving. Ronnie had had some non-alcoholic beers brought to the table. Gary and I had had cups of tea.

'How much?' I asked.

'Ronnie's asked for a few extra beers, for his room,' the orderly said.

'OK. How much?' I asked again.

'That'll be twenty pounds, please.'

The thieving git. How's that for a charming master criminal? Managed to mug me from inside a high-security facility – and left me laughing at it.

The Note

Ronnie got a message to me and Gary after the film came out. He told us that he'd really enjoyed the film but there was one detail that disappointed him.

There's a scene where Gary and I go into the Royal Oak, casually lift up a twin set of machine guns and, in glorious slow motion, shoot the whole pub up in a shower of sparks and shattered glass.

Ronnie's note? 'We never would have gone in there with machine guns. We would have used machetes.'

Like I say, London gangsters are the pickiest critics in the game.

Berlin

The descent into West Berlin was always terrifying. I'm sure an aviation engineer or air-traffic controller could explain why, but the moment you crossed over that wall and into the Western half of the city, the plane suddenly started going down steep. Fingernails in the armrest steep.

The Eastern territory was always so bleak looking. From above it was just greyness. An ocean of concrete. Square blocks all crammed together, with no space or light. Even from 10,000 feet you got a palpable feeling of claustrophobia.

West Berlin looked like a fairground in comparison. I'm sure they did it on purpose. An exaggerated display of decadence and defiance, to show the encircling Soviets how life should be lived. To keep a fire burning – however small – in the centre of things.

Spandau were here to play the Internationales Congress Centrum as part of our *Heart Like a Sky* tour, one of the last gigs we performed before the band finally broke down. There was something we wanted to see first, though.

I remember deciding we should go to Checkpoint Charlie. It was the major crossing point along the Wall; the place you needed to go in if you wanted to pass into East Berlin. I had been before, but now the Wall was falling.

As we got closer, I could hear the sound of hammers and chisels, although I didn't immediately recognise it as that. Instead, it was almost like birdsong. High, clipped, quick. Tchk-tchk-tchk. Tchk-tchk-tchk.

I suppose I thought to take down a wall you would need mallets. Jackhammers. Serious industrial equipment that would make the sound of it being dismantled as hard and heavy as roadworks. It turns out you don't. Not if you have an entire city willing to pitch in.

This wasn't the official demolition. That wouldn't happen for months. What we were watching was the work of the people, chipping away at the wall that had carved up their city for decades. All this time it had been holding them back; now they were ripping it down.

A spirit of freedom filled the air with every crack. Cheers of celebration. Tears of joy. A mammoth task before them, but an endless well of optimism and enthusiasm to see it through.

The entrepreneurial, capitalist spirit of the 80s was on full display too. As well as hiring out hammers to anyone wanting to strike a blow for freedom, enterprising locals were laying out chunks of freshly carved wall for sale on billowed-out bedsheets. They didn't care that anyone could go and rip out their own just a few feet away. There would soon be nearly a hundred miles' worth of rubble harvested from the Wall, flooding the market for chunks to saturation point, but that didn't stop them.

They knew they had history for sale and that there would always be buyers. I was one of them.

I looked up at the Wall and recalled memories of the armed guards I'd seen there on patrol on previous trips. The ones with binoculars, looking out over the two sides, not afraid to lift a gun if they thought anyone was loitering too long.

Something similar had happened to me, Gary and Tony in Belfast once. A hideously early morning radio promo meant we were the only car on the road when an armoured Royal Ulster Constabulary vehicle pulled up and three guards jumped out, two pointing machine guns at our windows. Our driver told us to relax, that he would sort everything out – but it's easier said than done. Especially after what had happened to Kidso.

Now the people of Berlin would no longer have to face down those guns in the centre of their city. They were free.

Looking back now, it's strange to join the dots and see how long a shadow the Second World War had cast on us all. Not just in growing up around all those old bomb sites, or suffering the after-effects of a national economy trying to recoup the cost of its war effort. It wasn't just the chill of the Cold War either.

The club we had all come of age in was named after a relentless bombing campaign. Wartime iconography was everywhere in that place. All our early outfits were bought from army surplus stock at Laurence Corner. Our band named itself after the nearby Berlin neighbourhood of Spandau and its notorious prison; demolished shortly before the Wall after its final and most famous prisoner, Rudolf Hess, Hitler's deputy, died.

All these remnants of a long-since-won war, which none of us had even been alive to see, had always been hanging around us. Now they were starting to vanish.

For all the bickering and bitterness in the band over the last few years, we couldn't have asked for a better moment to bow out with in Berlin than playing 'Through the Barricades'. Although it had been written about a very specific circumstance, the song had become an anthem to people trying to keep love alive across all sorts of borders – both physical and political.

In Belfast, where an end to the violence and bloodshed of the Troubles was still years off – but would soon be reached.

At Artists Against Apartheid, opposing the brutally segregated system that would end in South Africa in just a few months, as Nelson Mandela walked free.

In San Francisco, where the song had meant so much to the gay community there, suffering horrendously through the AIDS epidemic as their government and many fellow citizens ignored their plight.

And now here in Berlin, where an actual barricade was falling and where we invited East Berliners in for free to join in this incredible moment.

It wasn't until I was in the taxi headed back for the airport that the enormity of what we had witnessed hit me. The world had been changing before our eyes. Berlin, the city that had given us so much, had been a cornerstone of everything we had built – had given us our name – was healing. It was growing. Things would need to be razed before they could be rebuilt, but we knew that a beautiful, colourful future was possible.

That's what our last ten years had all been about.

The End

There was a song Rusty liked to finish on.

As a night of angular Japanese electro and mechanical German synth-rock drew to a close, he would pull one record from its sleeve and bring those Blitz nights to an end with a song from a musical. A waltz, in 3/4. 'Tomorrow Belongs to Me' from *Cabaret*.

I know what you're thinking. Martin, isn't that … the Nazi one?

It's true that, yes, of all the songs in *Cabaret*, 'Tomorrow Belongs to Me' is the only one performed by a member of the Hitler Youth. Every other number is performed by the gorgeously made-up, flamboyantly dressed, sexually liberated, gender-fluid misfits of the Kit Kat Club. So why did Rusty pick the only one that wasn't?

If he'd wanted to evoke feelings of the Berlin cabaret scene of the 30s in 80s London, he could have played 'Mein Herr', or 'Maybe This Time', or – most fitting of all – 'Money Makes the World Go Round'. But those songs were ours already. The one that needed reclaiming, that needed bringing into the clubs, was 'Tomorrow Belongs to Me'.

I should be completely clear that 'Tomorrow Belongs to Me' is not actually a Nazi anthem. It was written by two Jewish men – one of whom was gay – as a part of a show that is a total rebuke of fascism and all its trappings. The song was created specifically to be rousing and positive and uplifting (then used to utterly chilling effect in the show when you realise the ones who are feeling roused and positive and uplifted are the Nazis). But that's why repurposing that particular song at the end of a club night that celebrated everything those tyrants stood against felt so important.

Tomorrow didn't belong to them. The Berlin Wall was falling and we were the ones who were still here.

We hadn't all made it to see this moment. Some of the brightest, most brilliant lights among us had been lost to a devastating disease, and we would lose many more. They had been instrumental in helping build so much of the positive, optimistic new world onto which we were now looking out.

And now, as the Wall that had slashed the heart of that city – the city that had given us so much – finally tumbled, tomorrow belonged to us.

ACKNOWLEDGEMENTS

Massive thank yous go out to:

Steve Dagger, for his encouragement on this book and everything else I do!

Issy and Laura and everyone at Insanity Talent Management … Simply the best.

My A team: Shirlie, Harley and Roman, for their incredible love!

Everyone at HarperCollins and Chris Lochery, who all made this book possible.

And, of course, Ajda Vucicevic, who simply Rocks!